Donna Hamilton's
Gracious Country Inns
& Favorite Recipes

by
Donna Hamilton

**Featuring the Style, Ambience and Signature Recipes
Of North America's Greatest Romantic Hideaways**

*Illustrated by artist and designer Sheryl Schmidt, who creates treasures
large and small from her studio in Baltimore, MD.*

Grateful acknowledgment is made to the following for permission
to reprint previously published material:

Favorite Recipes from our Kitchen – The White Gull Inn
by Jan and Andy Coulson

High Hampton Hospitality Cookbook
by Lily Byrd

Shelburne Breakfasts
by Laurie Anderson and David Campiche

Cover and book design by Al Cunniff / Books Unlimited – Baltimore, MD
Cover Photo: Mark Daniels, Takoma Park, MD
Back Cover Photo: Kurt Kolaja, Kolaja Grain & Feed, Baltimore, MD

Cover Photo Location: The Inn at Perry Cabin, St. Michaels, MD
Donna Hamilton's clothes: Talbots

The Mockingbird Company
5115 Wetheredsville Rd.
Baltimore MD 21207

Manufactured in the United States of America
First printing November 1994
Second printing September 1995

About This Book

When Mary Ellen Iwata, Executive Producer for The Learning Channel, called me about hosting the television series Great Country Inns, I was instantly intrigued. To me, the adventure of packing my bag, getting on a plane and heading off for a destination I've never seen before is heaven. I travel, therefore, I am. Thus producer Carl Rutan, photographer Mark Daniels and I set off on a travel odyssey that would transport us to so many distant locales in North America.

Having stayed in more than my unfair share of large, impersonal hotels in my career, I love the warmth and intimacy that inns provide, the adventure of traveling with more than the comforts of home. That's what a lot of us seek when we travel, that feeling of being welcome, of hospitality being offered for its own sake. The people who run these "great" country inns genuinely like people and treat you as an honored guest, not a customer, whether you're miles from civilization or in the middle of a metropolis.

At every inn I've visited (and that's quite a few), the innkeepers are always extremely interested in food, as are their guests. Food is an integral component of the inn experience. Perhaps that's because food is the most obvious expression of solace and comfort, a way to show people that we're glad they came. Represented by the pineapple, food is the symbol of hospitality.

Country inn cooking ranges from the simple to haute cuisine, always lovingly prepared and served with the anticipation of pleasing you. Regional cuisine happily reigns supreme with wonderful recipes that have become oft, requested favorites by guests dying to know how to duplicate those glazed lamb shanks, that buttery banana bread or the pan-fried trout. Wait no longer.

Coming from a family that loves to eat and cook, I enjoyed experimenting with food even as a girl. Finding a recipe for a French fish stew in a magazine, I would dress up my little sister in old clothes and we would become "frugal French housewives" while cooking and serving the meal. We had a lot of fun in the kitchen and still do, thanks to my Mom, who is one of the best cooks I know.

A special thank you to all the inns who so graciously shared their time and recipes with me in this book. I should mention the fact that no one paid to be included in this book, which I have learned is not an uncommon practice in other guide books. If you have any doubts that I exaggerate about theses places, tune in to Great Country Inns on Saturday nights and weekday afternoons on The Learning Channel and see for yourself. I have often been asked, "Which one is your favorite?" or "Which one is the best?" Those questions are impossible to answer because the inns are all so different. That is the charm of inn travel. While varying widely in style and services offered, each one is unique.

I hope you enjoy traveling with me through this book to the Colorado Rockies, a little island in the Florida keys, the desert Southwest, the mountains of Tennessee, the Pacific Ocean in California, the St. Lawrence River in Canada or the Mississippi River way down South. But most of all, I hope that one day you'll experience these magical places and their hospitality for yourself. I guarantee you a wonderful journey. Bon voyage and good eating.

— *Donna Hamilton*

For Cada and Jesse, whose patience and understanding made this book possible. And for David, my editor, production manager and partner in just about everything else, who had a great deal to do with maintaining our children's patience and understanding.

And to Mom and Dad – thank you for your love and guidance.

TABLE OF CONTENTS

ROCKIES

C Lazy U Ranch

GRANBY, COLORADO

Peering at the view from the second floor balcony of C Lazy U's main lodge early one morning, I see a couple of glossy chestnut horses trot by, riderless. Then come a couple more until a full scale stampede of frisky looking steeds of every color and description gallop past. My jaw agape, I think first to sound the alarm – the horses are loose! Save yourselves! But before I claim the chance to embarrass myself, a couple of the ranch's wranglers trot along behind, rounding up stragglers, whistling, and shouting cowboy things like "Giddy-up." The morning roundup is over. It happens every day at C Lazy U, except when the horses get a day off. I can feel that cowboy magic rubbing off on me– I'm part of a real working ranch.

Thirteen pastures cover about 5,000 acres and produce 300 tons of hay a year to feed 145 horses.

WIDE OPEN

And it's not only a bona fide horse ranch, it's a big one. If your sense of pleasure is proportional to the amount of wide open space, you're gonna be mighty happy at the C Lazy U perched high on the western slopes of the Colorado Rockies. Thirteen pastures cover about 5,000 acres and produce 300 tons of hay a year to feed 145 horses.

That means each spring the wranglers head out to repair about 25 miles of barbed wire fence.

Yep, it's the real thing, and has been since 1925 when a rodeo cowboy named Jack Smillie opened the F Slash Ranch. Jack offered bear hunting, steaks and fresh baked pies, plus the unheard-of luxury of a bath house with his *and* her showers. Guest rates ran about $40 a week for room and board. Adjusted for inflation, that price hasn't changed much, but the service certainly has.

COWBOY TRADITION

*Immediately
suspicious, I keep my
doubts to myself.
Square dancing? You
can count this girl out.
A good book will do
just fine.*

The ranch passed through a succession of owners over the years. They were all folks who felt that cowboy magic and fell in love with the ranch's rustic charm and spectacular mountain views. Each added their own guest ranch refinements. The name was changed to the C Lazy U in the '40s, but a little ole' name change meant nothing to guests who continued answering the call of the range year after year, bringing their families along for the adventure.

One of those families was Peg and Clark Murray of Kansas City, who began their love affair with the C Lazy U in 1958. Immediately succumbing to its western charms, the Murrays journeyed back almost every summer. It became a second home, and through serendipitous fate, they bought the ranch thirty years after their first visit. A cowboy fairy tale.

The Murrays' aim? To keep up standards set before them such as the prestigious AAA five-diamond rating, and the Mobil five-star rating. Keep the great food, the fun on the range, and give guests what Clark Murray terms "the vacation of a lifetime."

The two story main lodge, built in 1947, is the social hub of the C Lazy U world. People still gather in the living room around the roaring fireplace downstairs to chat after a day on the range. This magnificent pine log structure is a great setting for the Navajo rugs and Native American art collection that fills the room. Floor to ceiling book shelves flank the fireplace, and the soft leather sofas beg you to stay a while and have a drink in the cozy bar just three steps away.

Upstairs is the dining room where breakfast, lunch and dinner are served family-style each day. The furniture is simple and solid, yet the snow-white napkins are starchy crisp. Fresh flower arrangements lend an elegant mountain touch. Pine beams run across the ceiling supported by tree trunks that emerge from the floor. A stone fireplace burns when the weather is cool, and more Navajo rugs grace the walls, plus oil paintings by Peg Murray. She lends her considerable talent to still lifes, landscapes and flowers that bring lively touches of reds, pinks and greens to the room. Step out onto the balcony where the air is sweet with the fragrance of hanging flower baskets and tubs of red geraniums. Here you can get a panoramic view of Peaceful Valley with the Never-Summer Mountain Range and its eternal snow-caps in the distance.

"Let's get you settled in," smiles one of the many helpful staff members. Multi-room cottages of various sizes surround the lodge. On the way to mine we pass the Patio House, a glass enclosed structure by the pool. Feeling the cool air while eyeing the swimming pool, I'm told that it's spring fed and assured that it's heated. Inside the pool house are a whirlpool, sauna, racquetball court, game room, bar, TV room and locker rooms with showers. I spy a large empty room. "What's that for?" I wonder out loud. The answer is a quick, "Square dancing and western swing dances held each week." Immediately suspicious, I keep my doubts to myself. Square dancing? You can count *this* girl out. A good book will do just fine.

I perk up considerably when shown to my room. A big stone fireplace already laid and ready to blaze (Good. I'm not much at getting 'em started myself), a mantle adorned with appropriate folk art birdhouses and wreaths, pine furniture, a queen sized bed, quilts, a large bathroom with heaps of toiletries that thoughtfully include a strong sunscreen and a monogrammed terry-cloth robe. A couple of soft armchairs sit by a big picture window overlooking the pine and fir trees right outside. An ample supply of fire logs is neatly stacked just outside the door.

Luckily in time for breakfast, I mosey back over to the lodge. This is where families begin the day at the C Lazy U, having breakfast together before they all head off in opposite directions for various activities. Folks already know each other a bit as they laugh and chat about yesterday or the day ahead.

"Sore, are you?"

"Well, just a bit. I stayed out riding longer than I meant to."

"Good granola. They make it themselves."

"Pass those biscuits, please."

Waffles, eggs, blueberry or chocolate chip pancakes with bacon are offered in the mornings. You need a hearty breakfast for the day before you. Just one more sip of that coffee and, "See ya'll later. Have a good day."

RIDIN' INTO THE WEST

Lots of folks head straight for the corral, where the wranglers have already saddled up many of the mounts for the morning ride. All guests who ride are assigned a horse and saddle for the week. Rides are offered twice a day for all riding levels. "Basic instruction" is from the hooves up, so to speak. This makes the novice more comfy. Then there's the "slow and scenic" – maybe you *could* go faster but you'd just as soon not, thank you. And then you have "fast." The word just about says it all. This level requires advanced experience. The wrangler allows fast riders the freedom to ride in and out of the line. A 10,000 sq. ft. indoor arena allows intense instruction for those serious about improving their horse skills regardless of the weather.

"Alright Ma'am, just put your left foot right here – no, your other left foot – and swing that other leg over Red's back. One, two, three – up you go." And here I am, sitting taller than I'm used to and on an immense auburn horse to boot. He seems not to mind me being there. Maybe we'll get along.

The group heads off, passing the 3 to 5 year olds; tiny kids on horses not much smaller than mine. Their little legs seem to stick straight out from the saddles. They're deliriously happy to have their own horse and teacher.

Over a small bridge and into a green pasture we move on past a red rock formation called Garden of the Gods. We have our choice of trails called Keyhole, Curtis Ridge and the Yellow Brick Road, named for the yellow aspen leaves which blanket the trail in the autumn. Now the wrangler surprises me. "Would you like to try a trot?" he asks innocently. I surprise myself by answering in the affirmative. Who said that?

"OK, just give Red a squeeze with your legs so he knows you're ready to go. And let your legs take some of the bounce." I squeeze, Red complies by quickening the pace - and - I'm - trotting-ing-ing-ing. Before I quite know whether I like this or not, Red moves cheekily into the lope. Now the meadow grass is flashing past, and I'm hanging on for dear, sweet life. Without really meaning to, I pull in the reins and Red slows and stops. My heart is hammering in my throat. Let's do it again.

"Shoot, you might be ready for the Shodeo with a little work," my wrangler drawls as we eventually head back for the C Lazy U. The shodeo is the guest rodeo held at the end of the week. Games of pole bending, barrel racing, and musical cones let the greenhorns test just how far they're advanced this week. "Everyone loves it," laughs Clark Murray. "The kids get involved, and imagine the kick they get out of seeing their parents trying to race around the barrels." Thank God my kids ain't here.

All guests who ride are assigned a horse and saddle for the week. Rides are offered twice a day for all riding levels.

OTHER WESTERN DELIGHTS

In the afternoon, everyone has headed in various directions. Many are off again for the afternoon ride. But if some degree of stiffness seems to be afflicting you, how about fly fishing? The ranch offers Gold Medal fly fishing and complimentary guide service on the ranch itself, Willow Creek and the Colorado River. If you're lucky, or good, you can hook a rainbow, brook, or German brown trout to enjoy the next morning at breakfast, compliments of the ranch kitchen.

Laykold tennis courts are available, as are skeet and trap shooting, or perhaps a splash in that heated pool. The Pole Creek Golf course is just a 15 minute drive away, and the ranch is just minutes from the Rocky Mountain National Park and the Arapaho National Forest. Drive the famous Trail Ridge Pass (the highest continuous highway in the U.S.). Both parks offer hikes guided by rangers, and miles of hiking trails. Ranch staff can also arrange for you to raft the mighty Colorado River, if you're hankering for a whitewater adventure.

Winter brings a Rocky Mountain white wonderland with old-fashioned cutter sleigh rides, sledding and tubing (with a world class half-mile sled run), and ice skating on the groomed and lit pond (with nearby toasty firepit). The ranch has added winter horseback riding with hour-long rides twice a day which have been extremely popular with guests. Twenty-five miles of machine-groomed cross country trails, backcountry touring and telemarking mean you don't need to hit the same trail twice, and all equipment and instruction is complimentary. Or, if you prefer downhill skiing, the ranch runs free morning and afternoon shuttles to Winter Park (30 min.) and Silver Creek (15 min.). Both are family resorts.

SOME FANCY GRUB

The chef might marinate a couple of haunches of prime rib, and roast them until they're a lovely reddish-pink on the inside. Rib bones are carved off and barbecued by the pool.

Back at the C Lazy U, dinner is almost at hand, often served in the dining room, where you might enjoy artichoke-stuffed mountain trout with basil-shallot butter, breast of turkey with cranberries and sage or maybe rack of lamb with apricot-mint sauce. Cookouts are held at the Patio House by the pool twice a week in the summer. The chef might marinate a couple of haunches of prime rib, and roast them until they're a lovely reddish-pink on the inside. Rib bones are carved off and barbecued by the pool as a less-than-delicate but satisfying appetizer for guests enjoying cocktails as the sun slips behind the hills. With exercise-sharpened appetites we plunge into prime rib, herb-marinated shrimp brochettes, crisp green salad, hot homemade breads and luscious apple cashew tarts. What a contented posse we are.

HEEL KICKIN'

But the night is still young. The ranch foreman announces the square dance, which he will personally call. Grab yourself a partner, and we'll do the Virginia Reel. For me, this is normally when I quietly slip away and do some serious and not-so-serious reading. But inexplicably I remain. Someone grabs my hand and I'm in the thick of it. Music starts, someone is playing the fiddle. "Grab that girl and sashay down – now sashay back. Bow to your partner....bow to the girl next door. Now swing your partner." Laughing uncontrollably while sashaying and swinging is not quite the way it's done, but nonetheless, I'm square dancing. My heart is hammering. Let's do it again.

ROAST DUCKLING WITH RASPBERRY PEPPEROCHINIS

The C Lazy U usually serves this dish with wild rice sautéed with walnut and some hot peppers thrown in.

1 5–6 lb. duck
1 medium sized onion
1 orange
2 stalks celery
1 bay leaf
1 oz. orange juice concentrate

SAUCE:

1 cup fresh raspberries
1 cup raspberry liqueur
1 cup raspberry preserves
½ cup sliced pepperochinis (these peppers can be found in jars in most supermarkets)
duck stock or chicken stock

1. Cut onion, orange and celery into large chunks and stuff into washed cavity of duck.
2. Rub duck with orange juice concentrate. Roast breast side up 1½ to 2 hours in 375 degree oven until tender.
3. Cut breast meat off bones and leg and thigh portion off body. Keep covered
4. Cut up bones and place in sauce pan with the cavity mixture, cover with water and simmer for 2 hours to make duck stock.
5. Strain duck stock and add to it all the sauce ingredients together. Simmer 20 minutes uncovered and pour over warmed duck meat.

Serves 4

TOMATO-SHRIMP SOUP

This tomato based seafood soup is extremely quick to prepare. Make it when tomatoes are ripe and plentiful.

2 tablespoons butter
1 medium onion, chopped
2 stalks celery, chopped
7 ripe tomatoes, peeled, seeded and chopped
5 fresh basil leaves, chopped
1 clove garlic, chopped
½ lb. 16–20 shrimp
3½ qts. chicken stock, seasoned

1. Sauté onions, celery and garlic in the butter until translucent.
2. Add the tomatoes and basil, cook for 5 minutes, stirring occasionally.
3. Add the chicken stock and simmer 1/2 hour.
4. Stir in raw shrimp that have been cut into fifths. Simmer additional 2 minutes. Salt to taste. Garnish with fresh basil leaves.

Makes 1 gallon.

BOURBON GLAZED CARROTS

Maple syrup and bourbon give steamed carrots a real face-lift.

¾ cups 100% maple syrup
2 oz. unsalted butter
1 oz. bourbon
pinch ground thyme
chopped chives (for garnish)
1 pound of sliced carrots

1. Steam carrots until done but still crisp.
2. Mix maple syrup and bourbon in sauce pan and simmer for 5 minutes.
3. Swirl in the butter and thyme, and toss with crisp steamed carrots and top with chives.

Makes 1 cup of glaze.

CASHEW TART

Cashew lover alert! What an unusual combination, and after a day on the range, this tart is beloved by grownups and kids alike.

CRUST:

½ lb. unsalted butter
¾ cups sugar
½ teaspoon salt
½ teaspoon baking powder
2½ cups flour

1. Mix well the dry ingredients.
2. Mix in the butter with hands until you have a corn-meal consistency.
3. Press into Pam-sprayed tart pan until pastry is ¼–⅜ inch thick. Wrap edges with foil Bake for 15 minutes in preheated 375 degree oven. (*This recipe makes enough dough for 2 tarts. If you desire to only make one, you can divide the dough in half and freeze the remainder until needed.*)

FILLING:
(HALVE INGREDIENTS IF MAKING ONLY ONE TART)

2 cups sour cream
4 egg yolks
1 cup brown sugar
1 teaspoon vanilla
1 teaspoon cinnamon
1 cup chopped cashews
4–5 Granny Smith apples, cored and sliced

1. Place sliced apples in the tart crust.
2. Mix sour cream, egg yolks, brown sugar, vanilla, and cinnamon together. Pour over sliced apples.
3. Bake at 325 degrees for 30 minutes.
Makes two 9" tarts.

Home Ranch

CLARK, COLORADO

Is there a place more perfect than the Home Ranch? Maybe "perfection" is too stingy a term. Heaven on a Rocky Mountain high is more like it. Ken and Cile Jones have created a rustic, western retreat with which one cannot find fault. Unless you frown upon an elegantly casual mountain inn, gourmet cowboy food, horses that like you, and a staff that feels likewise. They don't call it Home Ranch for nothin'.

That "boy this is a great place" feeling begins the moment you first open your eyes in the morning. A fan whirls lazily overhead in the vaulted ceiling crisscrossed with wooden beams. Through a high Palladian window I view blue sky with a few puffy clouds floating by. The sunshine streams onto the bed. I stir under the down comforter, think about snatching another 40 winks, but remember that cowboy coffee is waiting downstairs for early risers. I could make my own. There's a coffee maker in the room, but.... I get up, turn off the humidifier (useful in the dry mountain air), and pull on a pair of jeans, which are de regieur here, for the first walk of the day.

I stir under the down comforter, think about snatching another 40 winks, but remember that cowboy coffee is waiting downstairs for early risers.

BRIGHT-EYED AND BUSHY-TAILED

All is quiet at Home Ranch this early. Downstairs I pass through the lovely sitting rooms furnished with soft leather sofas and chairs. Rainbow-hued quilts, Navajo rugs underfoot and on the natural log walls add bits of color. A riverstone fireplace stretches up some 25 feet and game tables wait with intricate puzzles to be solved. A baby grand piano and bass fiddle (who plays that?) stand in one corner, an overhead library-loft lined with bookshelves stuffed with books, vases of mountain wildflowers and cowboy knickknacks complete the scene.

There it is, the dining room. On the sideboard is strong coffee with a supply of china "cowboy" cups. Westward Ho Rodeo is the name of the pattern with a cowboy on horseback, his lasso in the air. Hilarious! I pour myself a steaming cupful and the smell is life giving. Adding a dollop of cream, I'm off for the next morning walk.

It's early, but the day is never too young for the hummingbirds. As you step through the front door onto the flagstone porch, they are already dive-bombing the feeders hung there. This tiny bird, which many of us work so diligently to lure to our gardens back home, has lost its shyness here. They are everywhere. That humming noise from the rapid beat of their wings sings you on your way, but not before one or two hovers in mid-air about 12 inches from your head, sniffing out a possible feeding. Watch that rose cologne.

Breathing clean mountain air that still has a nip in it, I follow a flagstone walk from the lodge's front door past a split rail fence. Down at the corral, the horses (140 total, 90 riding mounts) are whinnying they are ready for breakfast. So am I.

Enough walking. Crunching my steps up the graveled road toward the ranch-house, the sun is almost up over the mountains highlighting their bright white snow-caps still prominent in June. Ken says they won't disappear until August. The ranch is nestled at the foot of these giants and with its multiple log rooms and green tin roof, the rambling main lodge has the appearance of a high country family home that kept growing from generation to generation, each new family getting its own addition.

MOUNTAIN COMFORTS

Ken explains the idea, saying, "We wanted a series of rooms that kind of zigged and zagged into each other, not a few huge rooms. We were looking for warmth and intimacy, like a real house, not a hotel."

The main lodge houses not only the common sitting rooms and dining room but also six guest bedrooms with western names such as Lonesome Cow, Baby Doe and Quick Draw. Other guests may stay in one of eight deliciously private cabins scattered through the white aspen groves. The cabins all have private hot tub/jacuzzis on the outside decks so that even in the winter with snow on the ground, a steaming soak is just outside your door. By design there are no TV's or telephones in the rooms. Ranging in size from the studio-loft cabin named Compromise to the largest and newest three bedroom, three bath Columbine, they are all decorated in variations of the elegant-roughing it-Ralph Laurenesque style of the main lodge. Antiques, big comfy beds with down comforters, Southwestern art and pottery, and large gleaming baths with hair dryers, fancy soaps and thick terry robes. And, each room is graced by a jar of truly wicked fresh baked chocolate chip cookies, magically replenished each day.

But please, only the naughty will indulge in a chocolate chip cookie before a Home Ranch breakfast. (*OK, but only one.*) Breakfast here is no hit and run meal. The oatmeal blackberry pancakes, fresh-from-the-oven morning-glory muffins, blintzes and apple sour cream cake, scrambled eggs dusted with fresh herbs, breakfast burritos with ranchero sauce, pitchers full of fresh-squeezed orange juice and milk on the coffee sideboard, all make for a memorable breakfast that is beyond satisfying. Perhaps guilt inspiring. But not according to Ken, who believes that the food here is an important part of the experience.

He sagely feels that it's all in our best interests. "Folks here get so much exercise, what's there to feel guilty about? They need to be well fed." You bet.

The cabins all have private hot tub/jacuzzis on the outside decks so that even in the winter with snow on the ground, a steaming soak is just outside your door.

And there is, indeed, as much to do as one could wish, or as little. While some guests will be content with taking in the sunshine by the heated pool and jacuzzi, you should already be heading down to the corral for the first ride of the day.

RODE HARD AND PUT UP WET

Guests at the Home Ranch are encouraged to stay for the week to really enjoy the whole experience. You'll be given your own horse for the week, assignments made according to your riding experience. Down at the corral they teach lessons on horse safety and saddling. If you don't cotton to throwing a heavy chunk of leather over a horse's back, and then yanking a strap tight under its belly, not to worry. There are a number of experienced, leather-chap wearing wranglers to do it for you.

Two hour morning rides are for greenhorns like me as I try building up to an all day ride and picnic. Ambling one thousand feet up to the top of Home Ranch Mountain is an alternately exhilarating and peaceful experience. You begin in meadows filled with the ranch's shaggy Scottish Highland cattle where the riding is easy. But once you get through the thick aspen groves and ascend into the colder fir tree territory, the ride and the terrain get rugged and for a couple of moments downright nerve-wracking. The horses know the trails well and though you may be uncertain, they aren't. The final eye-popping view of the Continental Divide in the distance and Home Ranch in the valley below more than make up for any bit of saddle soreness. Besides, you did it!

If you're into fly fishing or would like to be, there's a trout-stocked pond behind the main lodge plus the services of an expert to teach beginners or give advice to the experienced. Once mastering skills on the pond, the Elk River is just down the road. All the gear you need is yours for the asking at the lodge.

Try guided hikes into the wilderness, riding lessons and best of all for parents, a well planned children's program for kids over the age of five. Like you, they get their own mount, learn to ride and are kept splendidly entertained by special staff counselors.

In the winter, Home Ranch is a skier's paradise, with forty kilometers of tracked trails throughout the Elk River Valley and, all around the ranch, groomed areas for Telemark practice, and downhill skiing just a shuttle away in Steamboat Springs. Cross country equipment and lessons are available at the ranch. If you're looking for something even more exhilarating try dog sledding, snowmobiling and hot air ballooning. All can be arranged by Home Ranch staffers.

Try guided hikes into the wilderness, riding lessons and best of all for parents, a well planned children's program for kids over the age of five.

BUT NOT WITHOUT SUPPER

Meals at Home Ranch are frankly hedonistic journeys into the surprisingly wild and winsome world of Western cuisine. The only resemblance it bears to cowboy food is the use of a grill. The kitchen is ardent about fresh ingredients and variety. Rarely repeating meals in the course of a year, this is eclectic grub at its best. Cile explains, "The food has to be Western because we're a guest ranch in the Rockies but also sophisticated because we're a member of Relais and Chateaux. That's what our guests expect."

Lunch in the summer is often served buffet style on the veranda and guests gather to eat by the pool. On one day of my visit a long table is filled with a bounty of fresh baked hot breads, tomato-mint couscous, lentil salad, grilled duck sausages, baby lamb chops and dainty jewel-like fruit tarts for dessert.

Dinner is served family style on long, trestle tables in the log-walled dining room. I was presented with choices of grilled swordfish with mango salsa, warm scallop salad, veal chops with Hunter sauce, apple-smoked pork chops with peach and citrus chutney, or grilled whole beef tenderloin with ranch tomato sauce. Pass the potato biscuits, please. And save room for peach pie, apple berry crisp with bourbon sauce, banana crème brûlèe, or three flavors of homemade ice cream. Don't dress up. Jeans are fine.

Cile and Ken are completely charming dinner hosts. This Atlanta lady is completely at home on a horse, and her rodeo roping cowboy is a fun-time balladeer. True to Southern and Western tradition, they will have you feeling as though you've been friends forever.

Once a week, the kitchen packs up all the food and equipment in pickup trucks, puts guests on a haywagon, and you're off to the "llamasary"—where llamas used to roam as an attraction worth far less than the trouble they caused. Basically the llamasary is a big porch built into the mountainside a mile or so from the main lodge. Along with terrific valley views, you enjoy killer food and a golden-orange Rocky Mountain sunset.

Once you've eaten your fill, Ken Jones and his cowboy band break out the guitars and serenade you with poignant and rollicking Western tunes. Ken is the genuine article. A dry wit, a cowboy song and a beautiful gal by his side set a tone that keeps Home Ranch relaxed, fun and unforgettable.

It's no wonder you meet some people for whom a vacation at Home Ranch takes on a pilgrimage quality. Those folks believe in the proprietor's simple motto: "Big beds, good grub, and honest horses." You can flap your gums a heap, but that pretty much says it all.

And save room for peach pie, apple berry crisp with bourbon sauce, banana crème brulee, or three flavors of homemade ice cream. Don't dress up. Jeans are fine.

GRACIOUS COUNTRY INNS

GRILLED, BASIL-MARINATED VEGETABLES

Until you've had grilled vegetables, you haven't really had vegetables, and the basil dipping marinade adds a luscious flavor. The marinade will also keep for quite a while in the refrigerator. These vegetables are the ones they use at home ranch, but many others roast well, too. As they are delicious at room temperature, it's a great do-ahead recipe.

2 Japanese eggplants, halved
2 zucchini, halved
2 yellow summer squash, halved
2 red bell peppers, seeded, cut into thirds
2 yellow bell peppers, seeded, cut into thirds
1 small jicama, peeled and sliced ¼" thick
1 bunch green onions or Vidalia onions, sliced
8 stalks asparagus, trimmed of woody ends

BASIL DIPPING OIL OR MARINADE

1 quart virgin olive oil
¼ cup chopped shallots
2 tablespoons chopped garlic
1 cup packed fresh basil leaves
¼ cup parsley
½ teaspoon black pepper
8 sage leaves
¼ cup lemon juice
2 tablespoons Parmesan cheese
2 tablespoons pine nuts
1 tablespoon salt

1. Blend ingredients in processor or blender.
2. Pour over trimmed vegetables in a bowl. Marinate for several hours.
3. Grill over medium-hot coals just until tender. (*Some will cook quicker than others.*)
4. May be served hot from grill or at room temperature. Serve remainder of marinade in a bowl as a dipping sauce, surrounded by vegetables, arranged artfully.

HOME RANCH QUESADILLAS WITH BRIE, MANGO, AND CHILES

A delightfully different nosh food for before dinner drinks.

1 fresh Poblano chile (sometimes called a pasilla)
1 red bell pepper
½ cup water
1 medium onion, thinly sliced
2 tablespoon butter, melted
2 tablespoon vegetable oil
1 ripe mango, peeled, pitted, chopped
2 tablespoon chopped fresh cilantro
8 oz. chilled Brie cheese, rind trimmed, cut into
   ⅓-inch wide strips
4 8-inch flour tortillas

1. Char chili and bell pepper over gas flame or in broiler until blackened on all sides. Wrap in a paper bag and let stand 10 minutes to steam. Peel, core, and seed. Rinse, if necessary, pat dry and chop. Place in a small bowl.
2. Bring ½ cup water to a boil in a small, heavy saucepan. Add onion. Cover and remove from heat. Let stand until onion is wilted, about 10 minutes. Drain. Add onion to chili mixture. (Can be prepared 1 day ahead. Cover and refrigerate.)
3. Prepare barbecue (medium heat) or preheat broiler.
4. Blend melted butter and vegetable oil in a small bowl.
5. Add chopped mango and chopped fresh cilantro to chili mixture.
6. Place ¼ of Brie strips on half of each flour tortilla. Top each with ¼ cup chili mango mixture. Season with salt and pepper. Fold over empty half of each flour tortilla to enclose filling. (Can be prepared to this point and refrigerated for a few hours.)
7. Brush with butter mixture. Place quesadillas butter side down on grill or butter side up under broiler. Cook 30 seconds, turn 90 degrees and grill for 30 seconds longer. Butter uncooked side and turn over. Grill until cheese begins to melt, about 30 seconds.
8. Cut each quesadilla into 3 pieces. Arrange on a platter garnished with fresh cilantro.
Serves 4.

HOME RANCH GRILLED WHOLE BEEF TENDERLOIN WITH RANCH TOMATO SAUCE

This is traditionally served at the ranch's Saturday evening campfire cookout. A grill filled with roasting tenderloins over an open fire is really a sight to behold (and smell), as guests gather for a farewell dinner and evening of sentimental songs around the campfire.

1 whole beef tenderloin (Home Ranch uses Certified Angus dry aged beef), trimmed, approximately 1 lbs.

BBQ RUB

3 tablespoons kosher salt
3 tablespoons ground black pepper
2 tablespoons minced fresh garlic
1 tablespoons Hungarian paprika
2 teaspoons minced, diced bay leaf
1½ teaspoons dry mustard
½ cup chopped parsley, squeezed dry

1. Mix all ingredients together. Oil your hands and rub the dry seasoning into the tenderloin, coating well. Let stand 20 minutes.

BBQ MOP

1 cup beef stock
½ cup red wine
¼ cup Worcestershire sauce
⅛ cup oil
2 serrano chiles, crushed
2 garlic cloves, crushed
3 tablespoons bottled BBQ sauce
salt and pepper

2. Mix all ingredients together.

RANCH TOMATO SAUCE

2 tablespoons vegetable oil
1 red onion, chopped
2 garlic cloves, peeled
2 Poblano chiles, seeded, chopped
5 ripe tomatoes, peeled, seeded, and diced
1 teaspoon fresh oregano
1 teaspoon fresh basil
1 cup tomato sauce
1 tablespoon red wine vinegar
salt and pepper
2 tablespoons cold unsalted butter

3. To make the sauce, heat the oil in a medium saucepan over medium high heat. Add onion and garlic and sauté until translucent, about 5 minutes.

4. Add chiles, tomatoes, oregano, basil, tomato sauce and vinegar. Cook over low heat until sauce thickens, about 10 minutes. Season with salt and pepper.

5. Just before serving, whisk in butter over low heat.

6. Make a hot charcoal fire, and allow time to create a white ash on the coals, about 20-30 minutes.

7. Place tenderloin on the grill for 5 minutes. Brush with mopping sauce. Turn roast 90 degrees to make a criss-cross mark and grill for another 5 minutes. Turn roast over and grill another 5 minutes, continuing to mop every 5 minutes. Turn two more times to sear all sides. Move roast to a cooler part of the grill. Check internal temperature. When it reaches 120 degrees, move to even cooler part of grill, and cover loosely with foil. Allow to rest 10–15 minutes. Temperature should then be 125–130 degrees. For medium rare, cook until 135 degrees.

8. To serve, slice tenderloin and pass tomato sauce on the side.

Serves 8.

RiverSong Inn
ESTES PARK, COLORADO

Getting to Estes Park was more of an adventure than I'd reckoned. It's normally an easy 70 mile drive north of Denver, but I'm unfortunately coming from the opposite side of the mountains over the Continental Divide via Trail Ridge Road, the highest continuous highway in the country. Fine. June wildflowers are happily blooming all about in the lowlands. A slightly disturbing sign flashes by, something about the pass being closed by deep snow. But it's June, that can't possibly be a current sign. The road begins to go up – sharply. Soon fat white flakes are harbingers of doom: I'm driving into what is quickly becoming a serious late season snowfall. Soon all the evergreens are thickly blanketed. There it is, all my fears realized in a barred gate across the road: Closed For Snow – Detour. Forget it. Go back.

Devastated, I stare in disbelief for a few minutes, drag out the map, muttering bad things about the intelligence of someone who would ignore the signs. I'll just have go around. Way around.

Arriving in Estes Park hours later than planned, I find the road to RiverSong, a little country lane that follows along the most beautiful stream that is rushing and tumbling over water-smoothed boulders. That must be the Big Thompson River. Passing a few mule deer that bound off into the trees at my passing, I soon pull under a simple wooden arch with a small sign that announces that I have indeed, finally made it to RiverSong's 27 wooded acres.

There it is, all my fears realized in a barred gate across the road: Closed For Snow – Detour. Forget it. Go back.

ROCK AND RESTORATION

Resting on a riverstone foundation, the cream clapboard inn, trimmed in blue, is tucked into the evergreens as RiverSong sits at the base of Giant Track Mountain. A family of pale aspen wood walking sticks leans in the corner of the porch by the rocking chairs. Sitting in one of those rockers for a moment, I take the time to be thankful for getting here safely and for having such a respite at the end of my journey. From this spot, the rush of the Big Thompson is singing the inn's name, a few hummingbirds buzz by looking for sweets, but all else is quiet. The view of the Rockies gives my frayed spirit a new song.

RiverSong was built around 1920 as a private summer home. The '30s era garden plans show elaborate plantings of lilacs, daisies, rhododendrons and wild roses, some of which survive today. Gary and Sue Mansfield bought the place in 1985 with the idea of converting this gracious mountain retreat into an inn.

After renovating and redecorating, the inn was enlarged to include nine bedrooms, all with private bath and named after Rocky Mountain wildflowers – Mountain Rose, Indian Paintbrush, Pasqueflower. I am in Forget-Me-Not, a nostalgic room in the main house. The elaborately carved antique walnut bed and dresser belonged to Sue's grandparents when they set up housekeeping. Very comforting, this room. Sleep comes easy and runs deep under a fluffy comforter.

The elaborately carved antique walnut bed and dresser belonged to Sue's grandparents when they set up housekeeping. Very comforting, this room. Sleep comes easy.

Next morning I lift the shades on a sunny day and discover a view that peers all the way to the snow-capped Continental Divide (looks better from down here). I smell coffee. "Cowboy coffee," Gary tells me, "It'll put a giddy-up in your get-along." Roasted in Moose, Wyoming, this brew is predictably strong and delicious, served in generous mugs in the living room on a low pine table surrounded by a horseshoe shaped sofa topped with lots of pillows and soft knitted throws, perfect for a long read. A riverstone fireplace covers one wall; the opposite wall is a bank of windows looking at the mountains.

ARISE AND CLIMB

Soon lovely spicy smells are coming from the kitchen and dining room through the doorway. Guests can follow their noses. Breakfast changes daily and might be "mountain man" French toast, yogurt poppy seed muffins or Lee's bread pudding with rum sauce. Today, as I sit at a small table by the windows overlooking the grounds and numerous much-frequented birdfeeders, the day begins with a glass dish of ruby red sliced strawberries with a cap of crème fraiche and a sprig of mint. Soon what I've been hungrily sniffing arrives, RiverSong's premier much-requested breakfast dish: John Wayne Casserole. This eggy-jalapeno-cheese-tortilla concoction is totally satisfying. I begged for and received the recipe and now, you have it, too.

"Hey, how about a hike up the mountain out back?" calls Gary. I'm game, I think. Outside we grab two of those carved hiking sticks and head up the trail that begins just a few yards away. But not before he pauses, looks at the view and says softly, "Isn't this the most beautiful place in the world? You can see why we live here." Feeling a few pangs of envy for his good luck, I agree.

GRACIOUS COUNTRY INNS

We pass quite a few darting, black, bushy-tailed creatures that I presume to be squirrels. "Squabbits," we call them," laughs Gary. And they do look like a squirrely-bunny mixed breed. Past wildflowers and birds, the hike to the top takes only about 30 minutes to an elevation of 9,500 feet. Any fatigue you might experience may be relieved by weathered-stone benches installed long ago for Rocky rookies like me. From the top you look down on the Big Thompson, reduced to a tiny trickle by distance. Before you is the city of Estes Park, nestled in a valley carved out long ago by glaciers.

RiverSong and Estes Park are cheek-by-jowl with the Rocky Mountain National Park that encompasses over 250,000 wooded acres and 250 miles of hiking trails. Gary and Sue can point you in the right direction for endless recreation possibilities. Their sound advice: take a good sunscreen, plenty of film for the camera, and a large water bottle. Even though the mountain streams look harmless to the thirsty, a microscopic parasite that lives there may decide to ruin your vacation.

For cyclists, there's an adventurous ride to an elevation of 12,200 ft. at the top of Trail Ridge Road. No, you *don't* cycle up, though perhaps some hardy souls do. Special vans haul you and your mountain bike, then deposit you with helmet and water bottle. Now you just coast four hours down the mountain. Take a jacket. Up here it's markedly cooler. In fact, the snow I'm whizzing past on my right is several feet thick. To my left are cliffs and a view of green valleys below. Way below. Halfway down the mountain my group stops for a gourmet picnic lunch that has been brought by a trailing van. Downhill biking is, I think, a brilliant idea, when done right.

Horseback riding, white water rafting on the Colorado River, and trout fishing (artificial lures only, catch and release) on the Big Thompson – they're all there. If perhaps you've always wanted to be a rock climber but didn't know how to start, a nearby school offers beginning classes. You probably won't see me there. Golf is also available, the only inconvenience being an occasional waiting period for the elk to clear off the greens. ("Here, boy. Here elkie, elkie, elkie.")

In the winter, when things quiet down in Estes Park, they enjoy one of the fastest growing cold weather sports: snow-shoeing. If your knees aren't quite up to skiing and you'd like to get out in the park to where even cross-country skiers don't go, it's perfect. The shoes are no longer made from heavy wood but from anodized aluminum, weighted in back so the tips don't flop down every step. Sue Mansfield loves it, saying, "If you can walk, you can snow-shoe. The park is so quiet and peaceful, and you'll see the snow hares and ptarmigans, whose fur and feathers have turned from brown to snow white."

Back at RiverSong in the late afternoon, Sue tours me around their two newest accommodations just a short walk from the main house, across a wooden walkway that makes both rooms handicapped accessible.

"Wood Nymph" has a romantic fantasy of a bed that you won't find in any store. Constructed of tree branches soaked and curved into arching boughs that form a twig canopy, it was dreamed up and constructed right in this room. An arched wood-burning fireplace on the opposite wall is flanked by bookshelves filled with baskets, books, pictures, pottery and a small reading nook with lots of cushions. A yellow plaid loveseat offers fireside seating; brick floors are heated from underneath. Just through the door is a bathroom greenhouse with a two person whirlpool tub.

Sue describes "Meadow Bright" as a Colorado mountain suite. It's an apt description, with a handmade pine log four-postered bed and a double-sided fireplace that serves both this bedroom and the extravagant bathroom on the other side. The fireplace is set in a wall of buff colored riverstone, just by a double whirlpool tub. This is Romance. The rocks extend into a glass shower where a waterfall bubbles forth at a turn of the faucet.

Bare feet stay toasty on heated wooden floors. Both of these rooms have private decks overlooking a pond.

WELL EARNED FARE

Dinner is served several nights a week, by reservation only. Cream of carrot soup with fresh dill, avocado with tomato, red onion, feta cheese and vinaigrette or oriental soup with shiitake mushrooms might start your meal in the candlelight bay-windowed dining room. Decide between tenderloin of beef with capers and mushrooms, chicken breast with fresh basil-cream sauce, or a vegetarian Italian strudel with spinach, mushrooms, ricotta and Parmesan cheeses in phyllo pastry. Homemade desserts such as fudge walnut tart or Double Diablo – a chocolate-glazed, chocolate-almond torte – make me feel guilt for only a moment. I remember my long bike ride. "I'll have the Double Diablo, please."

After dinner, sit a spell outside on one of a dozen swings around the property. Or stroll down to the edge of the river, and plop into one of the Adirondack chairs that wait there. Lean your head back, breathe some Rocky Mountain air, and simply appreciate the river's song. I could live here, too.

MOUNTAIN MAN FRENCH TOAST

Sometimes a name says it all.

1 8-oz. package of brown and serve sausages, sliced
1 large loaf of French bread (16 inches or more)
¼ lb. sliced Monterey Jack cheese
4 large eggs
1 cup of milk
1 tablespoon sugar
salad oil
maple syrup

1. Cook the sausage, drain off the fat drippings and place on paper towel.
2. Cut 8 two-inch slices of French bread and into each slice, cut a pocket for the sausage and cheese. Carefully stuff the pockets with the meat and cheese, press together.
3. In a 9×13-inch baking dish, beat the eggs, milk and sugar with a fork until blended. Place the stuffed bread into the mixture and flip the bread over several times.
4. Bake each side on an oiled griddle until golden and the cheese begins to melt.
5. Sprinkle the toast with powdered sugar and sliced strawberries. Serve with warm maple sugar.

Makes 4 servings.

BANANA BLIZZARD SAUCE

This sauce served over any sliced fruit is a popular breakfast starter at RiverSong. Made in a few minutes, it waits overnight in the fridge.

1¼ cups sour cream
1¼ cups plain yogurt
10 tablespoons sugar
5 teaspoons orange zest
5 tablespoons orange juice

1. Mix all ingredients together in a bowl and set overnight in the refrigerator.
2. When ready to serve, slice ripe bananas on an angle into a dessert dish and spoon on the blizzard sauce.
3. Garnish with a little viola flower (edible) and mint.

Serves 12 people.

YOGURT POPPY SEED MUFFINS

These tender muffins stay moist long after other muffins dry out.

1 cup sugar
3 large eggs
1 teaspoon vanilla
½ cup evaporated milk
½ cup of plain yogurt
1 cup of cooking oil
2½ cups of unsifted white flour
1½ teaspoon of baking powder
pinch of salt
¼ cup poppy seeds
1 tablespoon of Amaretto liqueur

1. Combine the sugar and eggs, evaporated milk, vanilla, Amaretto, poppy seeds, yogurt and cooking oil in a mixing bowl till blended well.
2. Sift together the flour, baking powder and salt.
3. Gradually add the flour mixture to the egg mixture. Don't overmix.
4. Put in buttered muffin tins and bake in a preheated oven at 400 degrees for 20–25 minutes. The tops will crack when done.

Makes 12–15 muffins.

GRAPE NUTS PUFF

½ cup of butter
¼ cup of honey
¼ cup of sugar
2 teaspoons of fresh lemon zest
4 egg yolks
5 tablespoons of lemon juice
4 tablespoons of white flour
½ cup of Grape Nuts cereal
2 cups of milk
4 egg whites

1. Cream the butter with the sugar, lemon zest and honey.

2. Add the egg yolks and beat until fluffy.

3. Blend in the lemon juice and milk, flour and Grape Nuts. The mixture will look curdled but the appearance will not affect the final dish.

4. Whip the egg whites until they are stiff and fold them into the mixture. Pour mixture into vegetable sprayed ramekins and place them in a hot water bath halfway up sides of ramekins .

5. Bake for 1 hour at 325 degrees until the tops spring back when you touch them.

6. Garnish with a little whipped cream and garnish with raspberries or blackberries with a sprig of mint.

Serves 6.

JOHN WAYNE CASSEROLE

This recipe makes 2 big dishes, enough to serve 18 people, so it's great for a big brunch. Trust me. It will all disappear. (And it's good reheated.)

2 large onions, chopped
1 large red bell pepper, chopped
2 green chiles (Anaheims are good)
1 jalepeno pepper, minced
2 cloves of garlic, minced
3 tablespoons of butter
2 tablespoons of ground black pepper
¾ cup white flour
½ cup of milk
3 cups of Monterey Jack cheese, shredded
3 cups of Cheddar cheese, shredded
12 eggs
32 oz. sour cream
¾ cup blue corn tortilla chips
2 teaspoons Dijon mustard

1. Sauté the chopped onions, green *chiles* and red pepper in the butter in a large skillet until tender. Add the garlic and jalepeno pepper, sauté a couple of minutes more. Remove from heat and set aside.

2. In a large mixing bowl put in 12 egg yolks, milk, flour and pepper, then add the sour cream, cheeses, tortilla chips and the now cooled vegetables and mix all together.

3. Beat the egg whites until they are stiff; fold into the mixture.

4. Pour the mixture into two 9 x 13 greased baking dishes and place in a preheated oven at 350 degrees for approximately 1 hour. The dish is done when the top is a little crusty and starts to crack.

5. Serve with a little sour cream on the side sprinkled with chopped chives and tomatoes, or some salsa.

Serves 18.

Stein Eriksen Lodge

PARK CITY, UTAH

Arriving at the Stein Eriksen Lodge is something akin to finding your way to a gnome's secret mountain hideaway. Make the turn onto Stein Way at the base of Bald Mountain and begin the steep ascent, 8,200 feet. Back and forth you turn following the guard rails higher and higher still. Views of snow festooned aspens and pines are breathtaking; keep your eyes on the road. There is the carved wood Stein Eriksen sign, a haven at last. Drive up to the little octagonal hut, where inside sits a lovely Nordic looking young woman, all blonde and pink cheeked. "May I help you?" Mission stated, you are motioned to a garage door painted with the word "Valkommen," welcome in Norwegian. The wide garage door raises automatically and you drive under the inn and into a subterranean aerie.

Up a flight of stairs (or elevator) is a main lobby as generous in proportions as you might now expect. Tall ceilings crossed with stout three foot thick wooden beams, wide open spaces with conversation groupings of sofas and chairs in imported European fabrics. One particularly inviting pair of melon colored sofas nestle up to a thirty-foot fireplace (one of 145 fireplaces throughout lodge) made of stone mined here in the massive Wasatch Mountain range. A gigantic pair of stag antlers hang about fifteen feet up. Perched on the side of Bald Mountain, expanses of glass frame the surrounding ski slopes covered by brightly dressed skiers darting along so effortlessly.

Stein Eriksen began skiing as soon as he could walk and grew up to become one of Norway's athletic heroes, winning gold and silver medals in the '52 Olympics, and three gold medals at the '54 World Championships.

Across one wall of the lobby are lighted cases full of silver and gold trophies and medals won in competition by the man who lends his name to this lodge. Stein Eriksen began skiing as soon as he could walk and grew up to become one of Norway's athletic heroes, winning gold and silver medals in the '52 Olympics, and three gold medals in slalom, giant slalom and downhill at the '54 World Championships. He then left Norway to pursue his fortune in the United States. Stein was instrumental in the development of Deer Valley (where he is the Director of Skiing) and the Stein Eriksen Lodge. Blonde, tanned and smiling, he reminisces about the beginning of the lodge, "I walked along this ridge high over Deer Valley and knew this was the spot where the lodge had to be."

And the dream came true when the Stein Eriksen Lodge opened in 1982, consisting of the main building which houses the lobby and two restaurants overlooking the slopes, shops and two wings of 44 suites and 76 deluxe rooms, all of which are privately owned. Those rooms vary in size and amenities, but all have spacious closets, gold-plated bath fixtures, terry cloth robes and satellite cable TV. At the apex is the opulent Stein Eriksen suite with three beautifully decorated bedrooms and bathrooms (one of which is a cerulean blue-tiled palace with its own steam room and spa), a fully equipped designer kitchen with Portuguese tiles I would love to beam home, living room with fireplace and a dining room that seats ten. French doors open onto two balconies with superb mountain and slope views.

I stay in what the lodge accurately calls a deluxe room. Done in crisp blue and white designer cottons, the room was lovely with two queen size beds, table and soft chairs, pine armoire, and marble bathroom with a jetted tub (oh so helpful after a few ski runs) and plenty of Neutrogena toiletries.

Having ordered a continental breakfast the night before, a soft tap on the door announces its early arrival along with the morning paper. A carafe of dark coffee, fresh squeezed orange juice and a basket of delectable pastries is just what I need to build up my stamina. The reason for this inn's existence is waiting just outside, some of the finest skiing to be found anywhere in the world.

And at Stein's lodge, it's so easy. Not the skiing, per se. That can be challenging anywhere.

"Where should we rent our skis and how do you get there?"

"Wait here, another comes along in thirty minutes."

"Don't put your skis there, over here on these racks."

I become exhausted just thinking about it, not to mention the fact that everyone seems to know exactly where to go and which shuttle to take except me.

Go downstairs into the underground garage. Just in front of you is a fully equipped ski shop to rent out all the equipment you need, properly fitted. Now step just through the wide hall next door with the sunshine at the end. OK. Ski. It's really just that simple. A small slope just outside propels you to the ski lift that is a 12-minute ride to the top of Bald Mountain. When you get off the lift, you have a choice of twelve ski runs from beginner to expert, and the views are alpine dreams.

At Deer Valley you can choose from sixty-six trails, of which 15% are designated "easiest," 50% "more difficult," and 35% "most difficult." The longest run is two miles. There is also a very gentle "trainer" slope which is accessible directly from Stein's with its own short lift back up to the lodge's front door.

Detailed maps of the runs are everywhere. But to really get a feel of the "different angles" of Deer Valley, the resort offers complimentary mountain tours for intermediate and advanced skiers led by guides who could probably ski all runs blindfolded. And when you're finished for the day, valets take your skis and tuck them away safely and easily for the night.

Go downstairs into the underground garage. Just in front of you is a fully equipped ski shop to rent out all the equipment you need, properly fitted.

Next piece of advice: make it back to Stein's for the skier's buffet. This lunch spread is no humble mountain-side repast. Beautifully arranged bowls of shrimps in vinaigrette, platters of rosy smoked salmon with mounds of capers and crème fraiche, silver pots of veal stew with wild mushrooms, potato lasagna, big baskets of fresh baked breads, irresistible wild game chili that I had to eat every day, and a dessert table that would make you cry comprise but a small listing of the restorative delicacies. If you can ski after a lunch like that, and many folks do, don't forget the lifts close at 4:00 PM. After everyone is off the mountain, all slopes are groomed so that the next morning it's as virginal as can be. Reconstructed, of course.

Skiers plunge down the slopes an average of four hours a day, according to Stein. So what do they do the rest of the time? Not far away is the Utah Winter Sports Park with recreational ski jumping available for those eager to risk pain and injury. This daring feat can be performed on telemark, traditional alpine or ski jumping equipment. A limited supply of jumping skis, boots and helmets (a requirement) is available.

Observers, like me, also view Nordic and Freestyle jumping on the 65 kilometer and 90 kilometer jumps and on the Freestyle Aerial Jump. This $40 million facility, which will one day have a bobsled run is designed to aid in the training of young athletes hoping for a bit of the gold Stein Eriksen earned back in 1952. Watching the jumpers up close, not on television, makes one realize that survival is the name of this game.

Not far away is the Utah Winter Sports Park with recreational ski jumping available for those eager to risk pain and injury.

SANS THE SLOPES

Snowmobiling, hot air ballooning, horse drawn sleigh and wagon rides are all popular diversions. And regular shuttles will cradle you from the lodge down the mountain to historic Park City, the quaint mining town that has done a bit of surviving itself.

Silver mining created several fortunes and a boom town in Park City. But after silver prices went south and a devastating fire destroyed large chunks of real estate in the early 1900s, Park City became a virtual ghost town. The 1950s population was only around 1,000 tenacious souls. But the city was rescued from near oblivion by elements that had been there all along – mountains and snow. Today people from around the world come to ski the pristine slopes with an 80 to 100 inch snow base and constant fresh powder. Walking along Park City's bustling streets crowded with boutiques, restaurants, museums and galleries in historic buildings and visitors garbed in glamorous ski suits, it's taxing to imagine this trendy little burg ever on hard times.

Catch the shuttle back up Bald Mountain, unpack the swimming suit and head for the pool. The steam rises mystically from the heated waters. Relax, kick back, and think of others taking that last run down the mountain as the long blue shadows follow them.

I have reservations (important) in the Glitretind restaurant tonight. Carved pine chairs and white naperied tables with shining silver and china contrast well against the black floral carpet. A large stone fireplace blazes warmth and cheer. The menu cheers me further. Crisp Asian quail with coconut curry sauce, barbecued lamb with wilted romaine leaves, black olives and feta couscous, or chilled ahi tuna with wasabi-lime vinaigrette could all start the meal most admirably. Entrees include peppered red deer with blackberry cassis sauce and two potato hash, seared Atlantic salmon with a warm spinach-corn-potato salad and purple basil butter sauce, or perhaps medallions of beef tenderloin with Gorgonzola potato purée and red wine peppercorn sauce. All are complimented by wines from a list that has twice won the *Wine Spectator* "Award of Excellence."

Rolling into bed most content with the meal and the day, I only feel profound gratitude that Stein Eriksen stood on this particular mountain ridge on that particular day so long ago.

STEIN'S SWEET POTATO SOUP

The humble sweet potato rises to new southwestern plateaus in this recipe. Don't forget when roasting and peeling chilis, either wear surgical gloves or make sure you wash hands well after handling. Don't touch your eyes!

⅛ cup salad oil
2 onions–diced
2 carrots–diced
2 lbs. peeled sweet potatoes (cut in quarters)
64 oz. chicken stock
2 roasted Anaheim chilies (peel and seed by blistering chilies over flame or under broiler, sweat 5 minutes in a paper bag)
Salt and pepper to taste

1. Sauté carrots andonions in oil until translucent.
2. Add sweet potatoes and chicken stock. Bring to a boil. Simmer until potatoes are cooked. Add salt and pepper to taste.
3. Add Anaheim chilis and simmer for 5-10 minutes. Cool slightly.
4. Purée soup in processor until smooth. If soup is too thick, thin with additional chicken stock.
5. Garnish with sour cream and chives.
Serves 8.

STEIN'S WILD GAME CHILI

½ cup salad oil
1 lb. venison meat–cubed
1 lb. wild boar–cubed
1 lb. buffalo–cubed
Flour for coating
2 red onions–diced
1 yellow bell pepper–diced
1 red bell pepper–diced
1 Anaheim chili–diced
4 cups beef stock
1 cup red zinfandel wine
6 cups diced tomatoes–canned
¼ cup fresh garlic–minced
1–2 tablespoons dark chili powder
1 tablespoon black pepper

Salt to taste

1. In a thick-bottom stock pot, add oil and heat until oil is hot but not smoking.
2. Toss cubed meat in flour, shake off excess flour and add to pot. Brown the meat in small batches so it isn't crowded in the pan, otherwise the meat will not brown properly.
3. Add onions, pepper, chilies, garlic, black pepper and chili powder.
Sauté until onions are translucent, about 5 minutes.
4. Add the zinfandel, stirring any bits up from the bottom of the pot, then reduce wine by half.
5. Add beef stock and tomatoes. Let simmer for 45 minutes.
6. Add salt to taste. and adjust seasonings. Serve with crème fraiche.
Makes 10 servings.

ORIENTAL BANANAS FOSTER

I first experienced Bananas Foster in New Orleans at Brennan's years ago, thinking it the best thing I'd ever tasted. This recipe updates the original with ginger, coconut and tropical fruits.

1 cup butter
1 cup honey
1 teaspoon cinnamon
5 teaspoon nutmeg
1 teaspoon ginger–ground
6 firm bananas
1 cup rum
coconut for garnish–toasted
papaya or mango for garnish–diced

1. In a deep skillet, melt butter over medium heat.
2. Stir in cinnamon, nutmeg, sugar and honey and blend well.
3. Cut bananas length wise, then in half to make quarters. Add to honey mixture. Baste bananas with sauce until well coated.
4. Carefully pour in rum, warm for a few seconds. Ignite carefully!
Baste the bananas until flame dies.
5. Serve over vanilla ice cream, garnished with toasted coconut and mango.
8 servings.

THE SOUTH

Cedar Grove Mansion

VICKSBURG, MISSISSIPPI

There is some degree of controversy as to exactly when folks in Vicksburg began cel-ebrating the Fourth of July. Some say it was right after World War II when then General Dwight D. Eisenhower visited and locals thought it would be rude not to have some sort of party. (Even then it was called Carnival of the Confederacy.) Others swear that it was not until the bicentennial in 1976 that Vicksburg gave the Fourth any sort of notice. Still others declare barbecues and fireworks didn't begin until the early '80s. Whatever version you believe, one thing is clear: Vicksburg held no truck with the Fourth of July for an awful long time, still doesn't really, because that was the day in 1863 the town fell to the damn, God-forsaken Yankees.

The real fighting of the Union siege of Vicksburg, the well fortified "Gibraltar of the Confederacy" began on May 17th, 1863 and went on for 47 days. Because of its strategic location on the bluffs of the Mississippi River, The Union Army was deter-mined to take Vicksburg after three previous failed attempts. Three-inch cannon balls had been falling for a year fired from gunboats on the Mississippi.

Two of those iron spheres crashed on Cedar Grove, a graceful Greek Revival mansion whose carefully tended Italian gardens extended down to the river's edge. The first lodged in the wall of the ladies' parlor, the second smashed through the parlor floor into the lodgings of the house slaves below. The damage done that day remains unre-paired. The parlor wall still holds a most intriguing conversation piece.

One thing is clear: Vicksburg held no truck with the Fourth of July for an awful long time, still doesn't really, because that was the day in 1863 the town fell to the damn, God-forsaken Yankees.

Cedar Grove was built in 1840 by wealthy businessman John Alexander Klein for his wife Elizabeth. After a year long honeymoon, during which they shipped back numerous pieces of European art and furniture, they sailed home to make Cedar Grove a showplace. Many of their treasures remain. Ruby red Bohemian glass panels from Czechoslovakia high above walnut doors, gold leaf mirrors from France some fifteen feet tall, and delicate porcelains that miraculously survived a war and a subsequent century.

The Devil incarnate, otherwise known as General Grant, slept in John and Elizabeth Klein's bedroom for three nights after the siege ended. And yet the couple dispensed with burning that rosewood bed made with stout six inch thick posters especially for the 6'2" Klein. In fact, that defiled furniture now serves its purpose in what is called the General Grant room. And, in the corner is a tiny mahogany bed in which all the Klein babies (ten of them) slept until they were moved to the nursery next door.

Downstairs is the General Lee Suite, one of my favorite rooms. Not because Lee slept here. He did not. But the green walls and deep red carpet accented with cream is a lovely canvas for the mahogany four poster bed, deep ruby velvet down-stuffed club chair and ottoman, soft cream sofa, gilt mirrors, and carved mantle. A wall of shelves hold TV, VCR and stereo with an accompanying bevy of remote controls. Just a step outside is a small lattice-enclosed private brick terrace. Lee would be pleased, but this giant of few words would not have let on.

Owned since 1983 by Ted and Estelle Mackey, this apex of the antebellum South has twenty guest bedrooms and suites, all of which are furnished with incredible period antiques, many original to the home. Born in Mississippi and expatriated for some time, Ted felt the pull of Mississippi mud. Looking at many antebellum mansions and houses in search of an indefinable something, they finally found it in Cedar Grove. As Estelle recalls, "It really needed us. The others didn't." And its past was undeniably fascinating.

I'm quartered in the capacious Klein Suite. I rattle around in this two room auctioneer's paradise admiring the nine foot mirrored armoires, a carved walnut bed with tasseled half canopy, marble topped empire tables and not one but two of the fifteen marble mantles the Kleins had shipped from their European honeymoon. Echoes of the past. Dusky shades of pink carpet, walls, and fourteen foot draperies provide a charming pastel setting which was the height of antebellum fashion. The suite opens onto a long second story porch with lots of chintz cushioned white wicker chairs and sofas for quietly admiring the view over the lawns.

I rattle around in this two room auctioneer's paradise admiring the nine foot mirrored armoires, a carved walnut bed with tasseled half canopy, marble topped empire tables.

Waking up early I pop downstairs for the early riser's coffee put out at 7:00 AM. It's comfortably warm outside, perfect for a pre-breakfast stroll in the gardens on brick paths that wander through red calla lilies, weeping willows and fifteen foot fuchsia crepe myrtles. Just to the side of the "big house" is an azure blue pool set in a patio of brick. A burgeoning orange blossoming trumpet vine spills over a wall. At each of the pool's four corners are lion fountains providing a gentle splash of water. The poolhouse, which houses two accommodations, was the kitchen in days gone by, placed away from the house because of the risk of fire. A nine-foot-deep brick fish pond on the other side of the mansion kept fresh catfish for the family dinner table. Time for breakfast.

I bank on having one of my favorites, grits. I understand that my strong Alabama-bred grits attraction may be unfathomable to some. Grits lovers will understand such devotion. Cedar Grove does not disappoint me. They appear on my breakfast plate, cheese anointed, along side scrambled eggs, sausage and real Southern biscuits. Yes, ma'am, that's breakfast. I clean that plate just in time for the house tour.

My guide is a Southern lady who is a marvel of Cedar Grove details. From the "million dollar piano," one of only 100 made by the parent company of Kimball for the

1876 centennial, to a low level petticoat mirror made to "see if it's snowing down south." Royalty were not only popular subjects for parlor paintings if you pretended to any social status at all, they also functioned as utilitarian curtain tiebacks in the form of brass replicas of Queen Victoria's hand. Intricate ceilings were made from plaster thickened with horsehair, sugar, molasses, Spanish moss and slave labor. A faded wedding invitation of the Klein's eldest daughter Susan is framed on the wall with the date May 7, 1872. Her beloved bridegroom was killed two short years later while attending a duel. Susan and her niece sold this house with most of its furnishings in 1919 for just over $9,000.

A SOUTHERN STROLL

Just down Washington Street a few blocks is main drag Vicksburg. Stop in at the Biedenharn Candy Co. Museum, where they first bottled the "ideal brain tonic," Coca-Cola. Four years after a Coke salesman plunked down a 5 gallon keg of cola syrup in 1890, candy merchant Biedenharn figured the stuff sold so well at the soda fountain, why not bottle and sell it in the countryside? The rest is soda history, documented with loads of Coke memorabilia through the years, a testament to successful marketing. Biedenhern sent his first two cases to then Coke president Asa Candler. Candler wrote back that it was "just fine," but Biedenharn recalled later, "You know, he never returned my bottles."

But the real draw to Vicksburg is the 1,858-acre Vicksburg National Military Park. One of the best preserved of all the Civil War battlefields, it is sobering to visit where 17,000 Union soldiers are buried, row after row. These green rolling lawns commemorate just one battle where far too many young men lost their lives in our nation's bloodiest war. Confederate men are buried in the Vicksburg city cemetery outside the park. Written on a monument, "Ours the fate of the vanquished, whose heartaches will never cease. Ours the tears, regrets and tears, theirs the eternal peace." No, wars like this one are not soon forgotten.

At the Old Courthouse, now a museum, Federal soldiers jubilantly lowered the Confederate flag and raised the Union banner on July 4, 1863. Grant then reviewed his victorious army. The museum is a treasure trove for Civil War buffs, stuffed with pictures, flags, uniforms, guns, ammunition and great stories. One is that of the reunion of Confederate and Union soldiers in 1917 labeled the "Peace Jubilee," but by nightfall arguing and fighting had broken out between the old men and the gathering became better known as the "battle of the walking sticks."

To get a real sense of the power and grandeur of the mighty Mississippi, take a river cruise in the late afternoon. The largest body of water in the country, 500 million gallons of water per *second* flow under the bridge far above that links Mississippi and Louisiana, along with you . Glittering casinos at the water's edge, a fairly recent addition along the Mississippi, are well within the riverboat tradition. These are juxtaposed against barges loaded with inky black coal, fishermen checking their live wells for catfish, and an occasional white heron looking for dinner. As am I.

"Ours the fate of the vanquished, whose heartaches will never cease. Ours the tears, regrets and tears, theirs the eternal peace." No, wars like this one are not soon forgotten.

VITTLES AMIDST FLORA

The Garden Room is a fitting name for the restaurant. Massive windows overlook gardens and fountains. "This was the smokehouse, "Ted explains, "and it looked just awful. The entire ceiling was caved in." Estelle agrees, saying, "I wouldn't set foot in it!"

But better times have many guests happily setting foot and opening mouth in the old smokehouse cum Garden Room to eat uptown Southern vittles that I doubt the Kleins ever witnessed. Spicy jambalaya, tender baby back ribs or barbecue-blackened shrimp might start your meal at a beautifully set table. Then choose from grilled salmon with capers and Hollandaise, blackened prime rib, or savory General Grant catfish, grilled and topped with garlic, capers and grapes. For dessert, you must order the brandy bread pudding. Light, fluffy and soooo yummy that it's almost a digestive. "Don't scrape your plate Scarlett, there's more in the kitchen."

BLOOD IS THICKER THAN...

I haven't told you what happened to the Kleins during the Vicksburg siege. As luck would have it, they weren't home. The family had been removed in a timely fashion to a plantation east of the action. After the siege was over they returned home to a mansion almost completely unharmed by the Federal occupation. With them was their new baby named after Elizabeth's first cousin, a man who was no stranger to fiery Southern nights. The infant was christened *William Sherman* Klein.

For dessert, you must order the brandy bread pudding. Light, fluffy and soooo yummy that it's almost a digestive. "Don't scrape your plate Scarlett, there's more in the kitchen."

GRACIOUS COUNTRY INNS

ANDRE JAMBALAYA

2 lbs. chicken pieces
½ teaspoon cayenne pepper
1 tablespoons olive oil
8 oz. smoked sausage (andouille or kielbasa) cut
   in ¼ inch slices
1 medium onion, chopped
1 medium bell pepper, seeded and chopped
1 stalk celery, sliced
3 garlic cloves, minced
1 teaspoon dried thyme
1 cup long-grain rice
1 16 oz. can whole tomatoes in juice
1 cup fish stock or bottled clam juice
½ to 1 cup water
1 bay leaf
½ lb. medium shrimp, shelled and deveined
4 green onions, sliced thin
½ teaspoon Tabasco, or to taste

1. Pat chicken dry. Sprinkle on all sides with cayenne. Heat oil on medium heat in a large pan. Add chicken and cook for 4 minutes on each side until browned, in batches if necessary.

2. Add the sausage and cook, stirring occasionally for about three minutes until it begins to brown.

3. Remove chicken and sausage, leaving any liquid in pan. Add the onions, bell peppers, celery and garlic to same pan and cook, stirring frequently for 3 to 4 minutes until vegetables begin to soften.

4. Add thyme and rice, stirring until rice is coated with oil.

5. Add the tomatoes with juice breaking them up with a spoon. Also stir in fish stock, ½ cup water and bay leaf. Add chicken and sausage back into pan.

6. Bring mixture to simmer over medium high heat. Reduce heat to low and cook covered for 15 minutes.

7. Place shrimps on top of rice and press in lightly. Cook covered for 15 minutes more or until chicken and rice are tender and liquid is absorbed. (If rice has absorbed all of liquid before it is tender, add up to ½ cup more water and cook a few minutes longer.)

8. Remove skillet from heat. Stir in green onions and season with hot pepper sauce to taste.

Serves four.

CEDAR GROVE BOURBON RIBS

4 lbs. beef or pork ribs

SAUCE:

1 medium onion
½ cup light molasses
½ cup ketchup
1 tablespoons orange peel
⅓ cup orange juice
2 tablespoons olive oil
1 tablespoon vinegar
1 tablespoon steak sauce
½ teaspoon prepared mustard
½ teaspoon Worcestershire sauce
¼ teaspoon garlic powder
¼ teaspoon salt
¼ teaspoon pepper
¼ teaspoon Tabasco
⅛ teaspoon ground cloves
¼ cup bourbon

1. Place ribs in a large Dutch oven of saucepan; add water to cover. Bring to a boil and reduce heat. Simmer uncovered 45–50 minutes or until ribs are tender. Remove and drain thoroughly. (*This can be done earlier in the day or up to several days before and refrigerated.*)

2. Combine all sauce ingredients in a saucepan. Bring to a boil and simmer gently uncovered for 15–20 minutes. (*The sauce can also be prepared in advance. It will keep indefinitely in the refrigerator.*)

3. Heat the grill and cook the ribs over slow coals about 45 minutes. Turn every 15 minutes and baste with sauce.

4. Serve ribs with extra sauce.

Serve 4–6.

CEDAR GROVE ORANGE GLAZED SOUTHERN HEN

2 Cornish game hens
¼ cup butter, melted
1 6-oz package long grain and wild rice mixture
1 4-oz. can chopped mushrooms
¼ cup orange peel, cut into julienne strips
3½ tablespoons light brown sugar
2¼ tablespoons corn starch
⅔ cup water
¾ cup orange juice
¼ teaspoon salt
1½ tablespoons brandy

1. Rinse hens and pat dry. Brush with butter and salt. Bake at 350 degrees for one hour, brushing with more butter halfway through cooking.

2. While hens are cooking, cook rice according to package directions. When rice in cooked, stir in mushrooms. Keep warm.

3. Simmer orange peel in ½ cup water in saucepan for 15 minutes. Drain well and set aside.

4. In another saucepan, combine brown sugar and corn starch. Blend in water and orange juice. Cook and stir over low heat until thickened, 2–3 minutes. Remove from heat and stir in orange peel and brandy.

5. Arrange hens on a platter and cover with sauce. Serve over the rice.

Serves two.

CEDAR GROVE MINT JULEP

Several mint sprigs, saving one for garnish
1 oz. bourbon
¼ teaspoon sugar
crushed ice

1. Crush the mint with a mortar and pestle.

2. Add the sugar and a sprinkle of water to make a sweet mint syrup.

3. Pour the syrup into a chilled julep cup. Add the bourbon and crushed ice.

4. Garnish with a mint sprig.

Serves one.

In the Garden Room, meals are begun with hot bread and a bottle of Andre's herb-infused olive oil. The waiter pours a puddle on the plate and adds fresh parmesan cheese.

Great bread dipping!

High Hampton Inn and Country Club

CASHIERS, NORTH CAROLINA

Are there still places where people say "Yes Sir" and "No Ma'am"? Where the gentlemen still stand up when a lady comes into the room, and families still eat fried chicken for Sunday dinner, with homemade biscuits? They do at High Hampton in Cashiers, North Carolina. And a marvelous way of life it is. Slower, gentler, and with a true appreciation for the finer things in life.

OLD SOUTH

That has always been true at High Hampton, tucked away in the Blue Ridge Mountains, just outside the little town of Cashiers in western North Carolina. This property was owned in the 1800s by the family of General Wade Hampton, the Confederate "Giant in Gray" and a man who did not personally favor secession. (Trivia fact: In the book "Gone with the Wind," Scarlett named her son after Wade Hampton.)

After the Civil War, the Hamptons lost their fortune and other homes, so they decamped to the mountain estate where there were vegetables and game to eat. No one went hungry. Gen. Hampton wrote to a sister-in-law, "We can live very cheaply there and you will come back in the fall as stout as Mrs. Floyd, as you will live on venison, pheasants, and trout."

After the Civil War, the Hamptons lost their fortune and other homes, so they all decamped to the mountain estate where there were plenty of vegetables and game to eat.

The General had a niece named Caroline, who went to Baltimore to earn her way as a nurse at Johns Hopkins Hospital. A famous surgeon by the name of William Stewart Halsted, who invented surgical gloves (for Caroline's delicate hands), fell in love with the fair Caroline. She took him home to North Carolina for their honeymoon, and he too fell under the spell of the Blue Ridge Mountains, so much so that he bought the Hampton homestead from Caroline's two surviving aunts.

Here they would spend their summers, Dr. Halsted traveling back and forth to Baltimore, while Caroline stayed until Thanksgiving. Their dahlia beds became famous, and they planted exotic trees and flowering bushes from all over the world, many of which flourish today. At Christmas time, the Halsteds would send bags of potatoes, apples and cured hams from High Hampton to their friends.

The main lodge sits on 1,400 of the most beautiful acres ever created. From the windows of the lodge, Rock Mountain and Chimney Mountain jut up over 4 thousand feet into the blue North Carolina skies. Hampton Lake is 40 acres of clear, cool waters. It is springfed and great for fishing, boating and swimming. The bright green lawns are dotted with towering specimens of those rare trees planted long ago by Dr. Halsted; the famous Halsted dahlia gardens still bloom 4 to 5 feet tall from July to October. Feel free to pick a bouquet for your dining table.

That long tradition of hospitality continued into 1922, when the property was bought by the McKee family, who own it today. The McKees added the lodge in 1933, the only resort in the country built during the depression's dark days. Cabins are scattered about the property, built like the main inn, of wormy chestnut with chestnut bark shingles on the exteriors. "You can't get these shingles any more," explains Will McKee. "Most American chestnut trees had been killed by a blight by the 1920s." The wormy chestnut comes from fallen trees whose trunks laid on the forest floor until worms had etched their pattern into the wood.

BY DESIGN

In the middle of the inn's great room stands a gigantic granite fireplace, twelve feet wide with a hearth on each of its four sides. One or all of these hearths will have cracking blazes going to chase off the chill of mountain air.

In the middle of the inn's great room stands a gigantic granite fireplace, twelve feet wide with a hearth on each of its four sides. The gray column rises fifteen feet into the ceiling. Most seasons, one or all of these hearths will have blazes cracking to chase off the chill of mountain air. Pine sofas, chairs and tables with fresh bouquets of rhododendrons and mountain laurel cluster around the striking hearths. Simple but comfortable. This is also the room where you find early morning coffee, then tea and pastries in the afternoon, and where guests chat over a cup of soup before suppertime. On the wall is a list of the guests' bird sightings over the years. There have been hooded mergansers, green-winged teals, Canada geese, white ibis, the great blue heron, marsh hawks, wild turkeys, bluebirds, and a Peregrine falcon was seen in 1992 by Will McKee. Across the room is the check-in desk, looking for all the world like a scene from an old Bogart movie.

You will be greeted with southern charm and courtesy by one of the staff members who will explain how meals work (coat and tie required at dinner, all meals buffet), explaining where everything is on the map (it is a large place), and lead you directly to your room or cottage.

In the main inn, there are two floors of rooms above the great room and dining room, perfect for those who may not wish to walk far for meals. An infinite variety of cottages overlook the lake and the renowned golf course designed by golf architect George W. Cobb. More about the course later.

The 130 rooms and cabins are so unique, describing them would take far too long. Most are very simple in design, serviceable and with their own definite charm, but not what one would call not plush. All the cottages have a deck or porch overlooking the lake or the lawns. Most are pine paneled, with pine furniture, pine framed mirrors, pine bathrooms, built-in reading lights over the beds made from, well, pine. Most cabins have fireplaces and handmade quilts from local artisans. Both are handy as the nights do get chilly. High Hampton's brochure says, "Over the years we've found that not everyone likes it here." Maybe, but that's kind of hard to imagine. With a cool mountain breeze flowing in the window at night, the crickets and frogs singing their songs, a fire crackling away, you can't picture a nicer place to be as you pull up that extra quilt.

The exception to the pine rule is the Honeymoon/Anniversary Cottage. Very private and nestled on a small pond, with a view of the golf course's 18th tee, the living room is done in crisp stripes, a cathedral ceiling, a sleeping loft (great for kids if you have 'em and care to bring 'em along on your honeymoon) and a cozy boudoir with a rustic, queen-sized bed below. There's a deck out back overlooking the water, and rockers on the front porch surrounded by mountain laurel.

Or there's the Log Cabin Cottage, a hand-hewn log cabin that belonged to Will McKee's aunt. It was dismantled in Dillsboro, North Carolina and reassembled here at High Hampton. With a fireplace, a sitting area, and two queen size beds with quilts, you won't stay in a place with more homey charm.

Yet if you're in the market for something more modern and upscale, they have that too. A number of beautifully decorated, privately owned 2, 3 and 4 bedroom homes are also available on the edge of the golf course. They have full kitchens, TV and maid service – all the required amenities.

JUST DO IT

But, what people really come to High Hampton for is outside, such as the golf course. Eighteen holes stretch through the hills and trees with beautiful views wherever you turn. There may be more difficult courses but surely few more enjoyable to play. The 8th green is a picturesque peninsula surrounded by Lake Hampton. As you might guess, there are enough golf balls dredged from the lake periodically to stock the driving range. You might enjoy the golf schools for both beginners and advanced players, and two senior golf tournaments per season.

Perhaps tennis is your game. High Hampton has six fast-dry clay tennis courts. The tennis pros offer private lessons, clinics and will arrange games and round robin mixers. For kids, there are free clinics twice a week.

One of the inn's most popular activities requires you to lace up those hiking boots and truck off onto miles of marked trails. You won't believe the variety of flowers seen in these forests. Bright orange wild azaleas, purple rhododendron, silver bells, trout lilies, ox-eye daisies, goat's beard, pink lady's-slipper, flowering raspberry, evening primrose and much more in bloom, depending on the season.

By far the most popular walks are to the top of Rock Mountain (4,370 ft. and an hour's walk), and Chimney Top (4,618 ft. and one and one half hour's hike). Escorted outings are scheduled weekly, and while you'll get a workout (let's not kid ourselves), the views of the valley below are worth the effort.

Casting a line for a chance at a prize bass or trout is also fun and no license is required. But please, be careful that you don't snag Mitch the Fish, a mega-granddaddy large mouth bass over two feet long. This is not likely to happen, as he is fed regularly by children and adults at his favorite hangout, the boathouse. His eyes boldly inquire about your worm supply, and he will happily dart halfway out of the water to have a bite. Watch your fingers!

Add to all this bird watching seminars, watercolor workshops for children and

With a cool mountain breeze flowing in the window at night, the crickets and frogs singing their songs, you can't picture a nicer place to be as you pull up that extra quilt.

adults, wildflower workshops, bridge tournaments, antique shows, outstanding summer children's and young adults' programs, and you come up with a place that has tremendous appeal for couples, families or anyone hoping for a change of pace.

DO GRITS GROW ON TREES?

When you first arrive at High Hampton you will be assigned your own table in the spacious pine paneled dining room, with multiple windows open to lawns, lake and the face of Rock Mountain. Light reflects off the polished wooden floor and tables are set with starched white linen. This table will be yours for the duration of your stay, which adds to the feeling of being at home. The menu is one of the reasons so many return time and again. Not at all fancy, but the kind of food lovingly called Southern home cookin'. Hampton fried chicken, rainbow trout, Hampton country ham, fried tomatoes, fresh creamed corn, green beans, hot cornbread and biscuits are among the delicacies that adorn the buffet table each evening, along with a salad bar and dessert table filled with many luscious sweets. Your head will spin! Lady Washburn chocolate cake, sweet potato cake, sunny silver pie, black bottom pie, blueberry pie. Don't bother trying to make a quick decision – it's impossible. So do as I did – take one of each. Wine and beer are available in the dining room, but mixed drinks are available only in the newly opened tavern from 6-10 PM.

For breakfast, grits. Always. That's the way it should be at High Hampton. If you've never tried them, now is the time. Seize the grits, scrambled eggs, fat little sausages, bacon, hot biscuits, hash browns (as a nod to those not from the South), all kinds of cereals and fresh fruit. A terrific way to start the day.

Lunch may be soups, sandwiches, sweet potato sticks (yummy), succotash, turkey with homemade cranberry sauce, layered salad, a shrimp stir-fry, french fries for the kids, fantastic barbecue, pork of course, and a variety of desserts to please the noon-time crowd.

FAMILY TRADITION

You will meet many guests who have been coming to High Hampton for 30 years and more. What most of them fear is that when they come next time, High Hampton will have been "modernized." But the McKee family is committed to preserving the original charm and feeling of this splendid inn. They have always understood that good things should remain the same.

The season at High Hampton ends with a Thanksgiving house party. You might arrive in time for a set of tennis or golf in anticipation of a traditional Thanksgiving feast. In addition to the turkey dinner, one night features a barbecue dinner cooked in the great stone fireplaces. Special events all weekend include a full children's program. What a way to spend your holiday, and no dishes!

Another welcome touch. No tipping, and no service charge is added to your bill. As they say, "It is our pleasure to serve you."

The menu is one of the reasons so many return time and again. Not at all fancy, but the kind of food lovingly called Southern home cookin'. Hampton fried chicken, rainbow trout, Hampton country ham, fried tomatoes, fresh creamed corn, green beans, hot cornbread and biscuits

HIGH HAMPTON OLD FASHIONED FRIED TOMATOES

I like using green tomatoes but you may use red ones (not too ripe). They may be layered in a casserole, frozen and reheated.

6 tomatoes
1/4 cup flour
Dash of pepper
1/4 cup dark brown sugar
1 teaspoon salt

   1. Slice tomatoes 1/4 inch thick.
   2. Dredge slices in combined flour, sugar, salt and pepper.
   3. Fry in bacon drippings (or olive oil if you're watching your cholesterol) over medium heat until a brown crust forms on tomato. Turn and brown on other side. Keep warm until served.
   Serves 8.

GRITS CASSEROLE

You knew I had to have at least one grits recipe in this collection. If you've never tried grits with cheese, please do this once, just for me. My other favorite way to serve grits is to cook them according to box directions, replacing water with cream. It is a dish worthy of the finest meal.

1 cup of quick grits
1 lb. grated sharp Cheddar cheese
1/2 lb. butter
3 eggs just beaten
1 teaspoon salt
Tabasco to taste.

   1. Cook grits according to box directions.
   2. Add the cheese, butter, eggs, salt and Tabasco. Pour mixture into buttered oven-proof casserole dish.
   3. Bake one hour in 300 degree oven until golden and set.
   Serves 8.

HIGH HAMPTON RAINBOW TROUT

It is said that a true gourmet never removes heads of delicious High Hampton trout. So leave 'em on.

4 rainbow trout
1–2 cups vegetable oil
flour for dredging
salt and pepper
lemon wedges

   1. Clean and thoroughly dry your trout. Sprinkle with salt and coarse pepper, then dust the trout with flour (outside only and not cavity).
   2. Pour vegetable oil into an electric fry pan and pre-heat until oil reaches temperature of 385 degrees. Oil must cover half of the fish.
   3. Lower trout into hot oil and cover. Cook this way for six to eight minutes.
   4. Turn with spatula being careful not to break the fish and finish cooking without cover. Drain on paper towels. Arrange on hot platter, garnish with parsley and lemon wedges.
   Serves 4.

HIGH HAMPTON SUNDAY FRIED CHICKEN

The thing that always bothered me about frying chicken was that it often burned before the thicker pieces cooked through. At High Hampton they know you wisely finish it in the oven so it's tender but never burned.

   1. Have chicken (or chickens) cut into quarters.
   2. Dip the quarters in Carnation Milk.
   3. Season a pan of flour with salt and pepper. Dip the chicken in this flour; roll the pieces around a bit.
   4. Fry in 1/4 inch of vegetable oil until nicely browned.
   5. Put chicken in pans with drip pans under them and put in slow oven (325 degrees) for an hour or so.

Serve with stewed corn, green beans, candied yams or rice for a down home southern meal.

HIGH HAMPTON VEGETABLE SOUP

Use a large covered cooking pot – this makes enough for about 20 servings. It's terrific on a cool fall day. This soup can be frozen in glass jars indefinitely.

2½ qt. water (½ water, ½ chicken stock
   if available)
1 beef soup bone
1 beef bouillon cube
2 lbs. cubed chuck beef, cut into bite size
1 chicken bouillon cube
1 tablespoon coarsely ground pepper

1. Bring to boil, then simmer for an hour.
2. Add all the following ingredients:
   2 # 2 cans tomatoes
   2 or 3 coarsely cut-up stalks of celery
   1 small package frozen okra
   2 diced onions
   1 two-lb. package frozen mixed vegetables
3. Simmer for 5 or 6 hours.
Serves 10.

HIGH HAMPTON INN SPANISH EGGPLANT

This dish reheats beautifully, and is even better the second day (and can be frozen). It always is served at High Hampton with roast beef.

2 good sized eggplants
1 cup of chopped onions
1 cup of chopped green peppers
2 small cans of stewed tomatoes, drained
½ cup of brown sugar
2 tablespoons Parmesan cheese
2 teaspoons fresh garlic

1. Peel, cube and parboil the eggplant in salted water until tender. Drain.
2. Add drained tomatoes to the eggplant. Season with sugar, cheese, salt, white pepper, and garlic.

3. Sauté onions and peppers in 1 tablespoon of butter or oil. Add the sautéed onions and pepper to the eggplant and tomatoes.
4. Place mixture into large oiled casserole; sprinkle with buttered bread crumbs and more Parmesan cheese. Bake until brown, about 20-25 minutes.
Serves 8.

SUNNY SILVER PIE

This is a favorite dessert at High Hampton and often appears on the groaning board of desserts there.

⅓ cup cold water
grated rind of 1 lemon
½ tablespoon of gelatin
1 cup sugar
4 eggs
pinch of salt
3 tablespoons lemon juice
1 cup whipping cream

1. Set gelatin to soak in ⅓ cup cold water.
2. Place the 4 egg yolks, lemon juice rind, and half cup of sugar in a rounded bottom enamel bowl. Set bowl in larger pan of boiling water. Keep boiling. Whip the egg mixture until it becomes quite firm and creamy.
3. When it reaches this stage, turn the heat down and fold in the gelatin. Remove from heat.
   In another bowl, beat the egg whites very stiff and combine with remaining ½ cup sugar. Then fold this into yolk mixture.
4. Pour the filling into a baked pie shell and set in refrigerator for at least 2 hours.
5. Whip cream stiff and spread over top of pie just before serving.
Makes 1 pie.

The Inn at Blackberry Farm

WALLAND, TENNESSEE

Walland, Tennessee. Gourmet food and sumptuous surroundings in the middle of that camping heaven we know as the Great Smoky Mountains? 'Tis true. Welcome to a world of Southern hospitality, grace and tradition. This is the Inn at Blackberry Farm, just south of Knoxville, and one of the latest lucky few to be tapped by the Parisian Relais and Chateaux group.

Some fifty years ago, a Chicago industrialist and his wife were combing the mountains for the perfect site for their country estate. While walking along this property of 1,100 acres, she snagged her silk stockings on a blackberry bramble, and that was the beginning of Blackberry Farm. They built the house of clapboard, stone and slate, and over the years entertained many blissful friends and relatives here. Happy for all of us, the tradition didn't stop there.

Today it is owned by Kreis and Sandy Beall, who not only appreciated the original beauty of the place, but have also transformed it into an elegant inn, furnished with antiques, paintings, flowers, and 25 bedrooms of exquisite details. But you feel as though you're a house-guest. "That's the way we planned it," says Kreis. "No money changes hands. We take a charge by phone before you come, and it's all handled without ever feeling as if you're in a hotel."

The main rooms are, quite simply, some of the most fetching rooms ever put together. Kreis lays the credit for the look of the inn at the feet of her mother, adding the inn was "done piece by piece, like a patchwork quilt." But Kreis' experience as a stylist at Southern Accents magazine shows in every room. Antiques came from all over the South, and the detail work done on each room, in each corner, is incredibly textured. An antique English chest stands out from a floral still-life in oils that hangs above a group of five silver vases of staggered height, each filled with roses, the signature flower at Blackberry. In the dining room, an intricately carved sideboard, ten feet long, is topped with two tall brass lamps and an antique quilt spilling out of a basket, with more dried roses and hydrangeas in front of an oil landscape. Behind glass on the wall, a silk and velvet crazy quilt made in 1886 by Lula Potts (a relative of Sandy Beall), with which she won first prize in New Orleans. Twenty feet of oak English boys' school table now holds a cascading fresh flower arrangement of wild roses and blackberry blooms, daisies, wild azaleas, yarrow and large pink roses. It is obvious that flowers are Kreis' passion.

The main house, enlarged in 1990, contains the original nine room structure. Kreis explains, "Our main corporate client had grown beyond what we could give them, so we just took a huge leap and enlarged the inn from 9 to 25 bedrooms, and built the guest house in the process." The original rooms serve the same functions as days gone by, although the present day library was once the family dining room, and the Teaberry Room upstairs, now a favorite guest bedroom, was once the upstairs living room.

The main house contains twelve bedrooms. Each has its own wildflower moniker: Lenten Rose, large and overlooking the woods; Hearts-a-Bustin, in blues overlooking the lawn and mountains; Passion Flower, with two queen size featherbeds. These three bedrooms are part of the Cardinal Suite, which has its own living room. Perfect for family gatherings, the bedrooms may be rented separately or as a group. Lady's Slipper, Fire Pink, Jack in the Pulpit, Dutchman's Pipe, Trillium. Each room is individual, each perfect with fat fluffy draperies you might see in an English country estate. To get just that look, Kreis had the curtains lined, and then interlined again with flannel. Effort and expense, yes but, the effect is one that draws closer inspection from guests wanting *just that look* at home.

Kreis says that when they planned the guest house expansion, they took the dimensions of the main house living room and duplicated it exactly. "We wanted people to feel just as at home in the guest house, to feel as though there's no discernible difference." Indeed, you'll be amazed to learn the guest house is a recent structure, as it seems to have always been there, with a weathered appearance and moss growing on the slate roof. It has a slate foyer, large sofas with down pillows, a television, stacks of colorful quilts, books, magazines and its own bar.

You may want to choose the Gate House or the Farm House if you need more room for a special gathering. The Gate House consists of a living room, kitchenette, and two bedrooms with king size featherbeds. The Farm House has three bedrooms and baths, cozy country-elegant living and dining room with a brick fireplace open to both rooms. Two verandas with rockers and porch swings encourage you to sit a spell.

One of the many ways Kreis makes you feel at home is the pantry areas tucked behind the library in the main house and just off the entrance in the guest house. You'll find a supply of bottled waters, soft drinks, juices and snacks. Peek inside the freezer. In the frosty depths are caches of ice cream treats – Dove Bars, Snickers and other goodies to tempt your willpower in the middle of the night. If the chocolate covered banana chips don't get you, there is always fresh fruit for those pure of flesh.

Each room is individual, each perfect with fat fluffy draperies you might see in an English country estate. Kreis had the curtains lined, and then interlined again with flannel.

Eleven more bedrooms grace the guest house. Mine was Fire Pink, a corner room with a large bank of windows, and its own little private slate terrace surrounded by evergreens. You too, will find it most difficult to arise from the feather beds and down comforters. But the Whip-Poor-Will is calling its tune, and the sun is up over the Smokies. Hot coffee has been brought in insulated carafes for early risers to enjoy out in the rockers on the terrace. Now you see why this mountain range got its name. The hills appear truly smoky, and the sun is beautiful rising through that ever present mist. Go for an early morning walk or run the 3 mile paved path along a nature trail, or pedal off on one of the 20 Schwinn 10-speed bikes provided for guests. Now you're ready for a big Southern breakfast!

FOOTHILLS CUISINE

Hot cornmeal pudding with maple cream cheese, homemade grain and nut cereal, blueberry-cornmeal, buckwheat or sourdough griddlecakes with honey pecan butter, eggs any way you like 'em, plus country ham or bacon await you in the dining room. You might choose to have a continental breakfast delivered to your room instead. Just ask.

The food at Blackberry Farm is an important part of the "Blackberry" experience. The chef has developed a set menu each night called "foothills cuisine." Kreis is also a food perfectionist. "We're part of the mountains and want our food to reflect that regional influence, but our guests are also sophisticated travelers who expect a certain dining experience." Thus urbane-Southern dishes such as ham hock consommé with corn and buckwheat ravioli, wild spring greens with ramp (a mountain grown wild onion) vinaigrette, peanut-crusted rack of lamb with mint pesto, buttermilk whipped potatoes, asparagus and morels, and a homemade "moonpie" with pistachio brownie and white chocolate ice cream. That particular dessert brought down the house in New York City at the James Beard Foundation's dinner called "Springtime in the Smokies." At the Blackberry, they succeed at making their food uptown chic and down-home fun!

Remember that Walland, Tennessee is in a dry county. That means no alcoholic beverages may be sold at the inn. So you may bring your own wine, beer, champagne or liquor. They will be stored for you in the pantry areas, labeled for identification and refrigerated if need be. Bring your wine selection with you to dinner.

Every evening, as your room is turned down and curtains drawn, a list of the next day's available activities is left for your perusal. Guided nature hikes with resident expert Paul Gamble, fly-fishing lessons, a bird watching expedition, afternoon tea, or hot chocolate and cider at a bonfire by the pool depend only on your energy level.

The Trunk Branch Trail provides access to the National Park trail system. Walking sticks, binoculars, and nature books are ready for any adventure you may have in mind.

STUMBLIN' AROUND

Don't miss the nature hikes. Paul Gamble is a soft-spoken native of the Tennessee foothills and he knows more about the wildflowers (Lady-Slippers, Trilliums, Fire Pinks, and Jack-in-the Pulpit) and history of the area than can be begun here. He is also an avid collector of Native American artifacts, which he stumbles across every now and again in his explorations. He will eagerly let you handle arrowheads found in the streambeds and the rare corn grinders or hammer heads carved from stone. Those are from the Cherokee tribes who lived in this area long before the hardy mountain people set up camp and carved a living from this lovely but difficult land. The Nature Trail that begins at the inn will also lead you past the beginning of the Trunk Branch Trail in the nature preserve of the same name. The Trunk Branch Trail provides access to the National Park trail system. Walking sticks, binoculars and nature books are ready for any adventure you may have in mind.

Obviously, the inn is just a few miles from the Great Smoky Mountain National Park, all 687.5 square miles of it. This unspoiled wilderness is the sixth largest national park in the country, with 1,500 kinds of flowering plants and miles of hiking and horse trails.

For bicyclists or motorists, take a leisurely trip through green, leafy Cades Cove. The eleven-mile loop takes you through gorgeous Smokies countryside with restored historic log cabins and barns and an old mill. Here you're also quite likely to see a variety of wildlife, including deer, beaver and even a bear or two. The park advises that bears are potentially dangerous and that if one approaches your car, stay inside with the windows closed. Do not feed them.

The Foothills Parkway, located right by Blackberry Farm, is a scenic drive that offers spectacular views of the mountains. Along the way is an observation tower for the real bird's-eye vista.

The inn has four tennis courts and an outdoor heated pool located by the guest house. Or you might cast a line for a trophy-sized trout in the Singing Brook trout pond. If catfish or bass are more to your taste, Old Walland Pond awaits. Where do you find racquets, balls, fishing equipment, life jackets and the like? Why in the "toy closet," of course.

Four 18-hole golf courses are within 30 minutes of Blackberry Farm. Horseback riding can be arranged at a nearby stable and of course, swimming when in season at the heated pool. During a cool morning dip, the steam rolls off the pool, and with the sun coming up over the Smokies, it is an unforgettable, some might say spiritual, experience.

The staff at the Inn at Blackberry Farm is young, able, extremely polite, and very eager to please. The farm's brochure says they are delighted to assist with any of your needs, and they mean it. Southern hospitality is hard to beat.

The 11-mile loop takes you through gorgeous Smokies countryside, with restored historic log cabins and barns and an old mill. Here you're also quite likely to see a variety of wildlife, including deer, beaver, and even a bear or two.

GRACIOUS COUNTRY INNS

CORNMEAL AND SPICE BLACKBERRY COBBLER

It would not be Blackberry Farm without a twist on the traditional summer celebration with Blackberry Cobbler. They serve it with bourbon sabayon, but ice cream will always work.

6 cups fresh blackberries
1½ cups sugar
¼ cup brown sugar
zest of 1 lemon finely chopped
1 teaspoon cinnamon
1 teaspoon nutmeg
1½ tablespoon cornstarch
1 tablespoon dark rum

Toss blackberries with remainder of first seven ingredients. Place in lightly greased 9×13-inch baking dish.

5 oz. butter
1½ cups confectioners sugar
3 eggs
2¼ cups buttermilk
1 ½ cups all purpose flour
1 ½ cups masa harina corn flour
1 cup cornmeal
2 tablespoons baking powder
1 teaspoon baking soda
½ teaspoon ground cloves

1. For cobbler topping, cream the butter and confectioners sugar together until light and fluffy. Add the eggs one at a time. Continue to cream eggs, butter and confectioners sugar together until well aerated.
2. Sift together dry ingredients. On slow speed of mixer add dry ingredients into butter mixture alternating with buttermilk.
3. Put batter into a piping bag with a straight tip. Pipe a border around the edge of the baking dish and then pipe the remainder of the batter in a lattice pattern on top of the blackberries.
4. Bake in a 350 degree oven for 25–30 minutes until blackberries are bubbling and crust is lightly browned. Let cool slightly before serving.
Serves 8.

CORNMEAL BREADED TROUT WITH COUNTRY HAM AND HOMINY HASH

Traditional Southern ingredients and preparation meet in this colorful Sunday brunch dish. Typically, the inn accompanies this pair with a poached egg and a lightly dressed salad of watercress. Blackberry Farm presents the hominy hash flowing out of the belly flaps of the trout.

4 8-oz. trout, bones removed, head on
1 cup buttermilk
1 cup cornmeal
1 cup flour
1 tablespoon Old Bay Seasoning
1 tablespoon onion powder
1 teaspoon celery salt

1. Combine cornmeal, flour, Old Bay, onion powder and celery salt to form breading mixture.
2. Dip trout in buttermilk then dredge in breading mixture. Shake trout lightly to remove excess breading.
3. To sauté, brown both sides of trout in clarified butter for one minute.
4. Finish cooking in 350 degree oven for approximately 6 minutes.

2 potatoes, peeled, diced, blanched until tender
1 medium onion, diced
½ cup celery, diced
¼ lb. country ham, diced
1 red pepper, diced
1 green pepper, diced
2 teaspoon jalapeno pepper, finely chopped
1 tablespoon parsley, chopped
1 tablespoon chives, chopped
2 cups canned hominy, drained
1 teaspoon kosher salt
½ teaspoon freshly cracked black pepper

1. For hash, heat pan until almost smoking with clarified butter. Add cooked potatoes and sauté until browned and crisp.
2. Add onions, celery, country ham and peppers; sauté until tender.
3. Add hominy, chives, parsley, salt, pepper. Sauté for one minute. Taste and adjust seasoning. Adjust spiciness to taste with jalapeno peppers or cracked black pepper.
Serves 4

BANANA PUDDING CHEESECAKE

This dessert is a good example of combining the familiar with the new in the Blackberry kitchen. Bananas, sour cream and vanilla wafers are a classic combination (at least in the South). The inn has turned this combination into a cheesecake. They serve it with a warm caramel sauce, but whipped cream would be nice too.

CRUST

3 cups vanilla wafer crumbs
¼ cup blanched hazelnuts
½ cup sugar
½ cup melted butter

1. Combine crumbs, hazelnuts and sugar in a food processor. Process until nuts are crumbed. Stir in melted butter.
2. Press mixture into a 9 inch springform pan covering the bottom and side of the pan.
3. Brown in a 350 degree oven for 5 minutes.

GANACHE

4 oz. bittersweet chocolate, chopped
4 oz. heavy cream

1. Bring cream to a simmer pour over chocolate and stir until melted together.
2. Pour ganache into bottom of browned crust. Spread evenly.
3. Place in refrigerator until set.

FILLING

2 cups sour cream
1 lb. cream cheese
1¼ cups sugar
3 eggs
2 egg yolks
2 teaspoon vanilla extract
¼ cup banana liqueur
1 Tablespoon crème de caco liqueur
¼ teaspoon salt
2 cups puréed ripe bananas (about 4) mixed
  with 3 Tablespoon of lemon juice

1. Combine sour cream, cream cheese, and sugar in mixer. Cream until smooth. Add eggs and yolks one at time. Add vanilla and liqueurs. Add 1½ cups banana purée mixture.
2. Pour filling mixture into chilled crust. Put dollops of banana purée on top of filling then swirl with a wooden skewer or a thin knife.
3. Wrap the bottom of the springform pan in aluminum foil so that water cannot leak in.
4. Bake at 350 degrees in a hot water bath for 1 hour. Turn off oven and let sit for 1 hour.
5. Remove from oven, cool to room temperature then refrigerate for at least 3 hours. Call me when it's suppertime.

Serves 12.

BLACK WALNUT VINAIGRETTE

In the winter black walnuts are an abundant and flavorful resource in the foothills. They have a more distinctive flavor than the more common English walnuts and make the kitchen smell great when they are roasting. We compose a salad of Romaine lettuce hearts, crisp Tennessee bacon, apples, roasted shallots and this vinaigrette. The vinaigrette makes a perfect accompaniment for many other winter time salads, especially those including winter fruits and sweet winter root vegetables like carrots and beets.

2 Tablespoon malt vinegar
2 teaspoon fresh rosemary, chopped or 1 tsp.
  dried rosemary
¾ cup apple cider vinegar
2 teaspoon. Dijon mustard
½ teaspoon freshly cracked black pepper
1 teaspoon salt
½ cup walnut oil
1½ cup vegetable oil
¾ cup toasted black walnuts, chopped

1. Bring malt vinegar and rosemary to a simmer, let stand 5 minutes. Cool.
2. Whisk malt vinegar rosemary mixture together with cider vinegar, mustard, pepper and salt. Slowly whisk in the walnut and vegetable oil.
3. Chop black walnuts. Toast for 5 minutes in a 350 degree oven. Add to vinaigrette while still warm.

Makes 3 cups.

Little Palm Island
LITTLE TORCH KEY, FLORIDA

To those of you who say there is no true tropical paradise to be found on the United States mainland, I say to you: Little Palm Island. From the moment you step from the private launch onto the weathered wooden dock, and that is the only way one *can* arrive, you will be coddled, cosseted, petted and generally spoiled rotten in lush, South Pacific-like surroundings just north of Key West. Sound good? You better believe it is.

The breezes are balmy, the sun blindingly brilliant when greeted by a staff member as you alight from the launch. You are immediately taken under a friendly wing and whisked off to be shown your accommodations, make dinner reservations, and generally get your bearings at this 4-star, 4-diamond, Relais and Chateaux gem of a resort.

THATCHED LUXURY

You will be staying in one of fourteen thatched-roof villas, each containing two suites, all suitably sybaritic. Done in pastel sunset shades, all have sitting rooms with comfortable sofas and chairs while the baths feature handmade tiles and a spacious two-person tub. And, while you will no doubt enjoy a bubble bath soak, even more hedonistic is the outside shower on the other side of your bathroom door. With a large pink conch shell on the wall to hold your coconut soap, your shower is surrounded by a bamboo curtain, just dense enough where you can peek out, but they can't peek in. A word to the wise: don't lock the bathroom door behind you, or the only way back in is

Even more hedonistic is the outside shower on the other side of your bathroom door. With a large pink conch shell on the wall to hold your coconut soap, your shower is surrounded by a bamboo curtain.

through the front door. I know. A special mention for the wonderfully exotic mango-coconut toiletries and sun products. Little Palm had them custom blended just for the resort. You won't find them anywhere else. Too bad.

Inside the bedroom, romance was obviously on the mind of the designer. King-size beds are surrounded by mosquito netting that cascades down from the palm thatched ceiling. A ceiling fan circles high above, but the breezes that come in via louvered walls will probably be all you desire. On a hot day, close the louvers, turn on the air conditioning and you're the boss of all you see, including the climate. To keep your experience far from the jarring jangle of modern life, televisions and telephones are verboten in the rooms. And the staff discourages the use of cellular phones.

RISE AND DINE

You awaken to the revelry and rejoicing of the Little Palm birds and decide not to have breakfast here in your room, but in the restaurant. Walking there by way of the pier on the back side of the island, you might see the most beautiful long-legged white crane fishing for his breakfast not 20 feet away. He makes his way gracefully into the mangroves, an odd tropical specimen that grows only in salty ocean water. Sending down roots from its branches, the mangrove has the peculiar look of being on stilts and were the actual beginning of Little Torch Key. As more and more soil gathers in the roots at the edges of the island, the key continues slowly growing. Interesting way to add to your property. On you go through the blooming magenta bougainvillaea, pink oleander and crimson hibiscus. Turn left at the little sign that points the way to Cuba, some 90 miles away, and there you are – food.

The restaurant is open air, with the view of blue waters from any table. Today the temperature is about 75 degrees on the veranda, and the gentle breezes rustle through 80 foot tall palm fronds. Hmmmm. Perhaps a French omelette with sautéed shallots, fresh herbs, scallions and Brie? Eggs Benedict or a Louisiana omelette with diced tasso ham, jalapenos and smoked mozzarella are also tempting. In the end my waitress delivers frothy bittersweet cappuccino and inch-thick French toast topped with toasted coconut and a little pitcher of warm maple syrup. This is the good life.

TRUE ROMANCE

Since 1988, the Little Palm experience is the vision of tall, suave Southerner Ben Woodson and his partners. He explains that when folks come here, they are seekers of romance. "This is a true romantic hideaway, with nothing to do but lay on the hammock (all twenty-six of them), or by the pool, or on the beach. The most strenuous exercise is a body massage." All activities are, indeed, off the island proper.

For snorkelers or scuba divers famous Looe Key Reef is right in your backyard, so to speak. Voted one of the "top ten dive spots in the world" by *Skin Diver* Magazine, this magnificent reef is perfect for beginners or advanced divers, with crystal waters ranging in depth from 6 inches to 35 feet. The most startling assortment of sapphire, canary and vivid red fish of every size and description give you mildly interested looks, but continue on their way through the ghostly white coral, which you have been duly warned is protected by law. Anyone caught damaging this living treasure will be fined. Just don't put your flippers down, keep your hands to yourself, and all will be well.

Key West tours, deep sea fishing, island nature excursions, sea plane tours, sunset sails, and backcountry fishing can also be yours, if you tire of being "horizontal."

You might see the most beautiful long-legged white crane fishing for his breakfast not 20 feet away. He makes his way gracefully into the mangroves, an odd tropical specimen that grows only in salty ocean water.

WHERE'S THE PRESIDENT?

Just a bit of the island's history. To use a telephone on Little Palm, you must walk to "Truman's Outhouse." Really. This little wooden hut used to be the only "facility" on the island, back in the days when Little Torch Key was a favorite angling retreat for Presidents Franklin D. Roosevelt and Harry Truman. President Truman kept the "little White House" in Key West, and dropping off his bags, he would head straight to the simple fishing camp built here in 1921, happily spending days fishing for the tarpon, bone-fish and various bill fish that frequent these waters.

And if you've ever seen the film "PT 109," based on the President John F. Kennedy's South Pacific WW II escapades, Little Torch was selected as the filming site because of its towering palms. The story goes that during filming, President Kennedy and his father Joseph came to witness movie magic and movie stars in action. Papa Joe insisted that power lines be run to the island, so that the President could get his sleep without the annoying sound of the generators. Voilà!—electricity. Little Torch is still today the only out island with power.

SLAVE TO INDULGENCE

Afternoons at Little Palm's beach may spoil you a bit for other beaches. The service on the sand is up to the exacting standards elsewhere on the island. Relaxing on your padded chaise, you have a mild craving for a piña colada, a "Slumber Gumby" (the bartender's specialty coconut drink), or perhaps pan-seared grouper on greens with red onion-grapefruit vinaigrette (these cravings do happen), maybe gourmet lettuce topped with fresh buffalo mozzarella and julienne of smoked salmon (now you're talking). All one must do is hoist the little pink flag by your side and any or all of it is yours.

The cuisine here at Little Palm is unique and exotically soulful. French, with unique Caribbean twists and ingredients, the menu makes for delectably difficult decisions. Maine lobster salad with mango and passion fruit salsa. Grilled peppered tuna loin carpaccio. Marinated sirloin with a fondue of leek and sautéed wild mushrooms with seared duck foie gras. Grilled veal chop with stone crab fritters and yellow tomato coulis. Chocolate ravioli stuffed with coconut cream and praline sauce. A trio of tropical fruit sorbets. Take my advice and dine at sunset, at a table right on the sand. You will always be grateful to me.

Walking back to your villa in the quiet of the evening, you may happen upon the tiny Key Deer that wade over from the next door key on low tides or swim over on high tides. In danger of extinction in the mid '70s, the three foot tall cuties are now a protected species and guests love them. Only the chef has mixed feelings about the island mascots, as the Key deer love nothing more than to munch on his carefully tended herb garden, showing little remorse for the crime.

Little Palm receives many famous guests longing for peace and quiet. They find it here. Ben Woodson told me of a week long respite by reporter and anchor Charles Kurault, who has spent more than his share of time "on the road." Departing, he looked back and said in that familiar molasses-gravel voice, "I've never gone back to anyplace, but I'm coming back to Little Palm." Just another rotten day in paradise.

To use a telephone on the island, you must walk to "Truman's Outhouse." Really. This little wooden hut used to be the only "facility" on the island, when Little Torch Key was a favorite angling retreat for Presidents Franklin D. Roosevelt and Harry Truman.

COCONUT SORBET WITH GRILLED TROPICAL FRUITS ON MANGO COULIS

Light yet luscious, this dessert. The tropical flavors of coconut and mango make you feel as if you're sunning on Little Palm Island – if you close your eyes.

COCONUT SORBET

2 cups water
1⅓ cups sugar
1 tablespoon lemon juice
7 oz. coconut milk
2 tablespoons rum
1 egg white, slightly beaten

1. Bring the water and sugar to boil and set aside to cool.
2. Stir in the lemon juice, coconut milk, rum and egg white. Refrigerate until chilled.
3. Freeze chilled mixture in the sorbet or ice cream freezer according to directions.
Makes about 5 cups.

1 pineapple
1 mango
1 papaya
1 banana
½ cup butter, melted
2 fresh mangos
¼ cup cream
½ cup sugar
8 mint leaves

1. Peel all the fruits and cut into slices. Brush with melted butter.
Place on hot grill until marked, 30 seconds; turn for another 30 seconds. Remove from grill.
2. Peel and seed mango.
3. Put cream, mango meat and sugar in blender. Process until puréed to make coulis.
4. Place mango coulis on plate, arrange fruit around the edges and serve with one scoop of coconut sorbet. Garnish with fresh mint leaves.
Serves 6.

PEPPERED FRESH TUNA LOIN CARPACCIO WITH YOGURT-CHIVE SAUCE

2 two-inch thick fresh, cleaned tuna loin steaks
1 tablespoon olive oil
⅓ cup crushed white peppercorn
⅓ cup crushed black peppercorn
⅓ cup crushed pink peppercorn
½ pound washed baby lettuces torn in pieces and mixed, (Mesculun) including if possible:
   Baby red oak
   Frisee
   Mache/lambs-lettuce
½ cup extra virgin olive oil
1½ cups plain yogurt
3 tablespoons chopped fresh chives

1. Combine yogurt and chives. Can prepare up to one week earlier.
2. Roll the tuna loin steaks in peppercorns, pressing peppercorns into tuna.
3. Heat medium non-stick frying pan until very hot, add 1 tablespoon olive oil and place tuna in pan. Sear each side for 20 to 30 seconds for rare. Remove from pan and let cool to room temperature.
4. Arrange the lettuces on plate, sprinkle the olive oil over.
5. Slice the tuna steaks in paper-thin slices and arrange slices in a circular pattern over salad, with teaspoon points of sauce at the end of each slice on the plate.
Serves 4.

TIAN OF SEA SCALLOPS, FRESH TOMATO, ITALIAN ZUCCHINI OVER JULIENNE OF RADICCHIO IN THYME VINAIGRETTE

A lovely fresh dish perfect for ripe tomato season. Simple ingredients with sophisticated presentation is the hallmark of Little Palm Island.

8 large sea scallops sliced in rounds
3 tomatoes thinly sliced
1 large Italian zucchini thinly sliced
1 tablespoon fresh thyme
salt and pepper
1 large radicchio washed, dried and cut in julienne
1 tablespoon chopped red onion
1 teaspoon chopped fresh thyme
½ cup red wine vinegar
1 cup extra virgin olive oil
salt and pepper to taste

1. Combine red onion, thyme, vinegar, olive oil and salt and pepper well. Set vinaigrette aside.
2. Lightly brush butter on medium baking pan. Arrange the zucchini slices in two circles of overlapping slices in 2 circles. Salt and pepper and sprinkle with part of the thyme.
3. Top each zucchini circle with tomatoes also done in an overlapping circle. Salt and pepper tomatoes and sprinkle with thyme.
4. Arrange scallop slices on tomatoes the same way. Salt and pepper to taste.
5. Bake in oven at 300 degrees F for 15 minutes or until cooked.
6. Place each tian in middle of plate, arrange radicchio around them and sprinkle with thyme vinaigrette.
Serves 2.

CHOCOLATE SIN CAKE WRAPPED IN PHYLLO DOUGH SERVED ON RASPBERRY SAUCE

Desserts featuring flaky phyllo pastry are lovely and really not difficult. And when that pastry is filled with chocolate? Serve it forth. Just remember that when working with phyllo dough, it dries out very quickly. Always keep the dough you're not yet using covered by a damp, not wet, cloth.

1 lb. semi-sweet chocolate
4 oz. butter
4 egg yolks
2 tablespoons sugar
4 egg whites
2 tablespoons sugar
1 tablespoon cornstarch
2 teaspoons vanilla extract
¼ teaspoon cream of tartar
1 package phyllo dough (in freezer section)
1 cup butter melted
1 cup powdered sugar

1. Melt chocolate and butter over double boiler. Cool slightly.
2. In another bowl, cream together egg yolks and 2 tablespoons sugar. Whip until nice and creamy.
3. In a separate bowl, whip the egg whites, sugar, cornstarch, vanilla extract and cream of tartar until stiff peaks form.
4. Mix melted and somewhat cooled chocolate with egg yolk mixture.
5. Fold the whipped egg whites into chocolate/egg yolk mix.
6. Butter and sugar a 10 inch cake pan or springform pan and pour in the batter. Bake in a preheated oven (325 degrees F) for about 45 minutes or until set. Let the cake cool in the pan. Refrigerate overnight.
7. When ready to finish, cut chocolate cake in eight pieces.
8. Take one sheet phyllo dough and brush with melted butter, dust with powdered sugar. Place the next sheet of phyllo dough on top of the first one, butter and sugar. Repeat until you have four layers of phyllo.

9. Place one piece of Chocolate Sin Cake into the center of the phyllo dough layers and wrap the cake. You may wrap it like a package or gather up all four corners and twist, leaving a topknot of pastry. Do the same with the other chocolate pieces. (*May be refrigerated at this point for several hours.*)

10. When ready to serve, bake for 5 minutes in 350 degrees F and place the cake on a plate surrounded by raspberry sauce.

RASPBERRY SAUCE:

3 cups fresh raspberries
½ cup sugar
⅓ cup water

Mix together in pan and cook for 5 minutes on medium-high heat. Put one tablespoon raspberry sauce on each plate with the cake and dust with powdered sugar.

Serves 8.

Dining room overlooking the inlet

The Aerie
MALAHAT, BRITISH COLUMBIA

Suite with jacuzzi and fireplace

Guest room overlooking the redwoods

Applewood, An Estate Inn
POCKET CANYON, CALIFORNIA

The dining room...

Photo: Chris Shorten

Guest quarters

Averill's Flathead Lake Lodge
BIGFORK, MONTANA

Pool overlooking Flathead Lake

South side of the main house...

Blantyre
LENOX, MASSACHUSETTS

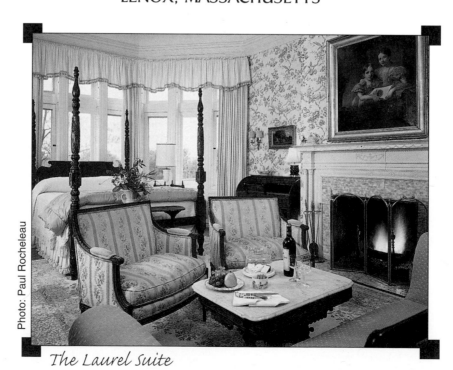

The Laurel Suite

The main lodge blends into the boulders…

The Boulders

CAREFREE, ARIZONA

The Latilla Dining Room

A casita — all have fireplaces

Photo: Craig Murray

The lodge in winter white...

C Lazy U Ranch
GRANBY, COLORADO

Photo: Nancy Fisher

Main living room

Italian boxwood gardens...

Cedar Grove Mansion
VICKSBURG, MISSISSIPPI

The parlour...

Smokehouse cum Garden Room

The main inn and summer house

Charlotte Inn
EDGARTOWN, MASSCHUSETTS

Room #17 in the summer house

Antique dressing table

Main lodge and lawns

High Hampton Inn and Country Club
CASHIERS, NORTH CAROLINA

*View of Hampton Lake and
Rock Mountain from lodge...*

The perfect mountain lodge...

The Home Ranch
CLARK, COLORADO

Stone fireplace in the living room

A rocking chair view of the Smokies…

Inn at Blackberry Farm

WALLAND, TENNESSEE

The living room

Fire Pink in the guest house

Main lodge
and gardens

The Inn at Manitou
McKELLAR, ONTARIO

The tea room

Chesapeake waterfront…

The Inn at Perry Cabin

ST. MICHAELS, MARYLAND

British dining…

Ashley bedrooms…

Photo: Marshall C. Webb

Overlooking Lake Champlain...

Inn at Shelburne Farms

SHELBURNE, VERMONT

Photo: Gary Clayton-Hall

Conservatory dining

Photo: Gary Clayton-Hall

The East room...

The sitting room. . .

Iroquois Hotel

MACKINAC ISLAND, MICHIGAN

Sitting right on the Straits of Mackinac

The Great Hall...

Keswick Hall

KESWICK, VIRGINIA

Room #48

Maison de Ville

NEW ORLEANS, LOUISIANA

"Traveling is a fool's paradise." That is the long ago sentiment of poet and essayist Ralph Waldo Emerson. If that be true then allow me to be a fool in New Orleans. I'm driving down I-10 near New Orleans and the highway beneath my wheels is making a familiar schwoop-schwoop-schwoop sound, the product of some degree of sinkage from the swampy ground (which is also why all graves are *above* ground here). Craggy cypress trees and wet-loving weeping willows dominate the roadsides, all draped with gray beards of Spanish moss. I take the Vieux Carre exit, the legal U-turn onto Toulouse, and enter what is unmistakably the French Quarter. Somnolent and sultry with a distinct female persona. Narrow streets are lined with picture-book two-story houses iced with lacy wrought-iron balconies.

CREOLE, CHOCOLATE AND SMILING HOSPITALITY

Pulling up in front of the Maison de Ville at 727 Toulouse, a staffer unloads my bags and a valet takes the car. I turn the old brass doorknob on the ornately carved walnut door – it's locked – so I peer through the etched frosted glass pane. Can't see much. I ring a small doorbell by the door and a shadowy figure appears. "Come in," says the smiling face. "Welcome to the Maison de Ville."

I abandon New Orleans' hot, noisy streets for an instant oasis of quiet, calm and elegance. This is the world hidden from so many who visit the Crescent City. Peeling

I abandon New Orleans' hot, noisy streets for an instant oasis of quiet, calm and elegance. This is the world hidden from so many who visit the Crescent City.

facades and fading paint are the exterior of many old Creole homes. Tourists peek through wrought-iron door barriers down long narrow brick halls to see just a hint of the beautiful forbidden courtyards and lovely homes beyond. At the Maison de Ville, you have your own Creole home. Just ring, and the door will open.

Dark chocolate-colored carpet with cafe au lait walls lead you down a hall that features a green marble topped empire table and five foot gold leaf Regency mirror reflecting an urn filled with pink Liatris and vivid Rhubrum lilies among curly willow branches. At the end of the hall is the intimate lobby, a salon really. Marble mantel, lovely antiques and muted fabrics, ancestral oil portraits all blend into a subtle tapestry of good taste.

Ten foot tall French doors open onto a weathered brick courtyard, enclosed by terra cotta colored walls and black balconies. In the center is a round multi-tiered fountain, gently splashing water around life size verdigris herons and water hyacinths. Several black iron tables and chairs sit here and there offering a spot to enjoy the beauty and a moment's relaxation.

"Shall I take you to your room now?" the same smiling face asks. Yes, that would be nice. We go just across the courtyard to the old carriage house. Suddenly I catch sight of an ornate wrought iron door with glimpses into the neighboring courtyard. Over the door the sign says Court of the Two Sisters. My mind reels back decades to when a little girl came to this famous courtyard restaurant with her parents and two sisters. It was our big night out in New Orleans and the world's fastest walk down Bourbon Street. "Mommy, what's that lady doing in her nightgown on that table?" The pace quickens. I remember flickering gas lamps and whispering to the waitress my order of fried shrimp in the Two Sisters' suitably proper atmosphere. It looks just the same.

The carriage house is a lovely two room apartment with a white tongue and groove paneled living room downstairs, a small bar area (the ice bucket is already filled), antique writing desk and sofa. A honey colored chest acts as the coffee table holding a small china bowl of softly scented potpourri. A framed Audubon print of a yellow-winged sparrow is on the wall. Upstairs is a sage green and white striped bedroom. It's like a tropical paradise beyond the French doors which open to the balcony surrounded by broad leaves of a banana tree. An unripe bunch of banana fruit grows just beyond reach.

A BITTER STREETCAR NAMED AUDUBON

At the other side of the courtyard is a two-storied building that is believed to be one of the oldest in New Orleans. History is fuzzy about its past – either slave quarters or garconierres, separate living quarters for a family's grown sons to accommodate their nocturnal habits. These are now four accommodations. Number 9 was where Tennessee Williams drank copious amounts of sazeracs and wrote his classic *A Streetcar Named Desire*. The Maison de Ville was also the home of pharmacist Antoine Peychaud, who concocted the famous Peychaud bitters still flavoring cocktails in bars worldwide.

Nearby on Rue Dauphine are the seven recently refurbished Audubon Cottages. These elegant antique-furnished suites, each with its own private brick terrace, have housed Liz Taylor, Julia Roberts and Tom Cruise. They followed in the footsteps of naturalist John James Audubon who lived in #1 while he created many of his *Birds of America* series in 1821. In the walled courtyard is a cool, blue swimming pool used by all Maison de Ville guests, of whatever fame, ill or otherwise.

By my watch it is late, but rather early by French Quarter standards where the party goes on all night. No wonder the Creoles long ago shut themselves away behind

Ten foot tall French doors open onto a weathered brick courtyard, enclosed by terra cotta colored walls and black balconies. In the center is a round multi-tiered fountain, gently splashing water around life size verdigris herons.

gates and gardens. Loud and racy on Bourbon Street, people of all ages and descriptions wander in search of something. I take a little more time than my mother allowed so long ago. But Royal Street is my more my pace, quiet and lined with antique shops shuttered for the night. What a fascinating mix of brash and genteel.

My bed has been turned down, a sugary pecan praline and cognac put by my bed. I sign the card that states a preference to have breakfast in the courtyard. I leave it, and a pair of shoes needing polish outside the door.

Breakfast comes precisely when it was requested. My door opens to the courtyard. The morning is warm, but pleasantly so and I find my shiny shoes in a brown bag at the doorstep. A silver tray bears flavorful chicory coffee, warm croissants and a moist carrot muffin. Nothing is saved.

SILVER, SATCHMO, SORROW AND ST. CHARLES

On the advice of the concierge, I head down Toulouse past Rue Royal and left onto Chartres heading for the Louisiana State Museum Cabildo. Slate sidewalks run past shops with silver asparagus tongs, epergnes and toothpick holders, finally arriving at a buff colored stucco building. The 1799 Cabildo has seen General Lafayette entertaining within its walls. The French, Spanish and Americans signed the Louisiana Purchase transfers here in 1803. You will quickly discover this city has a tough past. Antebellum New Orleans had the highest death rate of any American city due to cholera, smallpox and the prevalent yellow fever. Ask the Irish. Perhaps as many as 30,000 Irishmen lost their lives digging a swampy canal from Lake Ponchatrain to the French Quarter. No one knows for sure. An Irishman's life wasn't worth much in New Orleans in those days. Ghosts of the slaves could tell you of such sorrows. It was dreaded news to be headed to New Orleans' twenty-five markets which meant you were to be sold or traded at the South's largest slave trading center, with little regard for family relations.

But New Orleans never dwells on death and sorrow. An early 19th century visitor wrote, "the instant the luminary sets, animation begins to rise, the public walks are crowded, the billiard rooms resound, the music strikes up; life and activity resume their joyous career." Joyous is probably the most appropriate word for New Orleans. Crossing Jackson Square I pass by the famous Cafe du Monde smelling deliciously of hot sugared beignets and cafe au lait. The restored five block French market follows the Mississippi River, hawking Creole tomatoes, gator-on-a-stick, hot sauces, voodoo dolls and pralines, among other delicacies.

That joyous spirit is intensified every year during Mardi Gras, for some to almost painful proportions. If you choose not to visit then, you can still get a glimpse into the glittering and costumed world at the Mardi Gras Museum inside the Old U.S. Mint located next to the French Market. Across the hall is The Jazz Museum that revels in the one musical style to which America can claim sole ownership. Vintage photographs, instruments, stories and music document the beginnings and development of jazz. "Queen of the blues" Blanche Thomas, "Jelly Roll" Morton, Buddy Bolden and of course, the incomparable "Satchmo" are all featured here while their music provides testimony to their contributions to this city and its grateful nation.

At St. Charles and Canal Street, catch the olive green St. Charles streetcar. Built for steam in 1835, electrified in 1893, it is the oldest continually operated streetcar in the world. You'll rattle past Pearl's Oyster Bar and multiple shops to enter the cultured world of the Garden District. The street is lined with pastel peach, pink and yellow mansions looking like giant iced cakes. This was where the American elite lived after New Orleans became an American territory. The French Creoles dominated the Vieux

Breakfast comes precisely when it was requested. A silver tray bears flavorful chicory coffee, warm croissants and a moist carrot muffin.

Carre. Canal Street was the boundary between the two and called "neutral ground," a reference used for street medians in New Orleans to this day. At the end of the line is the leafy green Audubon Park and Zoo.

MORE THAN LAGNAIPPE

But it is the wise fool who returns to the French Quarter for dinner. Maison de Ville's restaurant, The Bistro, is an elegant yet casual dining experience. Walls of deep red with impressionist paintings, red leather banquettes, red roses and tealight candles on white linened tables provide intimate dining. This is not a tourist mecca. The Bistro is geared to locals who eat out well and often, with a seasonally changing menu of traditional recipes adapted with new twists. In New Orleans, food expectations are intense, as is the competition. This kitchen meets the challenge gladly.

At the table, lagniappe (a little extra) appears instantly as you're brought a small crock of cool, smooth pâté with warm chewy French bread. For the bold, begin with a Bistro Martini: Jordon Sparkling Wine with Ketel One Vodka and an essence of Peychaud bitters. Watch out.

Starters include sautéed chicken livers with grilled polenta and porcini, fried green tomatoes with lump crabmeat and saffron (which are unbelievable), or crawfish remoulade with croutons and tomatoes. Entrees might be pan roasted pork loin with five spice nectarine glaze, sautéed veal loin with foie gras butter and shiitake mushrooms or warm smoked tuna with kalamata olives, balsamic vinaigrette and baby red romaine. The chocolate bread pudding is a dark, brooding terrine of intense flavors, but if it's too much dessert, try the mango sorbet. Mon dieu!

The next morning I force myself from my shady retreat and pause a moment by the peaceful fountain as the sun streams through the banana leaves. A trumpet is moaning a jazzy tune that drifts across from an invisible courtyard. Emerson was wrong. I want to come back when the bananas are ripe to hear the end of the song.

At the table, lagniappe (a little extra) appears instantly as you're brought a small crock of cool, smooth pâté with warm chewy French bread. For the bold, begin with a Bistro Martini

GRACIOUS COUNTRY INNS

SHRIMP BISQUE

Shrimp bisque has always been a favorite of mine, but this one has a really unusual twist with the flavorings of vanilla and lavender.

¾ cup flour
¼ lb. butter
1 vanilla beans
1¼ qts. shrimp stock
¾ cup dry sherry
1½ cup tomato purée (strained of seeds)
½ cup veal demi-glaze or rich chicken stock
½ tablespoon lavender, finely chopped
2 cups shiitake mushrooms, julienned
1½ cups shrimp, raw, chopped
1 cup heavy cream

1. Melt butter in a Dutch oven. When melted, add flour over medium heat and whisk until smooth (a roux). Cook the roux until lightly toasted.
2. Slowly whisk in sherry and shrimp stock to avoid lumps. Add tomato purée and split vanilla bean (scrape inside of pods into soup, pods can be removed before serving).
3. Add heavy cream. Bring mixture to a boil and simmer 10 minutes. Skim off any scum that accumulates on top of the soup.
4. Finish the soup by adding the mushrooms, lavender and chopped shrimp. Cook an additional two minutes. Season to taste with salt and white pepper.

NOTE: The key to this soup is a good flavorful shrimp or shellfish stock.
For stock: Sear the shells (lobster, shrimp, crawfish, crab shells in any combination can be used) in a large pot. Add chopped garlic, and red pepper flakes. Sauté lightly. Add tomato scraps, chopped onions, carrots and celery, tarragon, thyme, bay leaf and peppercorns. Deglaze with white wine, cover with water and simmer. Skim the stock when necessary. Cook for several hours or until it tastes good, adding water when necessary.

CRISPY FRIED RAVIOLI WITH ONION VINAIGRETTE

A marvelous starter with flavors and textures of cheese, bacon and the tartness of the onion vinaigrette. Make the vinaigrette ahead to save time.

6 pasta squares or eggroll wrappers
6 slices apple smoked bacon, cooked until done but not too crispy (keep warm)
1½ cup marscapone cheese
⅓ cup grated Parmesan cheese
⅓ cup Gorgonzola cheese
salt and black pepper to taste
2–3 heads frisee lettuce (or endive)
1 recipe onion vinaigrette (recipe below)

1. Combine cheeses well, season and chill (can be prepared 2 days before).
2. Lay out pasta squares or eggroll wrappers. Moisten edges with a flour-water mixture. Lay a dollop of cheese mixture in the center, dividing mixture evenly between all six squares.
3. Fold pasta over in half, forming a triangle, squeezing out air pockets. Ravioli can be kept chilled for up to one day until ready to cook.
4. Deep fat fry the ravioli at 350 degrees for 30 seconds on one side and 30 seconds on the other. Keep flipping until lightly browned. Remove to paper towel to drain off excess fat.
5. On warm plates, spoon a portion of the vinaigrette on the front of the plate. Toss the frisee with some of the onion vinaigrette. Place frisee salad towards the back of the plate. Place fried ravioli in front. Lay one cooked bacon strip on top of each ravioli and garnish with some grated Parmesan cheese.

Serves 6.

ONION VINAIGRETTE:

3 onions, julienned
½ cup balsamic vinegar
2 tablespoons fresh basil, chopped
2 teaspoons brown sugar
⅓ cup olive oil
salt and black pepper to taste

1. Sauté onion in peanut oil until translucent.

2. Add brown sugar and balsamic vinegar. Cook one minute and remove from heat.

3. In a bowl, mix the onions with olive oil and basil. Season with salt and pepper to taste.

GELATO CAKE

The ultimate ice cream cake.

2 cups pecans, toasted (1 cup ground in food
    processor, or 1 cup coarsely chopped)
2 cups sugar
1 cup water
6 egg whites
6 egg yolks
1¼ cups milk
¾ cup heavy cream
3 oz. marzipan or almond paste
2 cups heavy cream

1. Boil sugar and water to 150 degrees.

2. Whip egg whites to soft peaks and drizzle in the hot syrup. Continue whipping until cool, about 15 minutes.

3. Mix yolks, milk and 3/4 cup heavy cream together in double boiler. Cook until thick and custard-like.

4. Add marzipan to hot custard and stir to incorporate. Cool.

5. Add cooled custard to egg white mixture. Whip the remaining 2 cups heavy cream to stiff peaks and fold into mixture, with ground pecans. Pour into a 10-inch springform pan and freeze. Serve frozen slices with toasted chopped pecans and fruit purées.

Serves 10.

APPLE, ENDIVE AND CELERY ROOT SALAD

FOR SALAD:

2 apples (granny smith, skins removed, juli-
    enned)
2 endive heads, julienned
½ celery root (skin removed, julienned)
6 radicchio leaves
1 red pepper, julienned
1 bunch watercress, cleaned
1 cup basil leaves
½ cup cilantro leaves
wonton wrappers, julienned and deep fried for
    garnish (optional)

FOR VINAIGRETTE:

4 tablespoons toasted sesame seeds
    (save 2 Tablespoons for garnish)
⅛ cup sesame oil
1½ cup peanut oil
½ cup rice wine vinegar
2 tablespoons cilantro, chopped
¼ cup lime juice
1 teaspoon garlic, minced
1 teaspoon orange peel, minced
2 teaspoon ginger, minced

1. Whisk vinaigrette ingredients. Season with fine ground sea salt and black pepper.

2. When ready to serve, toss all salad ingredients except wonton strips and 2 tablespoons sesame seeds in bowl with 1 oz. vinaigrette per person.

On six chilled plates, place one radicchio leaf. Fill with salad mixture. Garnish with wonton strips and sesame seeds.

The Marquesa Hotel

KEY WEST, FLORIDA

Your eyes are closed. Breezes rustle through the palm trees, birds scream out their tropical sounds, water splashes gently from the fountain, the sun is hot on your skin. "Can I get you some fresh iced tea?" a gentle voice asks.

"That would be lovely," you answer without moving your eyelids. After a moment, the sweating glass is placed on the table beside you. At this moment, you are profoundly grateful that the Marquesa Hotel was saved from destruction.

Built in 1884 as a single family home, the building narrowly missed the catastrophic fire of 1886 by some 200 feet. This charming Victorian structure then passed through an array of lives as a grocery store, a bicycle shop and a $5 a night boardinghouse. Oh, I'm being nice. It was a flophouse, really. But in 1988, The Marquesa Hotel became its latest and greatest reincarnation.

SAVING GRACE

After eight months of extensive sawing, hammering, painting, replacing and designing, a prominent corner in Key West's Historic District was now transformed by the birth of the Marquesa Hotel. The rich blue wooden building with dollops of cream gingerbread trim sits proudly, announcing to the world that preservation is good business.

The main goal of the renovation, according to general partner Eric DeBoer, was

This charming Victorian structure then passed through an array of lives as a grocery store, a bicycle shop and a $5 a night boardinghouse. Oh, I'm being nice. It was a flophouse, really.

not to freeze Victoriana, but to provide the comfort and amenities expected in a modern hotel within the setting of an historic building. They were eminently successful.

As you enter from the front porch, through the wood and glass double front doors, you sense a light, contemporary feel, with Key West sun pouring though tall windows and falling on the polished, North Carolina pine floors. You enter in the front hall, which is really a gallery, featuring glimpses of Key West and the Marquesa from days past. Look closely at one old photo taken from across the street. There's President Truman in a parade, and the window of the Marquesa behind him is filled with children's clothing for sale.

There are fifteen rooms and suites, all with large, modern, marble baths, beautiful furnishings and ceiling fans, a nice Key West touch, though the Marquesa is of course, air-conditioned. You'll find embroidered cotton robes in each room, Caswell-Massey toiletries, and each night your bed will be turned down cozily, with Godiva chocolates on your pillow. Some rooms have balconies that overlook the street outside, great for relaxing in the afternoon with a glass of wine.

You could choose the room that for James Bond fans, will always be the Timothy Dalton Room. To the owners, it is #15. Mr. Dalton must have valued the privacy afforded by this third floor suite while filming "Licence to Kill" in 1989. #15 is very quiet and spacious with dormer windows, a seating area done in cool white, and a king-sized bed. (I was able to dine with the cast, including Mr. Dalton, during the press previews of this film. He is indeed a charming fellow worthy of being anyone's Rhett.)

The honeymoon suite is on the ground floor with French doors that open onto the lush courtyard and pool area. Romance will germinate in this setting, designed with a big unfinished pine armoire, overstuffed chairs and a huge bed. A tropical flower arrangement made from antherium, beargrass, diffenbachia leaves and orchids. Wow.

THE HANGOUT

The courtyard is a very important part of the Marquesa. It is your haven away from the noise, heat, hustle and bustle of Key West streets. As owner and manager Carol Wightman points out, "People really wilt in Key West heat. After being out on Duval Street for a while, they love coming back to the pool!" Planted all around with traveler palms, orchids, bird of paradise, and the delicious smelling night-blooming jasmine, the solar heated pool is trimmed in blue and white checkerboard ceramic tiles. A tiled fountain off to one side provides the most soothing splash of water. What an exotic place to enjoy your breakfast, but you may have it sent to your room if you're anti-social in the mornings. Or, romantically secluded.

Regardless, enjoy frothy cappuccino or steaming dark espresso, served with fresh squeezed orange juice and some of Carol's buttery, blueberry-banana bread. Or try some of the Marquesa homemade granola, one of the nuttiest and crunchiest you've ever tasted. Breakfast Marquesa style is great wherever you have it.

HIT THE STREETS

After breakfast, Key West awaits your pleasure. Don't forget, everything in Key West is just a bike ride or walk away. Parking is difficult here, so ditch the car. Believe me, you'll enjoy strolling or biking through the colorful streets full of shops and lovely homes. And, you feel more a part of the Key West scene.

A must-see is of course, the Hemingway House. This fascinating museum is surrounded by ornate second story wrought iron railings. Ernest Hemingway loved Key West, the fishing, the drinking, the tropical lifestyle, the drinking. About 80% of his writing was done here in this, the first home he ever owned. His old typewriter, hunting trophies and books remain in his studio. As you may have heard, the place is crawling with cats, the six-toed polydactyl variety, mostly descendants from the cat given to Hemingway by an old sea captain. The old man and the sea, indeed.

For people who love the romance of shipwrecks and sunken treasure, try Mel Fisher's Maritime Heritage Society and Museum on Greene St. It contains some of the most spectacular pieces from the wreck of the Nuestra Senora de Atocha, a Spanish galleon that sank off the keys in 1622 in a storm. The once-rumored treasure stayed safely locked in its watery grave until 1985, when a determined fellow named Mel Fisher found the Atocha after a 16 year search. Displayed is an eight-foot solid gold chain, a six inch gold cross set with large emeralds, and a "cinta," the only one known to exist today. A necklace popular to noblewomen of the day, it is set with pearls, diamonds and rubies. Particularly haunting is the portrait of the daughter of Phillip II of Spain, seen wearing an identical necklace to one recovered from the wreckage and displayed underneath. Then there's the solid gold "poison cup," with the gallstone of a llama set in the bottom. Poisoning was common in those days, and the stone was thought to detect poison. The museum is open 365 days a year.

Duvall Street is the main drag in Key West. It is cheek by jowl with dozens of creative shops, trendy galleries and eclectic restaurants. But still in residence is "Papa Joe's," Hemingway's original hangout. Just as interesting is the people watching, with a colorful cast of characters filling all the roles on Duvall.

SAIL AWAY

If you'd prefer something a bit quieter, try a voyage on one of the wooden schooners. The 86-foot Appledore is a magnificent ship built in 1978. Get there about 5:00 or so, and everyone gets on board for the sunset cruise. The sails are up full, and guests enjoy light appetizers and a bit of bubbly as the sun slowly sinks over the water in a riot of red and gold. Gorgeous. You glide past Mallory Square (also worth a visit), and from sea, witness the human carnival. Jugglers, cats jumping through rings and musicians cavort alongside a 6-foot willowy Jamaican who bends double and squiggles through a 16 inch plexiglass tube.

For dinner, it's the Marquesa Cafe, which features bistro-style dining and "food of the Americas." Let's face it, in Key West you shouldn't expect or desire everyday food. Sesame-encrusted New Zealand rack of lamb with mint-basil pesto, seared lamb carpaccio with white bean salad, grilled portebello mushrooms with soft corn polenta and crumbled blue cheese, sweet potato bisque with smoked salmon or gulf red snapper sautéed with soy and ginger beurre blanc just fit the bill. All this is served in a very special dining room with smooth Cantera stone floors, a gleaming mahogany bar, and sponged apricot-gold walls – the colors of sunset. Best of all is the frenetic view into the kitchen through a trompe l'oeill framed opening.

But what you're really dreaming of is that moment by the pool. Your eyes are closed and the sun is hot on your skin. A gentle voice asks, "Can I get you..."

Then there's the solid gold "poison cup," with the gallstone of a llama set in the bottom. Poisoning was common in those days, and the stone was thought to detect poison.

CAFE MARQUESA'S GRANOLA

This is the crunchiest granola I've ever tasted, no doubt because of all the almonds. I fondly remember munching it in the Marquesa's courtyard pool.

6 cups rolled oats (health food variety)
3½ cups coarsely chopped almonds
4 cups sunflower seeds
¾ cups safflower or soy oil
¾ cups honey
¾ cups maple syrup
1½ tablespoons vanilla
¾ teaspoon almond extract
2 teaspoons cinnamon, freshly ground if possible
1½ cups (or more!) of any of these fruits: raisins, currants, dried apricots, figs, prunes, dates, blueberries, cranberries or cherries
pinch of salt

1. Put the oats, chopped almonds and sunflower seeds in a large bowl.

2. Combine the oil, sweeteners, vanilla, almond extract, spices and salt. Heat this mixture in a saucepan until it becomes watery (about 5 minutes on medium heat). Pour the oil mixture over the oats mixture. Stir until oats are coated.

3. Spread in a large baking pan or on cookie sheets. Bake in the middle of a 325 degree oven for about 30-50 minutes, or until the granola turns golden, stirring every 15 minutes so the mixture toasts uniformly.

4. Transfer to a large bowl or cool baking pan and toss occasionally until the granola is thoroughly cool and dry.

5. Add the dried fruit and toss to mix. Store in a airtight covered container.

GRILLED PORTOBELLO MUSHROOM WITH SOFT CORN POLENTA & CRUMBLED BLUE CHEESE

POLENTA:

2 cups milk
1 teaspoon garlic, minced
½ teaspoon white pepper
½ teaspoon nutmeg
¾ cup polenta meal or cornmeal
½ cup crème fraiche or sour cream
2 oz. Parmesan cheese, grated

1. In small saucepan bring milk, white pepper, nutmeg and garlic to boil.

2. In slow steady stream, pour cornmeal into boiling milk, whisking constantly. Reduce heat to simmer and continue stirring with wooden spoon till soft and pulling away from sides of pan.

3. Add crème fraiche or sour cream, stir vigorously till all is incorporated.

4. Adjust seasoning with salt, pepper and nutmeg. Keep warm.

MUSHROOMS:

4 whole portobello mushrooms
2 tablespoons balsamic vinegar
2 tablespoons basil, snipped
1 tablespoon thyme, snipped
1 tablespoon Worcestershire
2 teaspoons garlic, minced
1 cup chicken stock or water
1 cup olive oil
8 tablespoons Gorgonzola, grated fine or crumbled
2 ripe tomatoes, seeded, peeled and chopped fine

1. Trim mushrooms at bottom and brush away any sand (wash if necessary).

2. Whisk together vinegar, basil, thyme, Worcestershire, garlic, stock and olive oil. Pour over mushrooms and let marinate for 30 min. or up to 2 hours.

3. Prepare charcoal grill. Remove mushrooms from marinade, allow to drain on plate for 1-2 minutes. Place on rack over charcoal grill, turn occasionally. When mushrooms are soft, remove from heat.

4. Sprinkle 2 tablespoons of Gorgonzola on hot plates, (place in oven or microwave to heat plates). Spoon ¼ of polenta in center of each plate, place mushroom on top of polenta and sprinkle tomatoes around plate.
   Serves 4.

CAFE MARQUESA'S CARIBBEAN CURRY SHRIMP

Spicy, simple and spectacular. I have a particular fondness for Thai cuisine, but have never been sure how to approach it in my own kitchen. This recipe is really simple to prepare and takes no time at all. I've added basil leaves here for garnish as it goes so well with Thai food, and it's good with some added into the sauce, too.

2 lbs. shrimp, peeled and de-veined
3 tablespoons vegetable oil
2 teaspoon garlic, minced
2 tablespoons flour
1 cup coconut milk
2 tablespoons red curry paste (available in Thai
   food shops)
salt and pepper
fresh basil leaves for edible garnish

1. In a large sauté pan, heat vegetable oil. Add shrimp and garlic. Sauté for 1 minute.
2. Sprinkle flour over shrimp. Stir well.
3. Add coconut milk and red curry paste. Mix well.
4. Simmer till shrimp are done and sauce is thick. (If needed, thin sauce with white wine or water.) Season to taste with salt and pepper and garnish with basil.
   Serves 4 as an entree or 6 as an appetizer

SWEET POTATO BISQUE WITH SMOKED SALMON

The sweet potatoes and apples juxtaposed against the smoked salmon is wonderful. This soup can be made ahead and reheated, just add the salmon right before serving.

¼ cup olive oil
2 cups onion, peeled and diced
1 tablespoon garlic
1 cup leeks, split, washed and rough chop
2 lbs. sweet potatoes, peeled and rough chopped
2 each Granny Smith apples, peeled, seeded and
   rough chop
1 scotch bonnet pepper, seeded and diced
4 cups chicken stock or water and 2 bouillon cubes
salt/pepper to taste
chives snipped
6 ounces chopped smoked salmon

1. In large sauce pan or dutch oven, heat olive oil over medium high heat.
2. Add onions, garlic and leeks. Sauté till translucent.
3. Add sweet potatoes, apples and pepper, chicken stock or water. Simmer till potatoes are tender.
4. Purée in blender till smooth, strain back into pan and season with salt and pepper. Adjust the consistency with additional stock. (May be refrigerated at this point and reheated later.)
5. Sprinkle 1 oz. diced smoked salmon in each soup bowl, ladle soup over salmon and garnish with chives.
   Serves 6-8.

CAFE MARQUESA'S BLUEBERRY BANANA BREAD

A Marquesa favorite. You'll see why when you try it. A warning: Carol Wightman says she rues the day she first made it. Now no one will let her stop. Incidentally you can reduce the butter in the recipe from 8 tablespoons to 6 with no difference in the texture.

1 cup sugar
1 cup mashed bananas (approximately. 2
    medium-sized bananas)
½ cup butter or margarine, softened
¼ cup milk
1 teaspoon vanilla
2 eggs
2 cups bread flour
½ cup chopped nuts (walnuts, pecans)
1 teaspoon baking soda
½ teaspoon salt
½ cup whole frozen blueberries

1. Blend first six ingredients with electric mixer or by hand until thoroughly mixed.
2. Mix soda and salt with flour; stir flour mixture into banana mixture.
3. Fold in frozen blueberries.
4. Bake at 350 degrees for 40–50 minutes in greased standard loaf pan.

Makes 1 loaf.

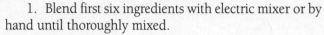

NORTHEAST

Blantyre
LENOX, MASSACHUSETTS

Driving between the eight foot tall brick pillars, up the long drive shaded by leafy copper beech trees that border emerald green lawns, my first reaction to seeing Blantyre is, "Wow!" It is truly splendid, drop-dead, take-your-breath gorgeous. Built in 1902 by a man named Patterson as a romantic gesture to his wife, Blantyre is an imposing Tudor brick and leaded glass structure that duplicates a grand Scottish manor. It is perched on 80 impeccably maintained acres in the Berkshire Mountains of Massachusetts.

That incredulous feeling continues inside the main hall. From the moment you pass through the ornately carved front door, you've entered the world of elegant perfection. Against walls of carved oak, the Persian rugs, Tiffany lamps, beautiful paintings, antiques and cascading fresh flower arrangements are a portrait of serene beauty. The ceiling panels, seventeen feet up, are intricately carved and crossed with oak beams. Ornate carving decorates the mahogany mantel. You will be hard pressed to find an inn more lovely than this one.

GRANDEUR REVISITED

Blantyre is run with computer-like precision by a largely European staff (all of whom are trained to accommodate with impunity) and a Scot named Roderick Anderson. He explains that Blantyre was labeled a "cottage," because the wealthy in the

Blantyre was labeled a "cottage," because the wealthy in the early 1900s wanted to live like British nobility (Don't we all?), with their own little "cottage in the country."

early 1900s wanted to live like British nobility (don't we all?), with their own little "cottage in the country." The family would visit in July and August only, and would spend the rest of the year in Georgia and New York. "Those *were* different days," Roderick dead pans. Indeed. But thank goodness they've been recreated for modern day romantics.

The bedrooms at Blantyre are as splendid as the main hall. From the bay windows in the Patterson Suite you can overlook the gardens filled with pink and white hollyhocks, deep purple Liatris, yellow and white Boston daisies and huge terra cotta urns bursting with salmon pink geraniums. There's more luxury inside with a carved four poster bed, two bathrooms, and a sitting area with chintz covered chairs and sofa.

The Cranwell Suite is delicately cream colored with vintage wallpaper, a carved four-poster bed, a seating area with camelback sofa and easy chairs and a sweep of large bay windows that overlook the lawns. Down a hall of closets is the dressing room with a chintz chaise lounge and dressing table. In the bathroom is a claw-foot tub, an antique marble lavatory, and an old-fashioned overhead water closet. Also in the main house are the Laurel Suite, The Ribbon Room, the Bouquet Room, each unique and beautifully appointed with antiques; some have fireplaces.

A short walk from the "big house" is the Carriage House, which contains twelve more accommodations, three of which are loft rooms. In Fernbrooke, you wind up a circular iron staircase to reach your antique furnished bed-chamber. Your sitting room, bath and balcony are down below, televisions and phones are upstairs and down. Spring Lawn and Hillside are one-level suites, each featuring a bedroom, living room, two baths and balcony. All guests are greeted in their quarters by a silver tray of just baked cookies, fresh fruit, cheese under a little silver dome, chocolates and bottled water, just in case you arrive a bit famished.

A NORMANDY TASTE, LOCALLY PRODUCED

The cuisine of Blantyre's kitchen is traditional French based but with a lighter twist, paying special attention to fresh, local produce. Chevre (goat cheese) from nearby Rawson Brook Farm, wild turkey from the Lusasik Game Farm in South Hadley and a multitude of other local delicacies show up regularly on the menu. Imagine having one supplier who grows 23 different kinds of lettuce just for you. Behind the kitchen is the herb garden which you're welcome to visit. Around a seven-foot eucalyptus tree grow fresh basil, lemon balm, hyssop, nasturtiums, rose campion, oregano, chervil, thyme and rosemary, all of which not only gloriously flavor Blantyre dishes, this pretty garden also furnishes many of the cut flowers for the inside arrangements.

A continental breakfast can be served in the privacy of your room. What a special treat. Not only was the orange juice fresh squeezed and the coffee dark and hot, but the linens and dishes charmingly changed each morning. I inquired about it and was shown shelves filled with various small stacks of pink, blue and yellow linens, and a variety of small sets of crockery. It's up to the server to arrange your tray as they wish. Delightful.

If you decide not to have breakfast delivered to your room, it is served on a glass enclosed terrace overlooking the vibrantly blooming flower gardens. Each table is set with crisp pink napery and fresh flowers. The china and silver gleam as the morning sun blazes across the room. Crispy potato cakes with chive sour cream, buttermilk waffles with strawberries and Irish bangers or, Merrimack smoked salmon with roma tomato, bagel and cream cheese all beg for your consideration. Whatever you do, don't miss the brioche fruit-stuffed French toast. One of Blantyre's signature dishes, it's so big, I defy you to finish it all.

In Fernbrooke, you wind up a circular iron staircase to reach your antique furnished bedchamber. Your sitting room, bath and balcony are down below, televisions and phones are upstairs and down.

OF ART AND MUSIC AND OTHER THINGS

So much to see and do is offered in this area, you'll be busy all day if you desire. Don't miss the new Norman Rockwell Museum, with the world's largest collection of paintings by America's best loved painter, who modestly referred to himself as an illustrator. What about the Tanglewood Music Festival, the Berkshire Botanical Gardens, or the Berkshire Theater Festival? Fine arts and lively arts are a big draw in the Berkshires.

For history lovers, down the road in Pittsfield is the restored Hancock Shaker Village with the largest collection of Shaker furniture and artifacts in an original Shaker site. This two-hundred year old village was called "the city of peace" by the Shakers and is today a living museum of their life, crafts and farming methods. The 1826 round stone barn is amazing in its architecture. And in the 1830 kitchen you can see (and smell) demonstrations of traditional Shaker cooking and baking in the brick ovens. Fascinating for children and adults.

If you're a tennis buff, there are four Har-true courts at Blantyre. The staff will be happy to trot a cooler of thirst-slaking bottled water or soft drinks courtside. Or if you're more inclined toward croquet, pack those whites. The inn has the only two bent grass tournament courts in Massachusetts. Lessons in either sport are available with Blantyre's resident professionals. Actually, I wasn't *too* bad at croquet, even though the rules are a tad more strict than those from my childhood backyard games. The only indisputable rule is that you must have a good time. Not a difficult edict.

Go on, you've earned it, a splash in Blantyre's azure blue pool surrounded by banks of orange tiger lilies. Soft towels, showers, lockers, sauna, and fresh iced tea are found right at the poolhouse.

Go on, you've earned it, a splash in Blantyre's azure blue pool surrounded by banks of orange tiger lilies. Soft towels, showers, lockers, sauna, and fresh iced tea are found right at the poolhouse. You don't mind being spoiled a bit, do you?

Around sixish, the guests saunter down to the main hall, where many nights you'll be entertained by local musicians. Listening to the harp played at sunset, with a glass of vintage wine in hand. I highly recommend it.

On to dinner. The dining room will transport you happily to a more opulent era. The room is darkly paneled and hung with delicate old world tapestries. The tables shine with damask, sterling silver, antique crystal and bone china and, of course, beautiful flowers. Dinner might begin with gratin of Maine crab on summer ratatouille with tomato-basil sabayon or open ravioli with braised squab, wild mushrooms and root vegetable brunoise. For the entree, choose from a "bible thick" veal chop with fresh truffles, Atlantic turbot in a potato crepe on young spinach and champagne-caviar sauce, or Maine Rock crab cakes with red and yellow pepper sauces, any and all complemented by a wine selection from more than 250 vineyards. Sit back and enjoy a spectacular meal, a la Blantyre.

For Sunday visitors, Blantyre orchestrates a couple of special treats. The first is the music of the bagpipes, piped by an authentically kilt-clad gentleman who strolls around the edge of the grounds. The haunting melody floating over velvety green lawns lends Scottish romance and atmosphere to the manor in the morning.

Then clippity-clop, off you go for a complimentary spin in a perfectly restored shiny black 1873 buggy, complete with fringe on the top. The driver is a charming man by the name of Bob Coakly, who has been touring guests around Blantyre's peaceful grounds for over a decade, with the help of his handsome brown Morgan horse named Felicity.

Once Blantyre and the Berkshire Mountains cast their Massachusetts magic on you, felicitous will be your state of mind. Please give Felicity my best regards.

MAINE ROCK CRAB CAKES WITH RED AND YELLOW PEPPER SAUCES

FOR CRAB CAKES:

1 lb. fresh crab meat, carefully picked over
2 eggs
½ cup onion, finely chopped
1 cup fine fresh bread crumbs
¼ teaspoon dry English mustard
2 tablespoons parsley, chopped
1 tablespoon mayonnaise
1 tablespoon Worcestershire sauce
½ teaspoon freshly ground white pepper
1 teaspoon salt
2 beaten eggs, flour and bread crumbs for dredging

1. Beat eggs slightly and combine with all the remaining ingredients.

2. Shape into 3-inch diameter patties, ½-inch thick.

3. Dredge in flour, then beaten egg, and lastly, fine bread crumbs.

4. Fry in vegetable oil over medium-high heat, adding a small nut of fresh butter to the pan when cakes have set. Turn carefully with a spatula, browning both sides.

5. Transfer to a baking sheet and finish in a preheated 375 degree F. oven. Bake until cakes puff a little, about 8 minutes.

Makes about 8 cakes.

RED AND YELLOW PEPPER SAUCES

1 red bell pepper
1 yellow bell pepper
2 egg yolks
1 cup vegetable oil
1 garlic clove, finely minced
salt and freshly ground white pepper
pinch of cayenne pepper
juice of ½ lemon

1. Rub the peppers lightly with vegetable oil, then char the skins over the flame of a gas stove or under a broiler until blistered. Place peppers in a brown paper bag closed for 10 minutes—this will loosen the skin.

2. In the meantime make a stiff mayonnaise by processing the egg yolks until frothy. Add lemon juice and in a slow steady stream, the vegetable oil. Season with garlic, salt, cayenne and fresh ground pepper.

3. Divide the mayonnaise between 2 small bowls.

4. Peel the peppers, cut them in half and discard the seeds and stems.

6. In a food processor, first purée the yellow pepper and whisk this into one of the bowls of mayonnaise.

7. Repeat with the red pepper, taste both sauces and adjust seasoning. The sauces should be pourable. (Whisk in a few drops of warm water to achieve the right consistency.)

8. Cover each bowl with cling film and reserve in a cool place or refrigerate until ready to serve. (The sauces can be made a day or two in advance and refrigerated. Gently rewarm in microwave when ready to serve.)

9. On a warm plate, place two puddles, one of yellow sauce and one of red. Top with one or two crab cakes.

Serves 4 as entree or 8 as appetizer.

MAINE LOBSTER, SPINACH & CUCUMBERS WITH GARLIC-HAZELNUT BUTTER

The lobster dish will require about 1/3 of the flavored butter—the remainder will be delicious on vegetables or fish. It freezes well.

2 tablespoons sea salt
4 live 1¼ to 1½ lb. lobsters (or buy them already steamed)
1 lb. fresh young spinach, stems removed, washed thoroughly and drained
1 European-style, burpless cucumber, cut into 2-inch lengths, quartered lengthwise again, and each segment "turned" into a barrel shape, leaving the firm outside flesh and a stripe of green skin.
1 tablespoon of sugar
3 tablespoon of unsalted butter
salt and freshly ground white pepper

GARLIC-HAZELNUT BUTTER

1 lb. unsalted butter, cut into small cubes
2 tablespoons garlic, finely minced
1 tablespoon shallots, finely minced
1 teaspoon salt
1 teaspoon white pepper
½ cup chopped parsley
1 tablespoon cognac
1 tablespoon Pernod
12 hazelnuts, toasted, peeled & finely chopped
pinch of freshly grated nutmeg

1. Place the room temperature butter into the bowl of a food processor or a mixer. Add all the ingredients and mix thoroughly. Reserve in a covered container. This butter keeps indefinitely frozen.

2. Bring 1 gallon of water to a boil. Add the sea salt, then plunge in the lobsters, cover tightly and return to a boil. Simmer 5 minutes, drain, and set the lobsters aside to cool.

3. To remove the lobster meat from the shell, detach the tail from the body with a twist, and do the same for the claws. Using scissors, cut down the length of the tail from the underside, and pull out the tail meat. Discard the black intestine which runs along the length of the tail. Gently crack open the claws and knuckles with a mallet and extract the meat.

4. Reserve the meat and discard the shells.

5. In a small sauté pan with a fitted lid, combine the cucumbers, sugar and 1 tablespoon of butter over moderate heat. Add a tablespoon of water and a pinch of salt, cover and cook until the cucumbers are tender-crisp. Set aside to cool.

6. In a covered skillet large enough to accept the spinach, melt 1 tablespoon of butter over medium heat, add the spinach, season with a pinch of salt and cover.

7. After about a minute, when the spinach is mostly cooked down, place the lobster meat atop the spinach, recover the pan and lower the heat.

8. While the lobster is heating, return the cucumbers to the stove to heat through gently.

9. Melt ⅓ of the garlic butter in a small pan, taking care to not let it burn.

10. Arrange a bed of spinach on each of 4 warmed plates. Divide the lobster atop the spinach mounds and put some of the cucumbers around each dish. When the garlic butter is foaming, spoon it over the lobster.

Serve with boiled new potatoes.

Serves 4.

FRUIT-STUFFED BRIOCHE FRENCH TOAST

FRUIT FILLING:

2 tablespoons butter
2 cooking apples, peeled, cored & diced
1 cup of diced fruit (pear, banana, pineapple or
    strawberries are suitable)
½ cup raisins or currants
zest and juice of 1 orange
½ cup light brown sugar
1 tablespoon dark rum (optional)

1. Place the raisins in a small pan with 2 cups of water, bring to a boil, remove from the heat leave aside while preparing the fruit. (Drain them just before starting to cook.)

2. Melt the butter in a skillet over medium-high heat. Add all the ingredients to the skillet, tossing gently, and cook until the apples are tender. Set the fruit filling aside to cool.

BRIOCHE FRENCH TOAST:

4 1-¾ inch thick slices of brioche, challah or
    homemade bread, cut from a large, unsliced
    rectangle loaf
3 eggs
¾ cup milk
1 teaspoon vanilla
1 teaspoon sugar
pinch of salt
2 tablespoons vegetable oil
powdered sugar

3. Preheat oven to 375 degrees F.

4. Lay the bread slices on a work surface, and using a sharp 5-inch paring knife, cut a pocket into each slice, entering from the top crust.

5. Fill each pocket with some of the fruit mixture, taking care not to tear the bread.

6. Combine the remaining ingredients in a wide bowl and soak the stuffed bread slices, turning often.

7. Add the vegetable oil to a large oven-proof skillet over medium-high heat. When the oil is fairly hot, add the soaked bread slices. (You may work in batches or use two pans.)

8. When the french toast slices are brown on both sides, place the skillet in the oven and bake for 10-12 minutes, turning once. The french toast should puff up slightly and be hot throughout.

9. Remove the slices from the oven, cut each in half diagonally and place on warm plates. Dust with powdered sugar and serve at once with warm maple syrup.

Serves 4.

The Charlotte Inn

MARTHA'S VINEYARD
EDGARTOWN, MASSACHUSETTS

Strolling idly by a young woman who was industriously applying a little elbow grease to a brass plaque garden gate that must not have met inspection, I remarked that this very activity seemed to go on almost continuously at The Charlotte Inn.

"How often do you polish the brass here?" I inquire, already suspecting the answer what with all the railings, knobs and numbers made of the stuff. "At least once a day, twice if the weather is humid," she said with a little sigh. Inwardly I wince, thinking of *my* neglected brass. This is the level of detail you will find at this New England white clapboard hostelry, constant and unwavering. Nothing languishes for lack of attention, least of all the guests at the Charlotte Inn.

VINES, FLOWERS AND RESTORATION

Explorer Bartholomew Gosnold first set foot on this island in 1602 and promptly named it for his infant daughter Martha and the grapevines growing there, and sailed on. "The Vineyard," as those in the know call this 100 square mile island, has become one of the most sought after holiday spots in the U.S. It has an aura of genteel glamour conferred upon it by the rich and famous off-islanders who come and camp in their summer houses.

One of the most sought after holiday spots in the U.S. It has an aura of genteel glamour conferred upon it by the rich and famous off-islanders who come and camp in their summer houses.

The Charlotte Inn is located on the island's northeast corner, in the old whaling port of Edgartown, and was itself built in 1860 as a sea captain's respite from ocean voyages. Converted to an inn in the early part of this century and purchased by Paula and Gary Conover in 1970, nothing could have foreshadowed for the captain the elegant life his house is living.

Upon check-in at the antique oak barrister's desk from Edinborough, Scotland, I am guided up a curving staircase carpeted in black, strewn with images of wild strawberries and their leaves. Some of the inn's 25 rooms are here in the main house, others are in the Carriage House, the Summer House (upon whose long side porch is served afternoon tea), the Garden House and the Coach House. A long narrow hall is suddenly widened by an unexpected five foot long window seat with a wide bay of small-paned windows looking down onto the courtyard. The alcove is artfully arranged with watering cans, brass bunnies, topiary herbs in pots and stacks of leather-bound books by Hawthorne and Dickens.

Room #12 is at the end of the hall. Thick beige carpet is topped by a Persian rug before the ready-laid marble fireplace over which hangs an English oil painting called "Country Gardens." It is flanked by a staring pair of china Staffordshire dogs. A muted pastel down loveseat sits in one corner, a pair of shiny black riding boots in another. A marble topped dresser offers silver combs and brushes, fresh flowers and a porcelain bowl filled with tiny dried pink rosebuds sending off their sweet scent. The bed is positively princely, a heavily carved four-poster with a wooden canopy "roof" overhead and made with a pristine white coverlet, monogrammed pillowcases and a fluffy duvet for your chilliest nights.

Across South Summer Street, made quiet and shaded by towering linden and horse chestnut trees, is the 1705 Garden House and one of my favorite rooms, #21. Not the largest or most opulent (surely the luxurious two-room Carriage House suite would win those honors), it too features English antiques, a four poster bed and armoire that engulfs one wall. With a green pinstripe wallpaper, it is perfectly suited for what is beyond those eight-foot French doors: your private brick terrace bordering a superb summer perennial garden that blooms with yellow daisies, hollyhocks, fuchsia loosestrife, and pink astilbes waving gently in the island breeze. A restorative setting.

All this has been lovingly crafted by two consummate antique hunters. Gary and Paula Conover shop for such treasures whenever the high summer season is over. London, New York and Philadelphia are some of their haunts. The Conovers' goal, now accomplished, was to replace any reproduction with an authentic antique. On every trip they pick up something from the past, whether a large burl walnut bureau or a delicate piece of porcelain that has miraculously survived breakage and is "Charlotte Inn" enough to rate purchase. "We don't really have a plan for anything we buy, which is why it's so much fun," Gary remarks. "We just cart our finds home and select just the right spot for them."

The Conovers are dedicated to gentler days gone by. Ask Gary for a peek into the office behind the barrister's desk. No computers. Really. Gary says firmly, "We do everything the way it would have been done at the turn of the century. All reservations are taken by pencil and paper. It works very well, you know, and it will always stay that way."

Although most rooms are equipped with air conditioning for the occasional steamy summer Vineyard night, a cool breeze drifts through the windows tonight making for a blissful deep sleep – with the duvet.

The alcove is artfully arranged with watering cans, brass bunnies, topiary herbs in pots and stacks of leather-bound books by Hawthorne and Dickens.

GRACIOUS COUNTRY INNS

ALL OR NOTHING

I look out the window the next morning to discover a classic New England day – crisp and clear. What a pretty garden nook below, one of many on the property. Brick topped and secluded, black urns filled with pale pink geraniums and glass tables stacked with glossy fat magazines for a quiet read in a cushioned chair.

Quelling the desire to skip down the hall, I proceed in a mannerly fashion to the first floor through the living room/art gallery into the dining conservatory for breakfast. Down four steps into a lovely glass atrium built onto the back of The Charlotte Inn, I see the back exterior, windows, shutters and all serve as a clapboard interior for the restaurant. Hung with original oil paintings, it is clever and eye-catching. The floor is flagstone and brick. Yes, it is the old terrace floor.

A choice of traditional breakfast dishes is available from eggs to waffles, but I am positively addicted to the "Morning Glory Muffins." They're moist and rich, studded with walnuts, raisins, carrots and coconut. Add fresh squeezed orange juice and coffee served in fine china constantly refilled by pleasant waitresses in smart summer frocks. A variety of newspapers await on a sideboard. The restaurant L'Etoile takes over here at night. I can't wait to see and taste it by candlelight.

Just outside The Charlotte Inn, Edgartown is your oyster, just one of many. A half block away is Main Street with shopping so diverse and tempting it's perilous to your bank account. Another block or two down the Edgartown Harbor stretches before you, festooned with lobster boats, dinghies and fishermen vying for position with sailors, yachts and powerboaters.

Plenty of various sized charters and rentals are available. I sail out on a 45-foot gaff-rigged sloop staring like any first timer at the infamous Chappaquidick Ferry, and gaping further at the waterfront houses along the island's edge. Modest shingle cottages sit with dignity beside gleaming monuments to success that must have cost a fortune in glass and railings alone. The fickle weather changes from gloriously clear to purple and threatening back to sunshine within 45 minutes.

An easy walk from the inn is the quaint, grey shingled, white-picket fenced Vineyard Museum. Maps, photos, legend and fact of the town's oldest buildings are here, along with the original Gay Head Fresnel light that steered many an 1860 ship to safety. They offer walking tours that are not only fascinating, but also provide the simple pleasure of strolling around Edgartown. The clapboard and shingle shuttered houses and shops are pristine with abundant flower gardens of Scotch broom, poppies and orange tiger lilies, ground oyster shell paths and driveways, trellises and picket fences loaded with climbing pink roses.

The Edgartown Beach – wide, clean and lifeguarded for your protection – is a five-minute drive away. Or rent a bike; paved bike trails alongside the roads seem to take you just about everywhere. Bird watching, hiking, horseback riding, fishing, picnicking can all be enjoyed on undeveloped preserves all over this island, quite of bit of which is waterfront. They belong to the Martha's Vineyard Land Bank. Monies collected from a 2% surcharge of real estate transfers go toward buying open space for the public's enjoyment. Get one of their free maps to find these conservation treasures.

FRESH AND FANCY

But get back to L'Etoile in time for your dinner reservation. Considered by most to be the island's finest restaurant, L'Etoile is owned by Michael Brisson – a talented chef of almost frenetic energy. He is adamant about the freshness of the foods they offer, especially the seafood. Words flow rapid fire as he busily dices and chops, laughing and

Down four steps into a lovely glass atrium built onto the back of The Charlotte Inn whose back exterior, windows, shutters and all serve as a clapboard interior for the restaurant.

giving directions to the equally energetic staff. "I can't stand seafood that has been processed. Have you ever tasted a sea scallop that tasted like chlorine? (Well, yes I have.) That's how some places preserve them for a few days. I get them straight from the source. That's the only way," he insists. I wouldn't argue if I could.

Inside the dining atrium, candles have been lit, the tables set with white linen, Limoges china and silver. For the most romantic table, ask for one of several outside by the wisteria arbor and a gently splashing fountain. Then order a glass of wine and enjoy the menu for a bit.

Though the offerings change seasonally, you might order such fantasies as chilled leek and northern white bean soup with crème fraiche and black American caviar, a warm galantine of chicken with black truffles and hazelnuts, summer cherry and onion compote, or seared and spiced yellowfin tuna with jicama, horseradish and frisée slaw, cilantro mayonnaise and flying fish roe.

For your entree, roasted lamb noisettes with a St. Andre cheese grape leaf custard and merlot-roasted garlic sauce. Or étuéee of native lobster with grilled *fresh* scallops, couscous salad and a chardonnay and vanilla sauce. Wow.

I retire to my room, set the fire to dancing and open a lovely book called *An Island Garden*. Celia Thaxter wrote it in 1894. Her words reflect so well my thoughts about The Charlotte Inn and Martha's Vineyard. "Though the tide is full it makes no murmur. I hear only the drowsy bees in the hollyhocks, the young fledgling song sparrows trying their voices...the season is divinely tranquil and sweet...and so it is with this little isle."

Candles have been lit, the tables set with white linen, Limoges china and silver. For the most romantic table, ask for one of several outside by the wisteria arbor and a gently splashing fountain. Then order a glass of wine.

WARM GALANTINE OF FREE RANGE CHICKEN WITH BLACK TRUFFLES & HAZELNUTS

In this dish the breast of a chicken is filled with a mousseline made from the leg meat and garnished with black truffles and roasted hazelnuts. While this looks difficult, it's not really. As Julia Child says, "It is a dish for those who enjoy cooking. A galantine is not built in a day."

one large free range chicken, about 3 lbs.
    (Ask your meat cutter to remove the breast
    whole–skin on–with the tenderloins spread to
    the side [still attached] to form a rectangle.
    The legs should be boned and cleaned to
    yield a total of ½ lb. meat.)
1 egg
½ cup each small dice carrot, celery, shiitake
    mushrooms, sautéed until tender and chilled.
2 tablespoons chopped black truffles (optional,
    depending on your bank account))
½ teaspoon salt
¼ teaspoon white pepper
pinch ground nutmeg
⅓ cup heavy cream, cold
3 quail eggs (hard boiled & peeled)

1. Butter a 12"×8" piece of parchment paper and place the chicken breast on it. Flatten the thick part of the breast by butterflying it to form a rectangle. Lightly salt & pepper the breast & chill.

2. In a food processor purée the ½ lb. of chicken meat with salt, pepper and nutmeg until smooth; add the egg and process until homogeneous; then add the cream slowly while pulsing the processor (do not overmix).

3. Place the mousseline into a stainless steel mixing bowl and fold in the diced vegetables, hazelnuts and truffles.

4. Place the chicken breast flat and line ½ of the mousseline down the middle, run your finger in the middle of the mousse to create a trench for the quail eggs.

5. Slice the quail eggs in ½ length wise and line the halves in the middle, close to each other. Cover the eggs with the remaining mousseline and smooth evenly.

6. Using the parchment paper fold the breasts over to meet each other and form an even package. The ends do not have to be covered by skin. Now with a larger piece of aluminum foil (shiny side up) wrap the parchment-wrapped stuffed chicken and twist the ends to seal and keep the galantine uniform while cooking.

7. Place the galantine in a bain marie (hot water bath). The water should be covering only ½ the galantine. Place in a preheated 350 degree oven for 45 minutes (internal temperature should read 140 degrees on a meat thermometer). Remove from water bath and let cool at least 10 minutes.

To serve: Unwrap galantine and heat a large sauté pan (on high) with 3 tablespoons olive oil. Slice the galantine in ½-inch slices with very sharp knife Sear the galantine slices turning frequently until golden. Serve on baby chickory with a warm fruit compote. Good luck!

Serves eight appetizer portions.

WARM VIDALIA ONION AND SUMMER CHERRY COMPOTE

This sweet yet savory compote also turns plain roast pork or roast chicken into a special meal. It is very versatile. You can add port and ginger if you like or any infused flavor to match an accompanying dish.

⅓ cup olive oil
2 cups vidalia onions sliced thin
1 cup bing cherries pitted and cut in half
¼ cup honey
⅓ cup sherry vinegar
¾ cup white wine (chardonnay)
¾ cup red wine (cabernet)

1. Using a large deep sided sauté pan or casserole pan, sauté the onions gently in the olive oil (cover to speed this up) until translucent.

2. Remove cover, add the honey and sherry vinegar and cook 5 minutes.

3. Add the cherries and the wines and one bay leaf, simmer 15 minutes.

4. Season with salt and pepper to taste and cook until liquid is thickened slightly. Let cool. Keep in refrigerator if not using immediately.

Makes about 2 cups of compote.

CHILLED SOUP OF NORTHERN WHITE BEANS & LEEKS WITH CRÈME FRAICHE AND BLACK AMERICAN CAVIAR

This variation on the classic vichyssoise is perfect for the warm summer months. The flavors are incredible.

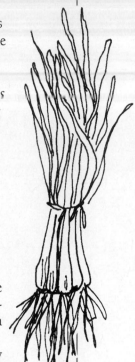

Overnight soak 3 cups white beans in 8 cups
    cool water, drain off the water before using
¼ cup olive oil
4 shallots minced (½ cup)
1 cup white wine
2 cups chopped & well rinsed leeks
4–6 cups chicken stock
1 cup heavy cream
½ cup crème fraiche
1 oz. black American caviar

1. In a heavy bottomed pot, heat the olive oil and gently sauté the shallots until translucent. Then add the white wine and reduce (on high) for 3 minutes.

2. Add the white beans and generously cover them with the chicken stock. Cover the pot and simmer on medium heat until the beans are tender (about 50 minutes).

3. Stir in the leeks, cover and cook five minutes until tender. Remove from heat and let cool a little.

4. Purée the soup in a blender until smooth (reserve some liquid to adjust texture later if needed). Season with salt and pepper.

5. Return to the pot and add the heavy cream; check the seasoning and texture. Add more stock if the soup is too thick, more heavy cream can be added if you like a richer soup.

6. Chill over a water bath or put it in the refrigerator and stir every ½ hour until cool.

7. Serve in chilled red wine glasses with three small dollops of crème fraiche and top the dollops with caviar. Garnish with chopped or whole chives.

Serves 10.

Inn at Shelburne Farms

SHELBURNE, VERMONT

Back in 1885, a stranger in a buckboard wagon appeared at the door of Vermont farmer Edward Saxton and offered to buy his farm, which sat right on Lake Champlain. The farmer eventually sold. A few years later, in the middle of what had been the apple orchard, stood the largest house in Vermont, a Y-shaped mansion of 100 rooms staffed by 30 servants, on a 4,000-acre farm. Shelburne Farms was a summer home for Dr. William Seward Webb and his wife Lila Vanderbilt Webb. Yes, *those* Vanderbilts.

Located just 15 minutes south of Burlington, Vermont, Shelburne was restored nine years ago by fourth generation Vanderbilts at a cost of $1.7 million. Beautiful? You bet, and I love staying at an inn that is really a living museum, with much of the original furniture, art and books. Some farm!

As soon as you step through the front door, you have a sense of being in a time when the pace was slower and living the genteel life was a cultivated art.

LABOUR OF LOVE

The inn is owned by modern day Shelburne Farms, a nonprofit environmental education organization, and run by Kevin O'Donnell and his wife Rhonda, who live nearby with their two young daughters. As Kevin puts it, "To be able to go to work every day in this incredible house filled with so many treasures is nothing but pleasure." You'll feel the same way without working.

As soon as you step through the front door into the oak-paneled entry room, you have a sense of being in a time when the pace was slower and living the genteel life was a cultivated art.

Stroll down the hall to the library. Virtually identical to what it looked like in Vanderbilt times with rich, mossy-green walls and restored gold leaf detailing, a collection of white marble busts line the room over the bookshelves. They seem content with your taking the time to read a tome as you lounge on a green velvet sofa. Grab any volume. Many date back to the Civil War. All the staff asks is that you be careful and please don't take them out by their bindings.

The twenty-four bedrooms range in size from cozy with a shared bath, which used to be the "bachelors' wing," to the roomiest quarters facing the lake. The Webb Room was Dr. Webb's bedroom, containing the ornately carved bed of William Henry Vanderbilt, Lila's father and one of the industrialist core that built the Vandy fortune. The bed was shipped here from New York after his death. Dr. Webb cocooned for weeks at a time in this beautiful room, where later in life he battled his cocaine addiction. The wealthy have their own crosses to bear.

"Overlook" was Lila Webb's airy bedchamber, and today it can be yours. Done in pink silks, it commands a beautiful view overlooking her beloved gardens.

Overlook was Lila Webb's airy bedchamber, and today it can be yours. Done in pink silks, it commands a beautiful view overlooking her beloved gardens. Lila's furniture remains, including a graceful white desk in the corner where she would sit and write in her journals for hours.

Don't miss the playroom on the thirrd floor that the Webb family created for their children. You'll find a four foot high playhouse and barn so large a five year old can crawl in and out.

At one end of the house is the game room, filled with pool tables and hunting trophies, including a Kodiak bear bagged by Webb on a month long tour of Russia in 1898. The game room is where the gentlemen would retire after dinner. With its large stone fireplace and big green leather chairs, one can almost smell the cigars and taste the brandy that were served here. The brandy you may have and this is the only room in the inn where smoking is allowed. Seems fitting.

DIVINE DAIRY DELIGHTS

Of course, Shelburne was built to be a home and a state of the art farm, with the latest agricultural technology. It is still a working farm today and runs a variety of educational programs for adults and children. You can see cows milked and horses shod in the "farm barn," a sprawling five story structure encircling a courtyard that somewhat resembles a castle with turrets. But most interesting is the transformation of unprocessed milk, from the Shelburne's Brown Swiss cows, into cheese. Shelburne Farmhouse Cheddar was voted the best specialty cheese in the U.S. by the American Cheese Society. Don't forget to take some home. It's the best I've ever tasted.

There's plenty to keep you busy in the Burlington area, beginning with an absolute "must-see," the Shelburne Museum, about 7 miles away in Shelburne Village. The museum covers 45 acres and includes 37 exhibit buildings where you'll find a general store, a covered bridge, the best collection of quilts in the country, and the Lake Champlain steamboat Ticonderoga. Renowned for its collection of Americana and folk art, it takes a while to see all that this museum offers but, it's time well spent.

For ice cream fans, don't miss the #1 tourist attraction in Vermont, Ben and Jerry's factory and ice cream parlor, just down the road in Waterbury. Take a guided tour to see how their ice cream is made, and grab a taste for yourself. I had my first taste of Chunky Monkey there, a memorable experience.

To work off those Chunky Monkey fat grams, take a swim in the clean, cold waters of Lake Champlain at the small beach just a short stroll from the Shelburne Inn. If that doesn't get your blood moving, you're in worse shape than you thought. Yup, it's that cold, even in August. Take a towel, or better yet take a warm robe, to wrap yourself in after your...well, let's call it an invigorating swim. I dare you to stay in more than 10 minutes. Or, if you decide not to swim (coward), at least enjoy the ferry ride that crosses Lake Champlain regularly to New York state.

Before dinner, guests are invited to wander downstairs, where cocktails are served along with that famous farmhouse Cheddar. Through the screen doors to the back terrace, enjoy your drink while taking in the view of Lake Champlain. It's also a perfect time to explore the elegantly restored gardens on which Lila Webb lavished so much thought and attention. You'll be filled with gardening envy at the delphiniums, lilies, peonies, lambs-ear, yarrow, and foxglove that thrive in flowerbeds laid out as they were in Lila's day. (It has also been the site of many a romantic wedding.) The lawns slope down to the lake and comfortable benches beckon from underneath shade trees. Ooops, time for dinner.

Meals are served in the conservatory, perhaps my favorite room at Shelburne. The floor is black and white checkerboard marble, with red walls, white woodwork, and crisp white napery, all overlooking the gardens and the lake. Very romantic.

The food must shine to match this setting, but the kitchen is up to the task. The chef is a firm believer in using fresh, local ingredients and the menus reflect classic flavors with a New England twist. Many meals are delightfully enhanced by vine-ripened, greenhouse tomatoes grown on the property by resident farmer David Miskell. Their flavor is simply unbelievable. Once you taste one, it'll be hard to accept grocery store tomatoes. Which is why some true tomato fans have them shipped to their homes year-round.

Breakfast might be ethereal buttermilk griddle cakes served with real Shelburne maple syrup and Vermont Marscapone, five-grain pancakes with local apple cider and dried cherries compote, poached local eggs with Miskell tomatoes and garden herb Hollandaise. Or maybe a farmhouse cheddar omelet with a rasher of cob-smoked bacon or apple sausage. Stop it, I tell you.

For dinner, start with Miskell tomato salad, Vermont goat cheese and red onions (my favorite), Maine crab-meat terrine with grain mustard and crème fraiche, or saffron linguine with locally smoked shrimp, asparagus and spring greens. Then move to Shelburne's pork tenderloin medallions with Long Trail Ale (a local micro-brewery) and Shelburne Cheddar sauce or pan-seared fillet of salmon with roasted garlic and garden herb cream. Consider the braised Vermont rabbit with locally smoked bacon and wild mushrooms.

Save space and energy for divinely indulgent sweets. Farmhouse strawberry shortcake with flaky biscuits and maple-sweetened Vermont cream. A frozen terrine of white, dark and milk chocolate mousse served on a fresh berry sauce. Lemon marscapone cheesecake baked on chocolate pastry garnished with berries. Surely Lila Vanderbilt never ate this well.

DOWN IN THE CELLAR

If you have time, ask permission to visit the archives in the basement of the mansion. It's heaven for history buffs, crammed with loads of old photos of the Webbs during their heyday, entertaining the crème de la crème of society. Even the guest books from the late 1800s survived. I could sit for hours reading the dipped ink pen entries of ghostly guests from days past. One tribute written in a large spiderweb-like Spencerian script, when penmanship truly mattered, wrote "It is easy to come and easy to stay, for a week or a fortnight, when asked for a day. But wherever I've wandered, I beg you'll believe, I've never found a place that was harder to leave."

Meals are served in the conservatory, perhaps my favorite room at Shelburne. The floor is black and white checkerboard marble, with red walls, white woodwork, and crisp white napery, all overlooking the gardens and the lake. Very romantic.

SHELBURNE FARMS CRÈME BRÛLÈE

Cream, vanilla, eggs, sugar. Simple, but oh, so divine. These can be made a day or two before serving, refrigerated and topped with sugar to caramelize just before serving.

1 quart heavy cream
1 vanilla bean
¾ cup (6 oz.) granulated sugar
10 egg yolks
3 tablespoons Demerara or dried brown sugar

1. Slice vanilla bean in half lengthwise and scrape out pulp. Add bean pod and pulp to heavy cream and sugar in a large saucepan. Stir to combine and heat to just above body temperature. Stir occasionally to dissolve sugar.

2. In a large bowl, whisk yolks to combine.

3. Temper the eggs by whisking in a small amount of the heated cream mixture. Continue slowly and gently whisking in cream. Avoid vigorous whisking to reduce air bubbles. Strain mixture through a fine mesh strainer.

4. Pour mixture into eight custard ramekins and place them into a hot water bath (not boiling) and set in a 300 degree oven. Bake for 50-70 minutes. Custards should be firm but not hard.

5. Remove from water bath and chill at least two hours or overnight.

6. When ready to serve, spread a fine layer of Demerara or brown sugar on top of custard. Place under pre-heated broiler to caramelize sugar to a golden brown. Remove and serve immediately.

Serves 8.

SHELBURNE WARM ASPARAGUS SALAD WITH ROASTED PEPPERS, PINENUTS AND LEMON

This is an especially good salad in the spring when asparagus is plentiful and fresh. With bright red peppers and green asparagus accented with the yellow lemon peel, this salad is quite festive. It's also excellent served at room temperature.

1 pound fresh asparagus
1 red bell pepper
1 yellow bell pepper
3 tablespoons pinenuts (pignoli), toasted golden
1 teaspoon grated lemon peel
½ cup extra virgin olive oil
2 cloves garlic, crushed

1. Rub peppers with small amount of olive oil. Place on grill or under broiler and turn frequently. When skin is blistered completely, place in a bowl and cover. After 10 minutes, remove from bowl and carefully remove skin. Cut off ends and open peppers into one long strip. Remove inside membranes and slice into 2–3 inch long strips.

2. While peppers are steaming in bowl, put olive oil into a saucepan with crushed garlic. Heat just to simmer and remove from heat.

3. Remove woody ends of asparagus, and steam asparagus to crisp-tender, about 5 to 8 minutes for medium size spears. If you poke the asparagus with a knife, it should be able to pierce the skin but give a little resistance.

4. In a hot sauté pan, add oil (without garlic) and pepper strips. Toss.

Add asparagus, pinenuts, and season to taste with salt and fresh ground black pepper. Heat through gently and finish by tossing in grated lemon peel.

Serves 4-6.

SHELBURNE PAN ROASTED BREAST OF CHICKEN WITH COGNAC AND BLACK PEPPERCORN SAUCE

A simple, classic dish that doesn't take hours to prepare, the flavor is elegant and memorable. Try serving this with wild rice and sautéed wild mushrooms.

4 8-oz. chicken breasts
2 tablespoons butter
1 tablespoon olive oil
2 cups chicken stock
1 tablespoon coarse, cracked black pepper
4 tablespoons cognac
salt to taste

1. Lightly salt and pepper chicken breasts.
2. Over high heat in large pan, heat oil. When oil is almost smoking, add 1 tablespoon butter.
3. Quickly sear chicken breasts to golden brown. Remove breasts when cooked thoroughly (do not overcook).
4. Remove pan from heat and pour off excess fat. Add cognac and return to heat. Be careful-cognac will flame up!
5. Reduce to simmer and reduce cognac by half, stirring up pan drippings from bottom of pan.
6. Add chicken stock and continue to reduce liquid, stirring occasionally. Add black pepper.
7. When sauce begins to thicken, return chicken breasts to pan to reheat. Remove when warm and finish reducing sauce. When sauce coats a spoon, stir in 1 tablespoon butter.
8. Spoon sauce over chicken and serve.
   Serves 4.

SHELBURNE VERMONT APPLE, SMOKE BACON AND ONION FRITTATA

This wonderful brunch or supper dish is best with Shelburne Farms Cheddar if you can find it (or order it). You may never go back to other Cheddars again.

4 large eggs
½ cup heavy cream
salt and pepper
½ cup smoked bacon, cooked and crumbled
½ cup finely diced red onion
½ cup diced Vermont apples
½ cup extra sharp Cheddar cheese
fresh chopped parsley
1 tablespoon butter

1. Combine eggs with cream, season with salt and pepper and whisk until combined.
2. In a very hot 10 inch oven-proof non-stick skillet, add the butter and melt until bubbling. Add the egg mixture and cook over medium-low heat until the bottom begins to cook but not the top, about 3 or four minutes.
3. Sprinkle eggs with the red onion, bacon and apples and top with the cheese. Place the pan in a 350 degree oven. Let the cheese melt and the rest of the egg mixture continue to cook just until firm, about 7–9 minutes.
4. Sprinkle with fresh parsley. Cut into wedges and serve hot or room temperature.
   Serves 4.

The Point

SARANAC LAKE, NEW YORK

Bouncing down a long unpaved road in the middle of nowhere, with nary a sign in sight, it's difficult to believe that this is the way to "the number one lakeshore resort in America." Believe it. Soon enough, you'll drive under a large marquee that uses whittled aspen branches to spell out "The Point" in true Adirondack style. Entering the property you see large and small log cabins with their original gabled slate roofs scattered throughout the pine trees, terra cotta pots of bright red and yellow flowers, flagstone walkways cradled between lush wild ferns, and Saranac Lake glittering like cut glass through the trees.

This is one of the former Great Camps of the Adirondack Mountains. Camp Wonundra was built in 1933 by William Avery Rockefeller (nephew of John D.) as a "modest" hunting lodge and escape from the city, complete with every comfort. This rustic compound was purchased in 1980 and restored to a new life as The Point. And it's a grand life as a place of warm hospitality, every conceivable luxury, sumptuous surroundings and superb food to robber barons in waiting.

ADIRONDACK ROMANCE

And boy, do Bill and Claudia Mcnamee know how to do it right. Staying at The Point can only be described as indulgent living in every sense of the word. The eleven rooms – four in the Main Lodge, three in the Eagle's Nest, and three in the Guest House – are all unique. Then there's The Boathouse, which is a real boathouse. In the Rockefeller days the children's playroom, today The Boathouse is the most unabashedly romantic room on the place, with windows on three sides and polished natural wood floors. You undoubtedly get the property's best view of the lake from the three-quarter deck that wraps around this second floor suite. Two beds swing on the porch in the lake breezes, just in case you tire of the huge bed in the center of the room. That bed is protected by extravagant yardage of gauzy mosquito netting draped down from the vaulted ceiling and tied at the four corners of the bed. A bottle of your best champagne, please.

Weatherwatch, Sentinel, Trappers and Mohawk. Some rooms are airy, some cozy, but all have fireplaces and sport a classic Adirondack look, with woodsy colors and buffalo plaids. Ralph Lauren lives here in spirit and style. I stayed in Algonquin, one wall lined with great old books, a stone fireplace at the end, and a bank of windows that looked out through the pine trees. My favorite touch was a puffy featherbed on top of the mattress that makes for some of the softest sleeping you'll ever experience. Your fire will be laid fresh each day so that the only effort expended for a warm blaze is striking a match. Bottled water, fresh fruit and imported wine await in your room. Spirits and wines are available (no charge) twenty-four hours a day in a small but extremely well-stocked bar just off the front entrance to the main lodge.

NO RESISTANCE, NO REGRET

And the food. Oh, the food. Executive chef Bill Mcnamee boasts that no one has ever left The Point claiming to have lost weight. That's surely understatement, because from breakfast through dinner, you are presented with a staggering array of delicious, original dishes paired with fine wines from around the world. Any willpower I had left was slipping further away at every meal. And I didn't care.

This level of expertise is no surprise, considering the fact that Bill was once a chef at the famous three-star restaurant Le Gavroche in London. He learned his lessons well. The Point makes everything fresh, from the fragrant breads to fabulous pastas. Bill admits that being in the middle of the Adirondacks provides a challenge to rival restaurants in New York or London, but whatever they can't get locally, they fly in. The Point has a continuing relationship with Le Gavroche, and young creative chefs travel over to work at The Point for six to twelve month periods.

You'll be awakened in the morning by a soft tap at your door. On the floor outside the door you find a tray with hot coffee. How did they know that's just what you wanted? In summer, breakfast is served alfresco on the stone terrace overlooking Saranac Lake, though the staff is more than happy to bring it to your room if you like. Your table might be set with a forest green tablecloth, plaid napkins and blue enameled tinware. How about banana walnut pancakes or eggs any way you like 'em, plus homemade sausage, country bacon, fresh mushrooms sautéed with herbs, grilled tomatoes and fresh baked breads, all served to the twitter of birds and the occasional distant roar of an early morning powerboat.

THE WILL TO MOVE

After breakfast, hiking, golfing, cycling on The Point's bikes, water skiing or fishing (equipment provided) might appeal to you. Let's face it, after a breakfast at The Point you may feel a real need for exercise. Saranac Lake offers many possibilities but one of the best is a ride in The Point's wonderful mahogany-hulled 1929 Hackercraft, which is a perfect way to see the other "great camps" around the lake. In the boathouse are canoes and small outboard motor boats for exploring the nooks of Saranac Lake, and a sunfish and sailboard. You can even hire an Adirondack guide to take you hunting, fishing or animal tracking on a hiking tour. Reservations are necessary.

You'll be awakened in the morning by a soft tap at your door. On the floor outside the door you find a tray with hot coffee. How did they know that's just what you wanted?

FROM MEAL TO MEAL

Lunch might be a barbecue, but probably not like any you've ever attended. Big round tables covered with red cloths sit on a point overlooking the lake. The grills are smoking, laden with swordfish and shrimp brochettes. There's also salmon in puff pastry, couscous, luscious salads made from everything from pink shrimp to red tomatoes, corn on the cob, homemade berry cobblers, with plenty of imported wines and beers to wash it all down. Try water-skiing after a lunch like this.

Everyone dresses for dinner at The Point, black tie Wednesdays and Saturdays, and it's truly an elegant affair. One splendid evening began with French champagne, hot and cold canapés and a sunset barge ride around the lake.

Chatting and laughing guests then move into the great hall, a magnificent log room with huge stone fireplaces at both ends. The walls are covered with hunting trophies from days gone by: deer in full antlered glory, antelope and moose. Leather sofas spread with zebra skins and fluffy down buffalo plaid pillows are arranged in intimate conversation groupings. This is Hemingway.

At one end, two round tables seating twelve each are magnificently set for dinner with bone china, sterling, and incredible flowers arranged by Claudia herself. Candles light the entire room. At The Point you dine with the other guests as you might have done in Rockefeller's day, dinner party style. Your dinner partners might be an industrialist, an up and coming writer, a well known designer or someone from the world of politics. Whoever they are, everyone is ready for good conversation and a four course gourmet feast that has kept the staff busy for most of the afternoon. Every dish will be matched with a carefully selected wine.

You might begin with soft shell crabs flown in from Maryland, sautéed with tomatoes and herbs, and served over homemade white truffle pasta or perhaps a soufflé Suisse – a light cheese soufflé with a Gruyère cheese sauce. Move on to rack of lamb with ratatouille, veal chop with baby vegetables, or roasted baby poulet with wild mushrooms and potatoes. Dessert could be a golden puffy Gran Marnier soufflé or a white and dark chocolate cream harlequin torte. Yes, it's as scrumptious as it sounds.

The Point is open year around, except for the boathouse which naturally gets just a bit chilly in winter. Cross-country skiing, ice skating, snow-shoeing, snow barbecues by roaring bonfires, or ice-fishing in a custom-made shanty on the frozen lake take over in the winter. Claudia Mcnamee says that it's her favorite season. "Everything is bit more quiet, and absolutely gorgeous." I can imagine. If you ever feel a need to totally indulge yourself in luxury, whatever the season, The Point is your place.

Everyone dresses for dinner at The Point, black tie Wednesdays and Saturdays. One splendid evening began with French champagne, hot and cold canapés and a sunset barge ride around the lake.

POINT ASPARAGUS AND MORELS IN PUFF PASTRY

This is an extravagant and very rich appetizer. When I found dried morels at $14 an ounce, I substituted various wild fresh mushrooms such as oyster, chanterelle, and porcinis. They were just as good, and my husband didn't leave me. Perhaps you know of a secret place where morels grow. If so, try them in this fabulous dish.

1 sheet of puff pastry (can be found in frozen food section)
2 ounces dried morels, rinsed, or 1 pound of other fresh mushrooms
12 asparagus spears, cut on an angle into 1-inch pieces
2 tablespoons of butter for sautéing
2 tomatoes, blanched, seeded and diced
4 cloves garlic
1 truffle, chopped (optional, depending on how rich you feel!)
3 ounces butter

1. Cut the puff pastry into six rectangles and cook as directed on package. Allow to rest.
2. Soak the dried mushrooms in hot water to cover for 10 minutes. Drain.
3. Dice the mushrooms and sauté in butter. Season with salt and pepper.
4. Repeat with the asparagus, cooking just until tender.
5. At this time melt the 3 ounces of butter. Crush the garlic with a knife, and add to the butter. Do not heat the butter too much, just enough to release the fragrance and taste of the garlic. Add the tomato and truffle, if using. Sauté for a minute, season, and remove garlic.

Place warm puff pastry on plate. Spoon the mushroom-asparagus mixture in center of pastry. Add the tomato butter around the plate and serve.

Six portions.

POINT POULET AUX LENTIL

This recipe is *so* "The Point." Simple yet very full flavored, it's an altogether satisfying dish on an autumn or winter evening by the fire. My family happens to be lentil lovers, so I was happy to get a new and different recipe from the traditional lentil soup. If you desire, sautéed carrots or zucchini may be added to the dish.

4 boneless and skinned chicken breasts
8 ounces of lentils (soaked in water for 1 hour)
1 carrot
2 shallots
2 stalks celery
4 tablespoons duck or bacon fat (or olive oil)
4 cups good veal or chicken stock
salt and pepper to taste
1 bay leaf
lardons (crisp bacon, chopped)
fresh thyme, chopped

1. Place fat in dutch oven and heat. Add all coarsely chopped vegetables and drained lentils. Sauté gently for 5 minutes.
2. Add the stock, cover and cook until done, about 45 minutes.
3. Roast chicken breasts at 400 degrees F for 10 minutes, or until done. Do not overcook. Slice breasts in diagonal strips and keep warm.
4. Place the lentils on the bottom of a large shallow bowl. Place sliced chicken breasts on lentils. Sprinkle with fresh chopped thyme and lardons. Add a little stock to lentils to keep them moist.

Serves four.

SALMON A LA NAGE

If you enjoy salmon as I do, try this rich but simple to prepare dish. I served it to guests for a leisurely Sunday lunch with a California chardonnay, accompanied by sautéed potatoes. There were no leftovers!

6 salmon fillets, about 6 oz. each
for poaching liquid:
  ½ bottle white wine
  3 star anise (or a few drops anise extract or Pernod)
  2 carrots
  2 leeks
  1 whole lemon, cut in half
  2 tablespoons sea salt

FOR SAUCE A LA NAGE:

4 shallots, finely chopped
1 cup cream
8 ounces butter
chopped chives

1. In a large pan or fish poacher, pour the wine and an equal amount of water. Add the star anise, carrots, leeks, lemon and sea salt. Bring to a boil, cover and simmer to combine the flavors for about 30 minutes.

2. Poach the fish in this mixture for about 10 minutes or until just done. Remove salmon from liquid (reserving 1 cup) and keep warm.

3. Gently sauté the chopped shallots in 1 tablespoon of the butter.

4. Add one cup of the poaching liquid. Reduce over high heat to a syrup.

5. Add the cream; then whisk in the butter 1 tablespoon at a time over low heat.

6. Add the chives and serve over the salmon.
   Serves 6.

POINT GRAND MARNIER SOUFFLE

Yes, we still all ooh and aah when a soufflé comes out of the oven, all golden and puffy, smelling like heaven. I've always been a little afraid of making them to tell the truth, but I can now say I've overcome that fear. Here is a soufflé recipe that is a favorite of guests at The Point made with candied oranges.

3 oranges
1 cup sugar
1 cup water
1 cup all-purpose flour
1 cup sugar
3 cups milk
1 vanilla bean
12 egg yolks
12 egg whites

1. Slice oranges with the rind and remove the seeds. Add 1 cup sugar and 1 cup water to the oranges in a large saucepan. Bring to a boil and simmer to a thick, syrup consistency. Cool and chop fine.

2. Mix together 1 cup flour and remaining 1 cup sugar. Bring half the milk to a boil and add the vanilla bean. Remove from heat and let stand 5 minutes.

3. Mix the remaining milk with the dry ingredients.

4. Remove the vanilla bean, and add the boiled milk to the milk, sugar and flour paste. Return this to the saucepan and cook over medium heat until thick, whisking constantly so as not to stick and burn. This will take about 3–5 minutes. Remove from heat. Cool slightly.

5. Add the egg yolks one at a time, whisking after each addition. Mix until smooth and all is incorporated.

6. Fold candied oranges to the custard.

7. Whip the egg whites until stiff. Add a little of the custard to the whites. Fold gently until incorporated. Then add the rest of the whites to the custard and fold again until almost incorporated.

8. Butter and sugar a soufflé mold that measures 12 inches across and 6 inches deep. Fill until ²/₃ full.

9. Bake at 400 degrees F for 35–40 minutes. Serve immediately.
   Serves 10–12.

The White Barn Inn

KENNEBUNKPORT, MAINE

When George Bush was elected President of the United States in 1988, the little seaside town of Kennebunkport was dramatically placed on the tourist map. Everyone wanted to see this place with the funny name where Barbara and George spent their holidays. But the curious also discovered what is not a well-kept local secret: Kennebunkport has been providing seaside New England family holidays for generations.

PLACE IN HISTORY

That sense of tradition is also the heritage of The White Barn Inn. Built as a farmhouse around 1872, it became the Forest Hill House about 20 years later, a respite for travelers making their way up the rugged coastline of Maine. An entry in a local paper:

> "They arrange the napkins every day differently at the Forest Hill House."   – *August 8, 1887.*

Or, how about this one.

> "Forest Hill House: Pleasantly located near ocean, river, and woodland. Table supplied with the best the market affords. Vegetables and pure milk from hotel farm. Sanitary conditions perfect."

The latter entry was a 1917 advertisement by innkeeper D. F. Toothaker (really)—old fashioned wording, but the facts haven't really changed, only the faces.

Today this respected establishment is called The White Barn Inn, owned and operated by a husband and wife team – native Australian Laurie Bonjourno, who runs his restaurant, and Laurie Cameron, who holds the reins at the inn. Together they manage a precision operation (one guest remarked that a Swiss watch had nothing on this place) that is indeed pleasantly located with a table most assuredly supplied with the best the market affords. A member of Relais and Chateaux, the inn was awarded four diamonds by Triple A. The White Barn Restaurant is the only five-diamond restaurant in New England.

Perched on Beach Street, just a short walk to the Atlantic, The White Barn is a blue-grey clapboard structure with white trim, very New England, with the Carriage House and Gatehouse just a few steps away. Inside the main building are several common living areas, stuffed sofas and chairs in period fabrics tucked into alcoves everywhere for private reading. The walls in the living room are a dark cranberry red, with polished wooden floors, a navy Chesterfield sofa and print chairs and tables full of magazines and fresh flowers. Cut glass decanters of port and brandy are on silver trays with fine crystal glasses for an evening nightcap. A rich Williamsburg blue room at the foot of the staircase offers a large TV hidden inside an armoire, with comfy chairs for viewing. Afternoon tea is also served in these rooms each day.

LUXURY FOR THE AGES

The walls in the living room are a dark cranberry red, with polished wooden floors, a navy Chesterfield sofa and print chairs and tables full of magazines and fresh flowers. Cut glass decanters of port and brandy are on silver trays.

My bedroom, one of twenty-five, is at the top of a maple staircase. It is sunny and peach colored with handpainted New England furniture. The corner armoire has a trompe l'oeill bottom drawer with several pieces of "clothing" painted to appear as if hanging over the edge. Inside is a thick terrycloth robe for the stay, and on the painted bureau across the room is a basket of fruit, a chilled bottle of wine and bottled water. A basket of toiletries thoughtfully includes a loofah and a small pot of strawberry lip balm. In the center of the bed is a flower and ribbon bedecked straw hat. Laurie Cameron and helpers make them in the winter when things are slower. She points out, "They're just another welcome sign, a little hello-we're-glad-you're-here for our guests."

For total, sumptuous, sybaritic luxury, take one of the Carriage House Suites just across the driveway. The Red Suite is my favorite with its deep red carpet, private covered porch and entrance. All suites have dark four poster king-sized beds, fireplaces with sitting areas of deep club chairs and ottomans, botanical prints on walls papered in period wall-coverings. Televisions hide in armoires and each suite has a private line telephone. The marble bathrooms are huge, with separate glass showers, double jacuzzi tubs for a good long soak, and tables full of toiletries. If you wish, your fire will be lit in the late evening while you are at dinner.

Retiring early, I find my towels have been magically replaced, my bed turned down, pillows fluffed, and by the bed a plate of sweets. I have been told these change daily at the chef's whim; tonight's poppy seed strudel-like pastries are more than welcome.

FOG AND LIGHT

The morning brings the usual Maine day – rather foggy and nicely cool. Deciding on a bicycle ride before breakfast, I put on a sweater to abscond with one of the inn's bikes ready for guests. Before I get on my way, a young staffer runs over from the herb and flower garden, breathless. "Let me wipe that off for you; it might be a bit damp with all this fog." She does, I thank her and am off. It takes me only two minutes to reach the ocean via flat Beach Road. Gooch's beach and whitecapping ocean sweep off to my left, and brown and gray shingled, shuttered houses are to my right. Most have window boxes of red and white geraniums or pink and purple petunias waving gaily colored heads, enjoying the light mist. Early morning walkers stride purposefully along the jagged coastline. The tide is out, deserting lonely, craggy, seaweed covered boulders. My only companions now are a few children out with their dog. The fog begins in earnest about 300 yards from shore, a few ghost boats hovering at its edge.

OK, now I'm really hungry. Back at The White Barn their ample version of a continental breakfast has been arranged in a sunny dining room off the lobby. The windows are draped with chintz and sheers, pretty chandeliers hang from the original pressed tin ceiling. I grab a newspaper over on a side table as I enter and stand frozen for a moment at the display. Silver trays of staggered height and platters are filled with chocolate chip and apple-pecan muffins, coconut scones, raisin rolls, apple filled pastries, rolls dusted with crushed walnuts, poppy seed twists, plain and chocolate croissants, blueberry-cranberry cake, chocolate pound cake and some plain baguettes for the disciplined. On another table is a big pottery crock of homemade granola which could be flavored with bourbon, cherries, kahlua or apricots, depending on the chef's mood. At my table, a waitress with a French accent (many of the staffers are from abroad) brings an artful plate of melon, pineapple, local blackberries and blueberries, and refills my coffee cup without being asked. I like that.

The four beaches of Kennebunkport are of course the big draw in the summer. Goose Rocks Beach (great for swimming and finding star fish and sand dollars), Gooch's Beach (closest to the inn and curved in a crescent), Middle Beach (you can see seven lighthouses from here at night), and secluded, quiet Parson's Beach (set in tall grasses – get there early to park) offer days of enchantment.

Can anyone go to Kennebunkport and not gawk at former President Bush's compound that has been in his family since 1903? Probably not. Just a five minute drive from the White Barn, it's on a rocky peninsula and you can see it easily from the road. "Hi, Barbara!"

Shopping is plentiful in Kennebunkport, both at Dock Square and the Lower Village, both just minutes from The White Barn. But real bargain hunters won't mind a little 45-minute drive to Freeport for the "mother ship" of L. L. Bean, open 24 hours a day, 365 days a year so scheduling is never a problem. It sits right in the middle of countless outlet stores. Something for me, something for Aunt Matilda. Something for me, something for Cousin Hortense.

Tennis, horseback riding, sailing, deep sea fishing, and three golf courses can all be arranged. And in the winter, Harris' Farm allows cross country skiing with miles of groomed trails. For any activities, if you tell the White Barn a day in advance, they will pack you a picnic lunch to take on your outing.

HEIGHT, DEPTH AND TASTE

I wander into the restaurant of The White Barn before the other guests. Constructed from two barns built in the 1800s, a dining atmosphere is created unlike anything I've ever experienced. At its apex, the three-story ceiling hits 50 feet, with lofts around the sides, filled with an old spinning wheel, decoys, crockery, well-traveled antique leather luggage, baskets, a hobby horse, the brass cash register, flags, a toy wooden train. At each end of the barn are windows, two stories high, letting in the day's last sunlight. The wait staff is already here, dressed formally in starched white jackets,

Early morning walkers stride purposefully along the jagged coastline. The tide is out, deserting lonely, craggy, seaweed covered boulders.

making sure that all tables are set perfectly with gleaming silver and china, napkins folded just so.

The White Barn restaurant is the domain of Laurie Bonjourno. He will oversee what will be one of the finest and most precise, yet joyful dining experiences I have ever had. Laurie moves around the room with the wait staff. The waiters have ascertained beforehand the answers to all pertinent questions about the people in their charge. Are they guests here? Have they been guests before? Are they celebrating a special evening? Associate waiters in their first year at The White Barn are never allowed to address the customer. Laurie explains, "It takes time to learn the subtleties of what we do here. They must learn about the menu and the wine list, the local history, about the other Relais and Chateaux properties in New England and their amenities."

Soon, guests begin to wander in. They pause at the piano bar, listening to live music played every night, the piano topped with a four foot arrangement of white lilies, delphinium and curly willow branches. The brass bar to the right glows from a perfect polishing.

The menu is a dream of culinary skill and imagination. Lobster minestrone with black beans, roasted tomatoes, olive oil croutons and a bacon pistou or a timbale of smoked salmon, Maine crab, artichoke and osetra caviar? I choose the grilled Hudson Valley foie gras with caramelized rhubarb, port wine and shoestring potatoes. I accidentally drop my napkin. Right as it hits the floor, a waiter swoops it discreetly away and murmurs "Let me get you a fresh one," before I even realize what has happened. Gee.

Entrees include grilled breast of duck with olive oil smashed potatoes, braised fennel and tomato petals in a red wine and calamata olive sauce or, grilled loin of yellowfin tuna with gingered basamati rice and cooled wasabi crème fraiche. Or, a grilled veal chop garnished with a ruby port poached pear in a pool of savory pear gastrique. Difficult choices but the waiter gracefully guides me through. These waiters are the best I've ever seen, with that delicate balance and impeccable sense of timing; when to come by; when to chat a moment; when to withdraw in silence.

And now the moment comes to serve the food. I hope you're sitting with a group to get the full effect. Each waiter bears a separate dish of food. They position themselves at the side of each guest. A slight nod, and in one graceful motion, all plates are served simultaneously. Bravo!

The foie gras is buttery and decadent, perfectly paired with the tart rhubarb and crunchy potatoes, a marvel of taste and texture. If you're feeling extravagant, try it with a half-bottle of Chateau d'Yquem sautérnes. Liquid gold. The tender duck breast and smashed potatoes are divine. I want to stand up and applaud, demand that the chef be brought from the kitchen for praise and honors. I do none of these things, of course. I finish a glass of Mersault, devour a light, airy lemon mousse, and think what a lucky stiff I am to have eaten at The White Barn Inn.

The tender duck breast and smashed potatoes are divine. I want to stand up and applaud, demand that the chef be brought from the kitchen for praise and honors.

PEAR MOUSSE

4 pears peeled and cut into 1/2" pieces
¼ cup white wine
1 tablespoon lemon juice
3 tablespoons honey
4 cloves
2 bay leaves
1 cinnamon stick
½ oz. gelatin dissolved in ¼ cup of water
½ cup heavy cream

1. Combine pears, wine, lemon juice and in a medium saucepan and toss well.
2. Add honey, cloves, bay leaves and cinnamon stick. Cover and simmer over low heat until pears are soft. Set aside to cool.
3. Remove and discard the bay leaf and cinnamon stick.
4. Purée the pears and add the gelatin mixture.
5. Whip cream until stiff and fold into pear mixture. Refrigerate for several hours or overnight until set. .
6. Garnish with fresh pear slices dipped in lemon juice so they will not turn dark.

Serves 4.

MAINE SUMMER RED FRUIT SOUP WITH BERRIES AND BUTTERMILK ICE CREAM

4 oz. strawberries
4 oz. raspberries
4 oz. blackberries
¼ cup cold water
1 tablespoon powdered sugar (depending on the
  natural sugar of the berries)
1 teaspoon lemon juice
4 oz. strawberries (for garnish)
4 oz. raspberries for garnish)
4 oz. blackberries (for garnish)

1. Liquefy 4 oz. of strawberries, raspberries and blackberries in a blender or processor. Pass through a fine strainer. Chill.

BUTTERMILK ICE CREAM

1½ cups heavy cream
2¾ cups buttermilk
1 teaspoon vanilla extract
1 small piece lemon zest
6 egg yolks
1 cup sugar

1. Combine buttermilk, heavy cream, vanilla extract, lemon zest and ½ cup sugar in a large saucepan. Bring to a boil over high heat, stirring constantly.
2. In a large mixing bowl combine the egg yolks and remaining ½ cup sugar and whip with a wire whisk until egg yolks are smooth and pale in color.
3. While constantly whisking, slowly pour the hot buttermilk into the egg yolks. Transfer mixture back into sauce pot and stir continuously with a wooden spoon over medium heat. (*Do not boil! If mixture boils, throw it in the garbage and go out for ice cream.*)
4. When mixture coats the back of the spoon, immediately strain and chill in an ice bath or in refrigerator. When mixture is cold to the touch put in an ice cream freezer and follow freezer directions until frozen.
5. Place equal amounts of reserved garnish berries into a soup plate. Pour red fruit soup over and around berries. Place a scoop of buttermilk ice cream in center.

Serves 6.

LOBSTER SPRING ROLL WITH SWEET AND SOUR SAUCE

1½ lb. lobster, steamed, shocked in an ice bath,
   all meat removed and cut into large dice (lobsters can be steamed for you at the market)
3 oz. carrot, julienne
3 oz. daikon radish, julienne
3 oz. snow peas, julienne
1 oz. savoy cabbage, julienne
½ teaspoon garlic, minced
½ teaspoon fresh ginger, minced
¼ cup soy sauce
3 tablespoon hoisin sauce
1 tablespoon vegetable oil
4 rice paper spring roll wrappers
1 egg, beaten with 1 teaspoon water and pinch
   of salt
Hot and Sour Sauce

1. Heat oil in sauté pan over high heat. Add ginger and garlic to hot oil and cook for a few seconds.

2. Add carrot and daikon to pan and stir fry for 1 minute.

3. Add snow peas and stir fry for 1 minute

4. Add cabbage to pan and stir fry for 30 seconds.

5. Stir in soy sauce and hoisin sauce to vegetable mixture and remove from heat. Place vegetable mixture on sheet pan and refrigerate to cool.

6. Combine diced lobster meat, with *half* of the cold, stir fried vegetables in a bowl.

7. Place square spring roll wrapper on the diagonal so that a diamond shape faces you. In center of diamond place ¼ of the lobster-vegetable mixture. Fold the corner close to you up to cover the mixture fold left and right corners in and gently roll mixture away from you. Place a small dab of egg wash mixture on top corner to seal and continue to roll.

8. Repeat with remaining 3 wrappers.

9. Allow spring rolls to dry in refrigerator uncovered for several hours for best results.

10. Deep fry spring rolls in 350 degree vegetable oil until brown. Drain on paper towels and keep warm.

11. Reheat the remaining half of the vegetable mixture. Place vegetables in center of a plate.

12. Cut all rolls in half on the bias. Arrange spring rolls on the plate of stir-fried vegetables.

13. Pour hot sauce over top of spring rolls and vegetables and garnish plate with fresh chopped cilantro.

Serves 4.

HOT AND SOUR SAUCE

1 cup water
1 cup sugar
¼ cup rice wine vinegar
1 tablespoon red pepper flakes

Bring sugar and water to a boil. Remove from heat and add remaining ingredients. Can be made ahead and reheated.

Makes 2 cups.

SOUTHWEST

The Boulders

CAREFREE, ARIZONA

I never realized there are so many elaborately shaped varieties of cactus. Beguilingly round – like lethal teddy bears or prickly fire hydrants. Or, multi-armed fifty-foot giants weighing as much as five cars with limbs outstretched to the sky. These water hoarding succulents are just a tiny albeit magnificent part of the diverse life here in the dessert. For those who think the desert a place where nothing survives, news flash. Some 2,500 different species of flowering plants, 300 types of birds and 100 different mammals call these Sonoran Desert foothills home sweet home. And so can you, with substantial style and grace.

In the middle of this ochre-tinted Arizona landscape, punctuated by cactus, brown and white rabbits scampering across the sand and 12-million-year-old granite rock formations providing welcome shade, you find The Boulders. Continually a top pick in the Zagat survey of the country's best hotels, The Boulders is barely distinguishable from its desert habitat. Sun hats off to the architect Robert Bacon, who lived on these 1,300 acres for a year before picking up a drawing pencil. His ascetic quest paid off. The natural terrain was left practically untouched during development and if any plant had to be moved, it was carefully dug up, tagged and replanted elsewhere on the property.

Sun hats off to the architect Robert Bacon, who lived on these 1,300 acres for a year before picking up a drawing pencil. The natural terrain was left practically untouched during development.

RISING FROM THE DESERT

The Boulders opened in 1985 just north of Scottsdale in Carefree, Arizona. The property consists of 160 truly well designed "casitas," a main lodge with two 4-star restaurants, two swimming pools, two 18-hole golf courses and six tennis courts. The surrounding tableau could not be improved upon by Van Gogh or Monet, and here they are blessed with 300 days of sunshine a year to enjoy it all.

6:00 AM, casita #219. Off in the distance is the lonely, early morning yelp of a coyote. Light is just beginning to peek through window shutters into my bedroom. My eyes wander over the room, designed in calming desert shades of tan and cream with muted southwestern art on the stucco walls, hand hewn beams crisscrossing the ceiling. The fireplace is stocked and ready to go fronted by chairs for lounging fireside in the evening. The bathroom is marvelous with Mexican tile floors and white handmade tile counters and walls, a dressing table with makeup lights (thank you), huge jacuzzi tub, separate glass shower, and walk-in closet. Every luxury for cocooning. It succeeds so well that I must force myself from bed and stumble outside to the balcony for a moment. The air is cool and fresh. The sun is coming up behind me throwing a brilliant spotlight onto the red granite boulders that tower over my room. Gorgeous. I hope they don't roll. Again the coyote howls, audible but invisible. I'd love to catch a glimpse and I search the desert foothills made golden by the sunrise, dotted with distant houses, mesquite and paloverde trees and cacti. What beauty – but no coyote. After brewing a cup of gourmet coffee in my little coffee maker, I slip into a pair of jeans. It's almost time for what I've been told is the best way to see the dessert.

Striding along the winding pathways through casitas and cacti, I pass by green #5. Early morning dew glistens on grass so green one marvels at the desert accomplishment. A few fat bunnies have this lush grassiness all to themselves for the moment, not at all concerned by my presence. Watching for a moment, I move on to the main lodge and duck through the massive stark front doors carved from four different hand-rubbed woods. Inside, skylights flood early morning sun onto the stone floors and light up walls adorned with original southwestern paintings and weavings of such quality and value that the inn offers art tours each week. All is quiet but even so, early morning coffee and tea are out for morning people or travelers still on east coast time.

Over across the fairway a small crowd has gathered, silhouetted against the sunrise. A huge flat balloon in patches of red, yellow, blue and purple is being rolled across the grass. By the time I get there, a fan is billowing air into the balloon's expansive interior. A couple of blasts of hot air and it's upright, a rainbow giant attached by ropes to a small, rather delicate looking wicker basket. Into this I'm encouraged to climb along with several other seemingly sanguine guests. Perhaps they don't sense the danger here. Clambering over the side none too gracefully, we get a few instructions from the pilot, then the flame thrower noisily belches heat up into the only thing that will soon keep us from dropping like stones. We lift almost imperceptibly from the ground.

I take a deep breath and concentrate on what I see. The still lake alongside the fairway is like a deep blue mirror. We pass by khaki tan casitas with their wooden lattice-topped balconies filled with snoozing guests, beside the main lodge the pools appear as two big sapphire misshapen eyes. Higher and higher we go, looking for just the right breeze. "Look, two coyotes just to the right." We all crane our necks, and sure enough, in a couple of seconds we spot some jackrabbits racing at breakneck speed and a couple of grayish coyotes loping along behind. You'll never catch breakfast that way, bub. Floating along in silence, broken only by the occasional blast of the propane torch is almost eerie, being so accustomed to associating rapid movement with sound of some sort, whether engine or animal. Could this be at all like what birds feel like flying?

A high-flying balloon-entranced woman arrives back at The Boulders just in time for breakfast in the Latilla Room. Large picture windows overlook a waterfall tumbling over massive rounded boulders. The ceiling is made from latilla wood, the thin ribs inside a saguaro cactus and a traditional desert building material. Sitting in one of the hand-sculpted booths, I come close to drooling on the menu. I could eat that jackrabbit myself. I begin with a "Boulders Sunrise" combination of orange juice, honey, yogurt, bananas, egg whites and a dash of nutmeg, just what the coyote hunter ordered. The menu staggers me with unusual options. Grilled Pacific salmon with marinated cucumbers, blue corn flapjacks with berries and mesquite honey, or an open faced omelette with Anaheim chilies, blue corn tortillas, ranchero sauce, sour cream and cilantro. But the breakfast burrito with eggs, chorizo sausage and tri-colored peppers is irresistible. And good.

DESERT OUTINGS

Sated with burritos and other delicacies, guests are now free to choose from many diversions. Golfers will delight in playing on two courses that won the Gold Medal Award from *Golf Magazine* as one of the nation's top golf resorts. Teeing off from the top of a boulder and hitting down vivid green fairways while fifty foot tall, 150 year old saguaro cacti act as sentinels is not your everyday golf outing.

If you don't mind driving for one and one-half hours, north of Carefree in Yavapai County is Montezuma's castle, a deserted monument to the ingenuity of a long departed tribe. Their homes and storage rooms were built one on top of each other reaching hundreds of feet up this limestone cliff. Seven hundred years later, these ruins are as fascinating to modern visitors as they must have been to Spanish explorers in the 16th and 17th centuries, plus the prospectors and cattle ranchers who followed.

It is intersting to ponder what this area now means to our country. Arizona was ceded to the United States after the Mexican War in 1848, at which time famed orator Daniel Webster described it as, "...a barren waste of prairie dogs, cactus and shifting sands, incapable of producing anything, and therefore not worth retaining." Time has proven otherwise.

Your activities at The Boulders will be bounded only by your imagination or your pocketbook. Rafting, Sedona day tours, Grand Canyon air tours, Llama treks into the desert and helicopter flights are among the more extravagant offerings. However, one of the most pleasurable will cost you nothing, save an hour or two. Nature walks on the property are provided to guests each week. Go. The naturalist will take you up into the granite boulders to show the incredible diversity of life that makes its home here. Saguaro cacti (the state flower), cholla cacti (watch out, don't touch), lovely yellow and orange wildflowers, thorny paloverde trees (the state tree) are in abundance. Did you know that the saguaro blooms its first white and yellow flowers at age fifty and at 150 years weighs around eight tons? The bright red fruit of the saguaro was so important to the local Papago Indians that they began their calendar year with the time of the spring fruit harvest. The many holes you see in the saguaros are from various birds who make their homes within – kind of a cactus boardinghouse.

SLIP INTO THE NIGHT

A refreshing dip in one of the pools, a quick drink on the balcony of my casita, and I'm ready for dinner. The walk from casita to lodge is so pleasant any time of day with the sun creating an ever changing landscape of colors and shadows that I enjoy it more each time out. Perhaps more and more as time for departure draws near.

Teeing off from the top of a boulder and hitting down vivid green fairways while fifty foot tall, 150 year old saguaro cacti act as sentinels is not your everyday golf outing.

Tonight I dine in the Palo Verde dining room, a bit less formal than The Latilla, and distinguished by an exhibition kitchen decorated with handpainted Mexican tiles. Through the opening you can watch as white hatted chefs concoct starters such as fire-roasted eggplant and Anasazi beans with nopal cactus salsa or, corn dough pizza with smoked duck, plum tomatoes, cilantro pesto and pepper jack cheese. Then they move on to achiote basted veal chop with pumpkin seed cream and red pepper orzo, southwestern bouillabaisse with grilled nopal cactus, or pecan-crusted rack of lamb with quinoa, seared sweet peppers and goat cheese.

As I walk back to my casita with waiting fireplace and cozy bed, the light is almost completely faded. As I pass by green #5 yet again the golfers are gone, the bunnies are back. They seem to look on me almost kindly, as if they know how much I enjoy this walk and how sad I'll be to leave tomorrow. But I'll be back.

You can watch as white hatted chefs concoct starters such as fire-roasted eggplant and Anasazi beans with nopal cactus salsa.

GRILLED SHRIMP WITH MANGO SALSA AND ANCHO CHILI MAYONNAISE

While the salsa and mayonnaise recipes here are great with the shrimp, they are also good on fish, sandwiches, grilled meats, just about anything but toast.

MANGO AND TOMATILLO SALSA

2 mangoes, peeled & cut into ½-inch cubes
6 medium tomatillos, rinsed & finely chopped
1 medium red onion, finely chopped
2 – 3 serrano chilies, finely chopped
1 small red bell pepper, finely chopped
1/8 cup olive oil
1 tablespoon lime juice
1 tablespoon lemon juice
Kosher salt, to taste
Freshly ground black pepper, to taste

1. Mix all ingredients, let sit 30 minutes and refrigerate.

ANCHO CHILI MAYONNAISE

3 egg yolks
2 teaspoons dijon mustard
¼ teaspoon kosher salt
3 cloves garlic
ancho chili purée*
½ cup olive oil
1 tablespoon balsamic vinegar
1 teaspoon lemon juice
Freshly ground black pepper, to taste

1. Combine egg yolks, mustard, salt, garlic and chili purée in food processor. With motor running, add the oil very slowly. Finish by adding vinegar, lemon juice and black pepper. Can be made a day or two ahead and refrigerated.

(*ANCHO CHILI PURÉE: 2 Ancho chilies, stems removed and broken into pieces. Soak in ½ cup hot water for about one hour or until soft. Purée in blender.)

12 large shrimp
Cilantro sprigs, for garnish

1. Peel and de-vein shrimp. Leave tails on. Toss shrimp in olive oil.
2. Grill shrimp over medium heat, turning frequently. Sprinkle with salt and pepper.
3. While shrimp are grilling, arrange the four warm plates as follows: Place a small pile of salsa near edge of plate. Place a spoon of chili mayonnaise near edge of plate a few inches away from salsa. Place three grilled shrimp on their sides on empty side of plate, tails facing out. Garnish with a sprig of cilantro

Serves 4

AHI FAJITAS

4 (6 oz.) ahi tuna steaks, cut in 1/2 inch strips
1 fajita marinade recipe (below)
2 tablespoons olive oil
1 red bell pepper, cut in strips
1 yellow bell pepper, cut in strips
1 small red onion, cut in half and sliced
2 roma tomatoes, cut into eighths
8 10-inch flour tortillas

1. Marinate fish in a glass or stainless container in marinade (recipe below) for at least one hour before cooking (maximum 3 hours), then drain.
2. Heat oil in a large skillet over high heat. Sear peppers and onions, keeping everything moving so as not to burn them.
3. When onions are translucent (about 3 minutes), add fish and tomatoes and cook another 2 minutes for medium rare. (Do not overcook fish.)
4. Warm tortillas on a dry griddle until they puff. Place on plates and divide the fajitas between them.

Serves 4.

FAJITA MARINADE

½ cup soy sauce
½ cup rice or white wine vinegar
¼ cup sherry
1 tablespoon sesame oil
2 cloves garlic
1 large shallot
1 chipotle chili
1 teaspoon freshly ground cumin
1 teaspoon chili powder
½ teaspoon cayenne
½ bunch cilantro, washed, stems removed

1. Mix all ingredients together.

SOUTHWESTERN GREEN CHILI CORN BREAD

In this girl's book, cornbread is good any meal, any season. Although my mother would never consider putting corn, chilies or cheese in her cornbread (and it is the best), try it. Not for nuthin' is this a Boulders favorite.

1 cup butter
½ cup sugar
4 eggs
½ cup green chilies, diced
1½ cup cream-style corn
½ cup Cheddar cheese, shredded
1 cup flour
1 cup yellow corn meal
2 tablespoon baking powder
1 teaspoon salt

1. Cream butter and sugar.
2. Add eggs slowly, one at a time.
3. Add remaining ingredients and mix well to incorporate.
4. Pour into a well buttered 9-inch square pan.
5. Bake in preheated oven at 325 degrees for approximately 1 hour.
   Serves 8.

SPICY PECANS

Great nibbles.

¼ teaspoon cayenne pepper
¼ teaspoon Kosher salt
2½ teaspoon chili powder
¼ cup water
1 tablespoon honey
¼ cup + 2 tablespoons sugar
1 cup whole pecan halves
2 cups peanut oil

1. In a small bowl, combine cayenne pepper, salt and chili powder; mix well to incorporate.
2. In a small skillet, combine the water, honey and sugar; boil until slightly thickened. Add pecans and cook 2 minutes; drain.
3. Heat peanut oil until it registers 350 degrees. Add nuts and cook a minute or two, stirring constantly. Remove with a wire skimmer and place in a stainless bowl.
4. Add chili seasonings and stir to coat. Pour out onto a baking sheet to cool.
   Makes 1 cup.

La Colombe d'Or

HOUSTON, TEXAS

Steel skyscrapers, oil fields, or get-along-little-doggie-cowboys may come to mind when you think of Houston, America's fourth largest city. Perhaps that's why a place like La Colombe d'Or is such a surprise. Belying Texas roots, it's small, only six bedrooms at this inn. It oozes European ambiance, nothing remotely western. And, given the fact there's almost nothing very old in Houston, that a little historic treasure like this to have been saved, restored, and opened to the public is a triple blessing. However, it does have a relationship with those pumping oil rigs. "Black gold" paid the bills.

IT WAS

Built in 1923 as the private residence of Walter Fondren, founder of Humble Oil (which became the much less humble Exxon), this prairie-style mansion was designed by noted Houston architect Alfred Finn. The Fondrens lived there until 1949, when the family awarded a 30-year grant to the Red Cross, who turned the graceful residence into a school and office. When Stephen Zimmerman bought this property from the family in 1979, he never expected to keep the house. Why would he? There were linoleum floors, acoustical tile ceilings, office cubicles littering the staircase and shelves on top of the bathtubs.

"I was so curious about what was underneath," says Zimmerman, who knew of architect Finn's reputation for beautiful detail, ornate ceilings, and carved woodwork. So he gave the house over to a fundraising group to use as a designer's showcase. Individual designers were amazed and delighted with what was underneath Red Cross efficiency. After all the painting, refinishing, papering and such, he didn't have the heart to sell it, much less tear it down.

Stephen Zimmerman decided instead to create a restaurant and inn with the southern French ambiance he had grown to love on wine-buying trips to France. He named his creation after La Colombe d'Or, a restaurant in a charming French Riviera village famous for its extensive art collection.

Right on the busy thoroughfare of Montrose Blvd. in the heart of Houston's Museum district, people go to La Colombe d'Or and this section of Houston for art, culture, museums, gourmet French food and blissful privacy.

A five foot wide herringbone brick sidewalk leads to the front doors of this mansion, edged by flower beds full of blooming purple and white pansies, red begonias, and potted topiary shrubs on the shady front porch. Inside the double front doors are dark, intricate parquet floors and a burl walnut grand piano. A large crystal chandelier glitters above a round table set in the middle of the floor, which supports an urn opulently filled with lilacs, delphiniums, peonies, tulips and tiger lilies.

One room over is the Bacchus bar. Painted a rich deep red with antique oil paintings on the walls and a walnut bar from Germany circa 1850. This is a great place for an aperitif. Or quaff an after dinner cognac, armagnac or port from the inn's formidable collection dating from 1892.

The staircase that leads up to La Colombe d'Or's six suites is just what an oil baron's staircase should be, extravagant and enormous with silky wooden banisters. At the top of the stairs, another wide hall is really another art gallery, filled with Stephen's rotating collections by various artists, from famous to lesser known.

ARTISTIC ACCOMMODATIONS

The Monet room is large, about twenty by twenty with 12-foot ceilings. Dark hardwood floors, oriental rugs, and peach walls are the frame for a Lucas Johnson painting. A seating area with burgundy quilted love-seats, a king-sized bed and antique lowboy are just sand colored silk curtains from your own private dining room, perfect for the continental breakfast that is always served in your room. Coffee, croissants and muffins, or a health breakfast of oat bran and fresh squeezed orange juice are brought up on crisp starched linens with china and silver.

When the Fondren mansion was built, air conditioning was a dream. So each of the five bedrooms on the second floor had sleeping porches, where available breezes could cool the snoozing inhabitants during the long summer months. Central air has allowed Steve Zimmerman to encase all the sleeping porches in glass, converting them into private dining areas for unique romantic retreats.

The Degas suite has emerged as the most popular honeymoon retreat. Resplendent in pink and lavender, it features "the boardroom," the largest private dining room. With its silk wall coverings and precious 17th century handpainted wood panels around which Zimmerman has constructed cabinets, double doors completely separate the boudoir from the dining room. One couple celebrated their anniversary here with a lavish French dinner in "the boardroom." The gentleman suddenly surprised his wife by simply opening the doors to the bedroom. Such romantic roguery!

But wait until you see the Penthouse upstairs. Occupying the entire third floor, this Shangri-la offers 2,000 square feet of luxury. The walls are gloriously painted with a Monet-style mural by a Houston artist. Burnished antiques, suede sofas, a tapestry covered king-sized bed and tapestry chairs add classic detail. With a wet bar, a small refrigerator, and a large jacuzzi tub in the marble bathroom, one could cloister here for days on end.

Inside the double front doors are dark, intricate parquet floors and a burl walnut grand piano. A large crystal chandelier glitters above a round table set in the middle of the floor.

ART & SPACE

But there is much to see and do here in this corner of Texas. Art galleries are just a stroll away here in the museum district, and down Montrose is one of the most interesting. The Contemporary Arts Museum, a huge stainless steel parallelogram, is the only Texas museum solely devoted to exhibitions of contemporary art. It has no permanent exhibits and specializes in emerging and regional talent. Great gift shop, too.

The Museum of Fine Arts, the Houston Museum of Natural Science (including a planetarium and IMAX theater), the Children's Museum of Houston (hands-on for children), Houston Zoological Gardens (with mammal marina and children's petting zoo) and the Japanese Garden in Herman Park (designed by world famous Ken Nakajima) are but a few of the available cultural attractions. "A Cultural Guide to Houston" is available at most museums, free of charge, and features maps and specific listings of all festivals, museums and theaters in the area. Grab it and go.

But come on, in Texas, you don't just walk. About a thirty-minute jaunt away is Space Center Houston, the new visitor center for the NASA Johnson Space Center. This is no walk-through-listen-while-we-talk-but-don't-touch place. Designed by Walt Disney Imageering, this $70 million 183,000-square-foot marvel lets you land a space shuttle (harder than I thought even after several tries). In the Space Center Theater is the world's best collection of space suits, and a five-story IMAX theater lets you experience space through an astronaut's eyes. Marvel at a Mercury capsule, a Gemini spacecraft and the Apollo 17 command module all displayed in simulated natural settings. A guided tram tour takes you for a behind the scenes at the Mission Control Center. "Apollo, this is Houston control, over."

Designed by Walt Disney Imageering, this $70 million 183,000-square-foot marvel lets you land a space shuttle (harder than I thought even after several tries).

TO DINE

After a full day, you'll be more than ready for that memorable dinner, La Colombe d'Or style. As Steve Zimmerman points out, "We've stayed true to what we are – French. Our chefs are always young and just over from France, so you eat what people in the south of France are eating today, not what was in vogue twenty years ago."

Is the cooking rich? "No 'aise' cooking here," retorts Steve. "No Hollandaise, no Bordelaise, no Bernaise. Just natural juices and fresh herbs, what a lot of French chefs today call the 'grandmere' style—cooking like their grandmothers."

There are three small elegant dining rooms, with a marble fireplace, sparkling chandeliers, beautiful paintings and tables set with fine china and silver. Once the living room, the music room and a sun-porch, they are now enjoying renewed life. Discerning eaters can admire the intricate gold leaf on the Alfred Finn ceilings while they enjoy young rabbit wrapped in leeks in a puff pastry, escargot and wild mushrooms wrapped in zucchini, a mosaic vegetable terrine with fresh tomato coulis, or roasted goat cheese with mixed greens.

Entrees change seasonally, but could include gulf fresh red snapper with caramelized oranges and lemon sauce, cherry-wood home-smoked Norwegian salmon with virgin olive oil and fresh herbs, or a roasted pheasant breast on a bed of caramelized green apples.

Desserts are wicked and luscious, such as a terrine of Roquefort with cognac marinated plums and pecans, chocolate marquise flavored with Gran Marnier, two pears poached in red wine and saffron, the red pear and white one fan-sliced and served with homemade pear sorbet. If only my grandmother had cooked like this.

LA COLOMBE D'OR PARSLEY DRESSING

1 cup extra virgin olive oil
2 cups of fresh leave parsley
2 teaspoons of balsamic vinegar
¼ teaspoon of white pepper
1 clove of garlic
¼ cup fresh lime juice

1. Place all ingredients in a blender or food processor. Mix at high speed until thick.
2. Pour over salad greens or cold cooked vegetables.
Makes 1½ cups dressing.

ROASTED HALIBUT WITH FRESH TOMATO COULIS

This recipe is best when tomatoes are ripe and flavorful. I also like adding a clove or two of garlic into the coulis, or some fresh basil.

4 8-oz. fillet of halibut
one pound asparagus
6 fresh Roma tomatoes, very ripe
Salt and pepper to taste
1 cup olive oil, extra virgin
Fresh basil for garnish

1. Steam asparagus until just tender and place in bowl of ice until it is cold. It is important to place the asparagus in ice to stop the cooking and to save the bright green color.
2. Make the coulis by first seeding the tomatoes. Slice tomatoes into small pieces, place in a food processor and pulse on and off until it becomes a purée. Put olive oil into the processor or blender with salt and pepper. Process just until mixed. Put mixture through a strainer, discard the juice (or save for soup) and the coulis is ready.
3. Take each filet of halibut and slice almost in half in preparation for stuffing with the asparagus later. Sauté in frying pan with olive oil over medium heat until golden. After halibut is sautéed, place in 350 degree oven to finish cooking just until done (about 10 minutes), when fish doesn't quite spring when pushed with a fork.

4. Place the halibut on paper towels; season with salt and pepper. Make a puddle of tomato coulis on a plate, then place the halibut on top – putting the asparagus spears inside the fish with the tips peeking outside the fish. Garnish with fresh basil.
Makes 4 servings.

SCALLOPS AND GREEN LENTILS WITH PARSLEY COULIS

Lentils are dried peas that do not need soaking before cooking. Just rinse them and cook. This lentil recipe is a really elegant presentation that tastes as good as it looks.

1 pound sea scallops
12 oz. green lentils
1 small onion, diced
1 carrot, diced
1 star aniseed
Salt and pepper to taste
1 package bacon, finely sliced
3 tablespoons olive oil
1 cup mineral water
2 cups fresh parsley leaves
½ teaspoon salt

1. Wash lentils and place in medium saucepan half-filled with water with onion, carrot, aniseed, salt and pepper . Bring lentils to a boil, reduce heat and simmer gently for 45 minutes. The lentils are done when you can easily crush a lentil with your fingers. Don't cook them to a mush.
2. In a skillet, fry the bacon until crisp. Blot with paper towels and combine with the lentils.
3. Heat the pan that cooked the bacon on medium high heat (be careful not to let the hot fat spatter and burn you). When very hot, sear scallops 3 minutes on one side, 2 minutes on the other side. Salt and pepper the scallops.
4. At the same time boil the mineral water with the parsley leaves and salt. Boil for 1 minute. Purée the parsley mixture in the processor to make a nice smooth consistency.
5. Place lentils in the center of a warmed plate, and pour parsley coulis around edge of plate. Place scallops on sauce and serve.
Serves 4.

Tanque Verde Ranch

TUCSON, ARIZONA

Bouncing along on the back of a horse through the Arizona desert across arroyos (gulches, silly), by Seguaro cacti much taller than me and Red, the wrangler just in front of me suddenly has to deal with a prancing, unhappy horse. He leaps off gracefully (I wish I could do that) and whips out...a pocket comb? The horse must be having a bad hair day. "Always bring a pocket comb with you when you're in the desert," the cowboy says laconically. Bending over he flicks the comb down the horse's rear leg. Off comes a small but lethal looking little spike-fuzz ball. "This here is a cholla cactus, looks kinda' cute, but if you try to get it off with your hand, it'll get stuck in your fingers or your whatever with little-bitty needles that feel pretty bad. The comb's the answer." With that sage bit of wisdom he mounts up again just as easily and we're off.

HEAT, HORSES AND AN HONEST RIDE

That's the kind of place the Tanque Verde Ranch is. Learning about and respecting the desert, and the plants and animals that inhabit it, is the ranch's creed. They live it, they teach it and they eat it (even some plentiful cactus species). Nestled in the Rincon Mountain foothills near Tucson is a dude ranch that makes the most of its location. The Tanque Verde Ranch has served up Southwestern hospitality since 1928. Tanque Verde is Spanish for green tank or green pool for the large pools of water that once formed part of the creek running through the property. What began as a Spanish

Tanque Verde is Spanish for green tank or green pool for the large pools of water that once formed part of the creek running through the property.

land-grant cattle ranch in the 1860s now grants a real western experience to travelers worldwide.

Truly worldwide. In the summer when the thermometer routinely hits well over 100 degrees, most guests are not from the U.S. but from Europe, especially Scandinavian countries. Owner Bob Cote, whose family bought Tanque Verde in 1957, seems puzzled by it himself saying, "They really like the sunshine, can't seem to get enough of it. Tucson gets over 300 days of sunshine a year. So they know they're gonna get tans here."

The ranch has 65 patio casitas and rooms that are designed comfortably with rustic Southwestern furniture and artifacts, clustered around the rambling collection of buildings that make up the main lodge. Many of the casitas have fireplaces and beautiful views from patios and picture windows overlooking the mountains. The living room just inside the main lodge's front door is filled with Western and Native American art and memorabilia. A large riverstone fireplace offers a gathering spot in the winter months.

Walk down the long weathered veranda that hasn't changed much since the early part of the century. The wooden slat hammocks sway in the breeze, ready to provide a moment's respite. The front lawn is brilliantly green with islands of thorned paloverde trees, yuccas and all varieties of cactus. The walks are lined with little tin-shaded night lights that have the signature initials "TV" cut through on one side and a cactus on the other. Down at the end of the veranda is a door leading to common living areas filled with rugged sofas and chairs where young people gather for videos and, for all ages, talks on hiking or Native American culture, artists presenting their crafts and wildlife educational programs. The dining room is a bit further back. But what really draws people to Tanque Verde is outside.

They run over 100 horses at the ranch – Appaloosas, Arabs, quarter-horses, and saddlebreds of all shapes and colors. There is always a horse for everyone on every ride. And boy do Tanque Verdeans ride. And ride. Breakfast rides, all day pack trip rides, hour rides, loping rides, walking rides, picnic rides, overnight rides and barrel racing rides. Owner Bob Cote explains the now obvious, "To a lot of folks Tanque Verde means riding. It's our specialty." And it's done with an exuberance that is contagious to the guests. "We get guests that have never ridden before, but they've always wanted to ride a horse ever since they were a kid, and now *they* have kids. So we teach 'em how to be comfortable around and on a horse. After a day or so, they may be a little sore but they can't wait to mount up in the morning."

The breakfast ride does leave early, 8:00 AM sharp. I throw a little cold water on my face, put on some jeans and boots (anything with a heel will do, no sneakers) and lope on over to the mesquite wood corral. People are already getting mounted up on horses that have been assigned to them for the week according to riding ability. Most people wear a hat as the sun is looking for you all year.

One firm rule – your hat must have chin-strings for the safety of the rider behind you. All a horse needs to spook is a baseball cap flying through the air. Likewise when on the trail, the wrangler explains, don't take off a sweater or jacket without letting him know beforehand. Horses don't like it. Everyone laughs and nervously checks their hat strings but none are daunted. "Don't forget to let the horse know what you want," says the wrangler as we head out of the gate, "You can't expect him to guess."

BLUEBERRIES IN THE DESERT

The ride is spectacular. The desert in the southern part of Arizona is an austere landscape with brushlands and rock outcroppings, paloverde trees and the flanks of red

They run over 100 horses at the ranch – Appaloosas, Arabs, quarter-horses, and saddlebreds. There is always a horse for everyone on every ride.

hills in the distance. After forty minutes or so we clip-clop into the breakfast encampment that we sniffed much earlier. Blueberry pancakes? You bet. The griddle is smoking, sausage and bacon are sizzling, pancakes are flipping, and huge trays of luscious eggs cooked with spicy chilies and sour cream are ready for chowing down. A cup of cowboy coffee and we all settle down contentedly for a well-earned (at least in our minds) breakfast.

Hiking is another popular mode of getting about the landscape. That's right, using your own two hoofers. The Rincon Mountain foothills provide miles of trails surrounding the ranch. Each morning the Tanque Verde offers two different guided hikes, one that means business to your cardiovascular system, the other is a nature hike to teach guests some of the intricacies of the desert ecosystem. (No matter which hike you take, or especially if you go alone, *always* take plenty of water.)

"Do you know why the cactus has thorns?" our naturalist-guide asks.

"To keep animals from eating it," is one tentative guess. We all nod agreeably. Sounds reasonable.

"It is an air-conditioning system. When a breeze floats by, no matter how small, the spines catch it and hold the slightly cooler temperature. Just a degree or two can keep the cactus cooler." I need some of those thorns, in spite of what my husband thinks.

THE BIRDS AND THEIR FRIENDS

Buzzards fly overhead, a gila woodpecker perches on a candelabra-shaped saguaro cactus; hummingbirds (eleven species live on the Sonoran desert) flit about. This corner of Arizona is one of the top birding areas in the Americas, kind of a "natural innkeeper" for migrating species on their journeys between Central and South America and Canada. The ranch offers occasional week-long programs for those who want to learn more about the avifauna (birds, natch) with excursions to hot birding spots like Ramsey Canyon, Sabino Canyon and Madera Canyon.

Each Thursday morning at the crack of dawn (if one must), you can join licensed bird-banders who capture birds in "mist nets" to record their vital statistics and local movements by placing a tiny aluminum band on one leg. I watch one morning as they are extremely careful with a tiny elf owl. Over 70,000 birds have been banded over the years, with over 170 species of avifauna (remember?) seen at Tanque Verde.

Fishing for bass or catfish in Lake Gambusi (equipment available), five tennis courts with a mountain backdrop and tennis pro November through April, swimming, shuffleboard or croquet on the front lawn await your pleasure at the ranch. But doubtless you'll want to see some of the magnificent sights in the area.

Tanque Verde runs a terrific children's program Thanksgiving through April 30th for darlings age four to eleven. They ride, take tennis "shorty swatter" lessons, nature lessons and hikes, swimming and in general lead the good life. Usually, all kids eat together. Not only do the children make good friends with each other, parents get to vacation on their vacation.

Off the ranch, the Seguaro National Monument is something you have to see to believe. These protected giants, some 150 years old, fifty feet tall with seven or eight arms and weighing as much as eight tons, stand firm and serene on the desert floor. A virtual forest of them. Some of these specimens are worth thousands of dollars and are so prized for landscaping that "cactus rustlers" illegally dig them up in the night. Here and there lay "ghost" saguaros. All that remains are the wooden ribs that supported them.

MUCH MORE THAN CHUCK WAGON STEW

At any ranch, mealtimes are crucial to hungry guests. Breakfast is normally served in the latilla-roofed dining room with large windows overlooking the pool and

Buzzards fly overhead, a gila woodpecker perches on a candelabra-shaped saguaro cactus; hummingbirds (eleven species live on the Sonoran desert) flit about.

patio. A bounteous buffet of cereals, homemade granolas, fresh fruits, baskets of breads and muffins, hot egg dishes, French toast, sausages and bacon, oatmeal, prickly pear cactus jelly, juices and plenty of coffee greet the early morning desert dweller. A far cry over the days of old, no doubt.

Dinner is chosen from the menu. Entrees might include lobster with guacamole sauce, mesquite broiled duckling glazed with prickly pear cactus syrup, or sea bass cabrilla Mexicana. But the night I look forward to the most is a desert barbecue down in the cottonwood grove. Aged steaks, an inch thick and grilled over mesquite wood give off a mighty powerful scent while we sip our cocktails and compare riding notes. ("Really, you rode all day?") Bonfires are blazing with checkered cloth tables grouped around. Homemade rolls are cooked in an old fashioned adobe oven, with all the fixin's. As everyone chows down on world-class steak, a geetar-man starts strumming gently over at the side. Soon, they'll have us all line-dancing. "Hey, any more steaks over there?"

But the night I look forward to the most is a desert barbecue down in the cottonwood grove. Aged steaks, an inch thick and grilled over mesquite wood give off a mighty powerful scent.

RANCH BREAD PUDDING

This bread pudding is unusual in several ways; it uses no cream or milk, and it calls for cheese. The almonds, pine nuts and walnuts give a nice crunchy texture.

1 cup firmly packed brown sugar
1 cup water
1 cinnamon stick
½ lb. French bread
½ cup toasted pine nuts
½ cup toasted slivered almonds
½ cup chopped walnuts
¾ cup raisins
½ lb. Monterey Jack cheese, cut in ½-inch cubes
1 tart apple, thinly sliced

1. Boil brown sugar, water and cinnamon stick until slightly thickened, about 5 minutes. Discard cinnamon stick.
2. Cut bread into ½-inch thick slices. Break bread into large pieces. Place half of bread in a buttered 9"×13" casserole.
3. Add half of the pine nuts in a layer, repeat with half of almonds and walnuts, raisins and cheese in layers. Top all with half of the sliced apples. Pour half of the cinnamon syrup over all.
4. Repeat layers, topping all with remaining cinnamon syrup.
5. Cover and bake in 350 degree oven for about 20 - 30 minutes. Remove cover for last 5 minutes.
6. Serve warm with whipped cream or ice cream.
Makes 8 to 10 servings

RANCH MESQUITE— SMOKED BEEF BRISKET

Serve with crusty home-made bread and barbecue sauce. Leftover brisket (if you have any) is excellent cold.

2 tablespoons liquid smoke
6 lbs. boneless beef brisket (well trimmed)
⅔ cup oil
⅓ cup white vinegar
4 bay leaves
2 teaspoons mesquite smoked salt
1 teaspoon garlic salt
1 teaspoon freshly ground black pepper
3 cups mesquite flavored barbecue sauce
1 large Spanish onion, thinly sliced

1. Rub liquid smoke over entire surface of brisket. Place meat in shallow pan. Blend oil, vinegar and bay leaves; pour over meat. Refrigerate for 2 hours, turning occasionally.
2. Before cooking, remove brisket from marinade and pat dry.
3. Blend seasonings and rub into both sides of beef.
4. When mesquite wood or charcoal fires are ready, toss in a layer of dampened mesquite chips and position grill 6 inches above coals. Sear brisket 6 to 8 minutes on each side.
5. Remove brisket from grill. Place on 2 layers of heavy duty aluminum foil, cover with 1 cup of mesquite flavored barbecue sauce and thinly sliced onion. Seal the foil, place on grill and roast about 50 minutes on each side or until done. Serve with additional barbecue sauce.
Serves 8.

BROILED FILET CABRILLA MEXICANA

Serve this avocado sauced fish with baby carrots sautéed with pecans and cinnamon, or jicama sticks (a root vegetable which maybe purchased in supermarkets) sautéed in butter.

3 to 4 pounds of boneless, skinned Mexican
   Cabrilla or sea bass, or other skinned fish
   filets such as red snapper.
¼ cup of butter
¼ cup olive oil
3 cloves of fresh garlic, finely minced.
3 tablespoons of minced parsley
2 tablespoons of fresh squeezed lime juice
1 recipe of avocado sauce (below)

1. Rinse fillets and pat dry. Place fillets on broiler pan or cookie sheet.
2. Melt butter in a small sauce pan. Add olive oil, garlic, parsley, and lime juice. Heat until bubbling and remove from heat.
3. Brush fish generously with garlic sauce. Season with salt and white pepper. Sprinkle tops lightly with paprika. Place under broiler or in a 375 degree oven until white and firm, about 20 minutes depending on the kind of fish used and thickness. Baste once or twice with garlic sauce while cooking.
4. Place fish on serving platter or plate. Put a spoon of avocado sauce over the top of each fillet. Garnish with diced fresh tomato and fresh cilantro.

Serve balance of avocado sauce in a side dish.

8 servings.

AVOCADO SAUCE

4 large ripe avocados
4 to 6 tablespoons of lime juice
4 tablespoons minced red onion
2 cloves garlic, minced
2 large tomatoes, peeled, seeded, and chopped
1 teaspoon ground coriander or 1 tablespoon
   chopped fresh cilantro
salt to taste
3 drops of Tabasco sauce

1. Peel avocados. Cut in half and remove pits. Place in bowl and mash pulp coarsely with fork, blending in lime juice at the same time.
2. Add onion, garlic, tomatoes, coriander or cilantro, Tabasco and salt to taste. Cover and chill if not using immediately.

TANQUE VERDE PECAN FRIED CHICKEN

Fried chicken, while one of my favorites by itself (my mom used to serve it every Sunday for lunch), is unbelievably good with the pecan-honey sauce. Hopefully you will have chicken left over. We kids always called cold fried chicken "picnic chicken." That's what always went along on outings to "Kiddieland" or family reunions.

2 frying chickens about 4 lbs. each cut into serving pieces
3 cups buttermilk
1 cup all purpose flour
¾ teaspoon salt
¼ teaspoon white pepper
Enough oil for frying
Honey-Pecan Sauce (below)

1. Place chicken pieces in a large bowl and cover with buttermilk. Place in refrigerator to soak for 2 hours.
2. Drain chicken and coat with flour seasoned with salt and pepper.
3. Fry chicken in ½-inch hot oil until golden brown. Bake the chicken pieces in the oven at 325 degrees on a drip pan for 45 minutes until done.
4. Place on serving platter and drizzle warm pecan sauce over chicken.

Serves 8.

PECAN SAUCE

½ cup butter
½ cup honey
½ cup chopped pecans

1. Place ingredients in small heavy pot and bring to a gentle boil. Remove from heat. This sauce can be made ahead and reheated.

NORTHWEST

Applewood, An Estate Inn

POCKET CANYON, CALIFORNIA

Heading up scenic Hwy. 1 along the northern California coast, the address itself sounds intriguing. Pocket Canyon, near Gurneville. In moments, the scenery has taken an interesting twist, with the sudden appearance of magnificent redwoods towering over the winding road. If you have never seen them before, prepare to be impressed. And these aren't even the big ones!

At last the sign – Applewood, An Estate Inn. Applewood appears as a cinematic version of a movie star home from the 1920s. Mission Revival style in pale pink stucco, with a tiled roof, graceful lines, sunporches and vast arched windows.

Built in 1922 by the Belden family, who had moved to Gurneville to open a bank, the house remained a private home until 1982, when it was purchased by a group of real estate developers. A three-year restoration later, Jimmy Caron and Darryl Notter were touring the wine country. Seeing the place for sale and having those "Gee, wouldn't it be great to run a country inn" feelings, they went inside on a lark and stayed as the owners, never looking back.

COZY INSIDE AND OUT

But as much as Applewood appears "grand dame" from the outside, the feeling through the front door is warm, friendly, and exceptionally unstuffy. Jimmy greets you almost immediately with a quick assessment of your needs and desires.

"Let me get those bags for you."

"How was your trip?"

"Are you hungry? (*Yes.*) Good, dinner is almost ready."

"Would you like a glass of chardonnay?" *This is just what I've been needing.*

The interiors are the creation of Jimmy's partner, Darryl Notter. You may find it almost impossible to believe that these everything-is-just-right rooms were completed in the space of one month, but Darryl swears it's true.

The first room you enter at Applewood is the formal living room, dominated by a massive riverstone fireplace with an oak Tudor style mantle. The ceiling is criss-crossed by heavy, dark beams. Four oversized down-stuffed armchairs covered in a hunter green pinstripe damask allow you to cozy up to the fire. Hanging on biscuit colored walls are antique iron sconces.

That fireplace also warms the conservatory on the other side. Lush fabrics cover the bamboo furniture that is bathed in sunlight from wall-to-wall windows. What a romantic place to enjoy breakfast or dinner.

There are ten accommodations, with plans for seven more. The uppermost room is on the third floor. Once the home's nursery, it is now a tree-house retreat, three stories up. Through a bank of windows on one wall you have a lofty view of redwoods. Cafe curtains are gray and white striped, and that fabric upholsters the opposite wall behind the bed. Against the other butter colored walls are a drop leaf desk made by Jim's father in 1918 and an art deco armoire artfully concealing the television.

Room # 10 has a private entrance from the outside. It too, has a sunny bank of windows, but these overlook the vineyard. This romantic room features a half-canopy bed and everything wrapped in colors of seafoam green and dusty rose, with apple blossoms on the draperies.

In the forest green and cabernet colored master suite, the most marvelous cherry sleigh bed faces a conversation area by large bay windows, with the redwoods once again, just outside. All beds have down comforters, and perhaps the most comfortable mattresses on which you'll ever snooze. Custom made to Darryl's specifications, this small touch shows exacting attention to comfort and detail. All rooms have private gleaming white tile baths with old fashioned pedestal sinks and are stocked with every convenience. Seven new rooms-to-be will all have jacuzzis and fireplaces.

Wandering through the French doors out back, you'll find a Caribbean blue jewel-like heated pool resplendent on the stone terrace, surrounded with pots of giant climbing roses, daisies and topiary pomegranates. Out on the lawn are century-old gnarled apple trees from a long ago orchard, thus the name Applewood. You are now on the turf of Applewood's two adorable and personable guardians. Balky is an affable black retriever and Norton an appealing dog with a most curious appearance and lineage.

Try breakfast out here in the mornings, enjoying your coffee as the California sun peeps over the redwoods. Just smelling that brew will make you feel better. Add "fresh-squozen" orange juice, buttermilk pancakes or perhaps a bacon, asparagus, and Gouda cheese omelet. You hear the twitter of the birds, maybe the sound of an early morning swimmer slicing though water. Now, you're ready for the day.

Just about whatever your relaxing heart demands is available in this verdant, Eden-like area. How one place can be so lush green, with flowers year-round is beyond comprehension.

WISTFUL WOODS, WINES AND OTHER WONDERS

Nearby is the Armstrong State Redwood Reserve where you can enjoy the magnificence and solitude of the ancient redwood giants while you're walking or on horse-

The forest green and cabernet colored master suite features the most marvelous cherry sleigh bed and conversation area by large bay windows, with the redwoods right, once again, just outside.

back. The stillness of this 700-acre preserve is both refreshing and unsettling, making me realize just how few reflective times we have in our rushed modern lives. Cool and dim inside the reserve, the trees shut out most of the sunlight from the paths that wind their way around elephantine trunks soaring 300 feet into the air. Thank goodness Colonel Armstrong, a timber magnate at the turn of the century, had the foresight and good sense to recognize and save this national treasure.

As you're smack dab in the middle of Sonoma/Russian River wine country, why miss such an opportunity to vineyard hop? Korbel, Alexander Valley, Murphy Goode, Dry Creek, Rodney Strong, and Belevedere are but a few of the famous names in wine that are just a short hop away. Honestly, if you're interested in wine, this is an area packed with excellent vineyards and wineries, most of which do tours and even better, tastings. You can get a map called the Russian River Wine Road, which can help you plan a personal tour, with locations and info for 54 award winning wineries of northern Sonoma County. Write them at P.O. Box 46, Healdsburg, CA 95448.

DIGESTIVES

After a busy day of seeing the sights, save an hour or so for the most unusual relaxation treatment you may have yet encountered. The Osmosis Enzyme Bath just down the Bohemian Highway (I'm not making this up), is a form of heat therapy from Japan that is reputed to eliminate toxins, cleanse the skin, improve circulation and metabolism.

Don't be nervous, just slip into your swimsuit, and then into a 5'x 7' foot box filled with fragrant Hinoki cedar fiber, rice bran, and over 600 different active plant enzymes. I counted them. The attendant takes a pitchfork and digs a trough large enough for you to lie in, and then covers you with the mixture. It's warm, yes "quite" warm. Oooh, my toes are on fire. All this enfeebling heat is generated biologically through fermentation. After 20 mind-melting minutes in the box, you brush off the cedar, shower, don a kimono, and enjoy a blanket wrap with "musical balancing," or a 75 minute therapeutic massage. The interlude ends with a soothing cup of enzyme tea in the Japanese garden. All unwanted kinks are gone now. Those you keep are your problem.

Floating back to wood on an enzyme cloud, I find a wine tasting in progress. During my visit, it was presented by Domaine Michel, one of Jimmy and Darryl's favorite vineyards. Comparing the attributes of the '89 and '90 chardonnays is a rather tough assignment, as they are both delightful. I'm not really in a mood to criticize anything, let alone a fruity glass of wine. The guests all happily compare notes on wines, travels, inns, food, and the other things that bring pleasure to life. Soon it will be dinner time.

Back in the kitchen, Applewood's dinner preparations are in full gear. Darryl has oiled and herbed the chickens, trussing them firmly but lovingly, Swiss chard will be sautéed in olive oil and garlic, shiitake mushrooms popped into Darry's famous risotto, all served with more of Domaine Michel's chardonnay. Dinner is pre-fixe and the set menu changes nightly. You might enjoy a rack of lamb marinated in Asian herbs and served with a peanut sauce, or shrimp and scallop cakes, fried and served with a chive vinaigrette. Try and save room for dessert, which tonight is a rich, creamy champagne zabaglione with fresh strawberries or Darryl's blackberry clafouti, a guest favorite. Once you've tasted the food here, it will be no surprise that Applewood's restaurant has become renowned for sumptuous cuisine.

A glass of a ruby colored pinot noir by the fire, a cuddly down comforter and the bed feels *sooo* comfortable. Szzzzzzzzzzz. Sweet dreams!

Korbel, Alexander Valley, Murphy Goode, Dry Creek, Rodney Strong, and Belevedere are but a few of the famous names in wine that are just a short hop away.

THAI COCONUT CREAM TART WITH MACADAMIA NUT CRUST

Darryl took a Thai cooking seminar at the famous Oriental Hotel in Bangkok several years ago, and now this luscious dessert frequently appears at the end of their special Thai dinners.

CRUST

²/₃ cup roasted, unsalted macadamia nuts
1½ cups unbleached flour
½ cup sugar
½ teaspoon salt
½ cup (1 stick) unsalted butter, cut into pieces
2 egg yolks

COCONUT CREAM

2 cups canned Thai coconut milk (available in specialty stores)
1½ teaspoon unflavored gelatin
1 tablespoon dark rum
8 large egg yolks
10 tablespoons sugar
pinch of salt
1 cup chilled chipping cream, whipped into soft peaks

GARNISH

¾ cup sweetened, shredded coconut, toasted
¾ cup coarsely chopped unsalted macadamia nuts toasted

1. For crust, finely chop nuts in processor, pulsing off and on. Add flour, sugar, salt and butter. Process until mixture resembles coarse meal. Mix in yolks. Press dough over bottom and up sides of 11-inch tart pan with removable bottom. Cover and place in freezer for 30 minutes.

2. Preheat over to 375 degrees. Bake crust until golden brown, about 30 minutes. Cool completely on rack.

3. For coconut cream, sprinkle gelatin over rum in small bowl. Whisk yolks, sugar and salt in medium bowl. Bring coconut milk to boil in heavy saucepan. Gradually whisk into the yolk mixture. Return mixture to saucepan and stir over medium low heat until custard thickens and coats the back of a spoon. Do not boil. Pour into a bowl. Add gelatin mixture and stir until dissolved.

4. Refrigerate until thickened but not set, stirring frequently.

5. Fold whipped cream into coconut filling. Pour into crust. Refrigerate until set, at least 2 hours and up to 6 hours.

6. Sprinkle toasted coconut and macadamias over tart. Cut and serve.

Serves 8.

APPLEWOOD ITALIAN WILD MUSHROOM SOUP WITH VERMOUTH

Very popular with Applewood guests, this aromatic soup couldn't be easier to make. Darryl gets his mushrooms just down the road in Sebastopol at Gourmet Mushrooms, a place that ships exotic fungi to famous restaurants all over the world, but many supermarkets now carry quite a few varieties of wild mushrooms.

6 tablespoons unsalted butter
2 medium onions, coarsely chopped
½ lb. fresh shiitakes
½ lb. fresh chanterelles
1 28-oz. can imported Italian plum tomatoes, drained and chopped
4 cups beef broth
6 tablespoons sweet vermouth (like Cinzano Rosso)
salt and Fresh ground pepper, to taste
chopped fresh Italian parsley and freshly grated Parmesan cheese for garnish

1. Heat 1 tablespoon butter in heavy, medium sauté pan over low heat. Add onions and cook until translucent. Set aside.

2. In same sauté pan, melt remaining 4 tablespoons butter and cook mushrooms until they give off most of their juices and soften.

3. In medium soup kettle, add onions, mushrooms and their juices, beef broth and tomatoes. Heat to boiling, then reduce heat and add salt, pepper, and vermouth.

4. Simmer 5 minutes and serve hot, with sprinkled parsley and grated Parmesan.

Serves 6–8.

APPLEWOOD POACHED EGGS AND TOMATOES ON BACON AND POTATO PANCAKES WITH BASIL HOLLANDAISE

This is a brunch show-stopper, and especially good when you have lots of basil and ripe tomatoes in the garden. What a combination!

½ cup chopped onion
1½ cups grated, peeled baking potatoes
½ teaspoon salt
¼ teaspoon pepper
2 slices cooked bacon, crumbled
4 large eggs poached
4 ¼-inch thick slices ripe tomatoes
1 cup basil Hollandaise (recipe follows)
4 basil sprigs as garnish

1. In a bowl, combine onion, potatoes, salt, pepper and bacon. For each pancake, spread ½ cup of mixture on an oiled skillet, keeping pancakes 2 inches apart. Cook over moderately low heat, undisturbed, for 20 minutes.

2. Increase heat to moderate, and cook for 5 or 10 minutes more until undersides are browned. Turn pancakes and cook 10 minutes more. (These may be kept warm in a 250 degree oven for up to 30 minutes, while you poach the eggs.)

3. Arrange pancakes on 4 heated plates, top each one with a tomato slice, top each slice with a hot poached egg. Spoon Hollandaise over eggs, garnish with basil.

Serves 4.

BASIL HOLLANDAISE

1 cup packed basil leaves
1 stick (½ cup) butter
2 large egg yolks
4 teaspoons fresh lemon juice
2 teaspoons Dijon mustard
salt and fresh pepper to taste

1. Melt butter over moderate heat and keep warm.

2. In a blender or food processor, blend egg yolks, lemon juice, mustard and basil leaves for 5 seconds. With motor running, add hot melted butter in a slow stream until mixed. Season with salt and pepper.

Makes 1 cup.

APPLEWOOD TORTA DI RISO (RICE TORTE)

Jimmy's mother has made this inexpensive and terrific appetizer for every family wedding, birthday, and funeral for years. Originated by his grandmother, it reflects their Northern Italian-Genovese traditions.

1⅓ cups rice
4 cups water
1 teaspoon salt
6 tablespoons olive oil
1 chicken bullion cube
3 tablespoons minced onion
3 tablespoons finely chopped Italian parsley
pinch of fresh oregano
pinch fresh thyme
2 minced garlic cloves
¾ cup freshly grated Parmesan cheese
4 eggs, slightly beaten (beat and reserve 1 egg separately)
½ cup milk
fresh bread crumbs

1. Bring 4 cups water to boil. Add rice, 2 tablespoons of the olive oil, salt, and bouillon. Cook for 15 minutes, and cool.

2. Preheat oven to 375 degrees. Add to the rice the chopped onion, parsley, garlic, thyme, oregano, all but 3 tablespoons of the cheese, the 3 beaten eggs, milk and 2 tablespoons olive oil. Stir well.

3. Oil the bottom and sides of a 9"×13" baking dish. Dust with bread crumbs. Pour in the rice mixture. Beat remaining egg with remaining 2 tablespoons olive oil and spread over top of the rice mixture. Sprinkle the remaining cheese over all. Bake for 30–40 minutes. Cut into 1½-inch squares and serve warm or cold.

Averill's Flathead Lake Lodge

BIGFORK, MONTANA

From the moment your plane touches down at the Kalispell, Montana airport you realize you're not wherever you came from anymore. The spot you deplane is where you also claim your bags, with a separate cache for fly rods or snowshoes, of course. The people around me seem to effuse big sky country. Their boots are dusty and scuffed; worn jeans seem to be old friends that know all the contours. This is western panache. I stare down at my pitiful shiny new boots, vowing they will look worse for wear by the end of the week.

Even though the vast majority of us will never own a piece of the Montana pie, we can eat a slice of it just by visiting Averill's Flathead Lake Lodge in the state's picturesque northwest corner. An old red stagecoach at the entrance lets you know this is the place. Split rail fences line a long dirt road past a bigger-than-life bronze of a man on horseback and an old wooden wagon. Its bed is planted with red, pink, yellow and orange petunias and marigolds. A smiling bear carved from a tree trunk holds a welcome sign.

BUFFALO, BEARSKINS AND BENEDICT

About 130 guests come for one or two week stays at this 2,000 acre tree-covered dude ranch, beginning Sunday nights. The kick-off is a Montana-style welcome buffet

This is western panache. I stare down at my pitiful shiny new boots, vowing they will look worse for wear by the end of the week.

with gigantic salads, spicy barbecued chicken and ribs. Anchoring the end of the table is a hulking seventy pound haunch of buffalo with Cajun barbecue sauce; what you might call a proper western howdy.

Owned by the Averill family since 1945, the ranch is now run by Doug Averill, a rodeo cowboy himself who grew up as one of eight brothers who had the run of Flathead Lake Lodge. He kindly extends the same privilege to his guests. Look around all you like.

After dinner, most of us wander (in a buffalo haze) around the lodge and property to get the lay of the land. There's a lot to see. The log cabin style main lodge was built in 1932, its 40-foot cathedral ceiling crossed by massive tree trunk beams. The focal point is a riverstone fireplace with a four foot hearth and stone mantle seven feet up. A little boy comes by and obligingly stokes the embers with what is surely the longest poker in the world, a full two feet taller than his four. Clustered around the hearth are rough-hewn sofas and chairs, tough enough to take cowboy boots and roughneck kids.

Behind the circle of sofas is the main dining area. Seven foot tables, each made from single pine slabs, seat ten. Long picture windows overlook the lawns but there's enough on the walls to keep your eyes busy for a while. Where there are no windows, walls proudly sport the trophies of outdoors-men and women: bearskins, antelope, big horn sheep, and a marlin (presumably not caught nearby). On a second floor railing are silver inlaid leather saddles, waiting for ghost riders from the big sky.

Wander out back, down the stone steps and past a terrace planted with red roses and purple pansies to lush green lawns. These in turn slope past a large picnic patio area towards a heated pool perched right on the edge of the lake, which is the feature that really transforms the ranch from a place where you ride horses into a first class resort. Flathead Lake is a thirty mile long-tall drink of pristine water, named after the Flathead Indians who live on their reservation at the lake's south end.

As night falls the guests are ensconced in 1, 2 or 3 bedroom accommodations grouped within cabins constructed from hand-hewn logs, paneled with pine and scattered through the trees. The furnishings are ranch style, sturdy and comfortable, no televisions or telephones but there are small refrigerators, wet bars and lots of space for families to spread out. Balconies or decks overlook the woods or the lake. It gets real quiet up here in Montana at night.

8:00 AM, Bigfork. Once we learn food follows, the clanging of the breakfast bell is usually enough to summon the laziest traveler. Roast beast seems a distant memory. Doug Averill takes a look at the kids (who dine first) in the side dining room, a bleached multi-antlered chandelier hanging over their little heads and a white mountain goat on the mantle. He nods and says, "Looks like they're about all here. Sometimes it takes a day or so for everybody to get in the swing of things."

At 8:30, the envious adults sit down in the main dining room to plates heaped with Eggs Benedict, thick-sliced bacon, hash browns with green, red and yellow peppers, and homemade applesauce cake. The coffee keeps on coming.

RIDIN' HIGH

After breakfast I check out the activity sheet on the wall. Obviously, no time is wasted in gearing up at Flathead Lake. 8:45-kids' horseback ride, 10:00-fly fishing lesson or sailing instruction, 10:30-adult horseback ride, 11:00-boat cruise, 12:00-lunch, 1:00-water sports, 4:30-more grownups on horses, 5:30-happy hour, 6:00-kids' dinner, 6:30-my dinner unless I wear pigtails, 6:45-kids on horses, 8:30-beachfire sing-a-long.

What? Nothing at 2:10? These are all options, mind you, but the quiet of the

Flathead Lake is a thirty mile long-tall drink of pristine water, named after the Flathead Indians who live on their reservation at the lake's south end.

lodge after breakfast attests to a high percentage of participation. Only one lone stray, his nose stuck in a book by the fireplace.

I mosey on down to the corral where the children (six years and up) are just heading out on their first horseback ride, faces full of delight and expectation. As Doug Averill watches them getting mounted up with the wranglers, he explains, "We don't just accept kids. We cater to them and plan our entire program around them." Indeed, the lodge runs a full children's program, with not only horse riding, hikes, and water activities, but arts and crafts as well.

The ranch runs about 70 horses, not as many as some ranches but as Doug points out, "We don't need as many horses because there are so many other things for guests to do here, not every guest rides every day." A few days of horsing around may make you welcome the respite of sailing, tennis, volleyball, water-skiing, canoeing, fishing or golf. And, if you wish, you can help with the everyday chores around the corral or the training of colts to feel as though you're really part of the ranch.

DUDES AND DUDETTES

That idea of living a part of the romantic west began in the 19th century when folks back east heard tales of sprawling cattle ranches. People with enough money were able to buy a visit to the ranch of a cattle baron, live the cowboy life, ride and even help out around the corral. They became known as "dudes." And that was the beginning of one of America's most unique vacations.

Watch the children's rodeo one afternoon and you'll understand the thrill of the dude ranch. Some of these kids have never ridden a horse before this week, but today, they're hopping aboard with abandon, riding to the end of the corral where hapless parents await. The kid dismounts, the parent clambers aboard and holds an egg precariously on a spoon, as the child leads the horse by the reins back to the starting point. After more riding games, the little ones are all loaded into the back of a long red fire engine and hauled off to get ice cream.

Red fire engines, stage coaches, old timey carriages. They abound at the Flathead Lake Lodge. The reason is that the Montana Carriage Company operates in a cavernous barn on the property, making and restoring all sorts of old-fashioned modes of transportation. It's fascinating just to stand around a while and watch them painstakingly paint shiny gold letters on a fire truck. "It's a bunch easier to make one from scratch than to restore an old one," says a fellow hunched over a wagon wheel. "Look at all the patching I'm having to do on these wheels. Much easier to make a new one. But it'll look like new when I'm finished."

Watch the children's rodeo one afternoon, and you'll understand the thrill of the dude ranch. Some of these kids have never ridden a horse before this week, but today, they're hopping aboard with abandon.

GET UP AND GO

But carriages are just are a part of their restoration efforts. Docked at the lodge's little marina are the only Q boats ever designed by L. Francis Herreshoff, two of less than a dozen Q class boats remaining in the world today. The Questa and the Nor'Easter were once the fifty-foot racing sloops of financier J.P. Morgan who raced them in 1924 on Long Island and Marblehead. Now these beauties are once again sailing together on different waters here at Flathead Lake.

While you might be tempted to cocoon at the lodge your entire stay, a trip this far into Montana almost demands that you visit the mountain region carved out by huge ice age glaciers, the 1,600-acre Glacier National Park. Today, about fifty small glaciers are still quietly shrinking as they have for the past one hundred years and probably longer. Some, like Jackson Glacier (about a quarter of the size it was at the time of the

Civil War) are visible from the road, while others can be reached only by trail. But the incredible mountains and valleys seen here are all the product of millions of years of grinding ice and rocks. Their future is anyone's guess. In another century they could be gone completely or growing back to massive proportions.

Hiking, rafting and biking are great ways to see the park, but the "jammer" buses have it hands down for old fashioned sightseeing. Built between 1936 and 1939, these red and black motor coaches feature roll back canvas tops to see the sweeping vistas. Their moniker comes from the days when the buses didn't have auto-transmission, and drivers would grind and jam the gears going up and down the mountain. That must have had passengers on the edge of their seats. Glacier National Park is such a worthwhile visit, many people allot extra days to explore it before or after their week at the lodge.

Back at Flathead Lake Lodge, water-skiing, hydro-sliding and swimming have been in full gear since early afternoon. Just in case anyone grows faint from lack of food, the small side dining room sideboard is filled with lemonade, iced tea, bowls of fruit, trays of cheesecake with fresh huckleberry sauce and home baked chocolate chip and butterscotch cookies. Help yourself.

SIT A SPELL

At 5:30, most bathing suits are drying on patios and everyone is dressed (casually) and heading over to the Saddle Sore (for some, this is no joke) Saloon. The sign says, "We sell no beer or wine or whiskey, or gin or rum to make you frisky. You bring the sinful stuff yourself, and put the bottle on the shelf." Not entirely factual, you can buy bottles of wine, but you take them to dinner. The rest is labeled with your name and the saloon provides fresh "ditch water" and set-ups.

A dinner of stuffed quail and grilled Flathead tenderloin of beef (the most tender I've ever eaten), a cruise under the mottled violet and orange sunset sky aboard the Questa, and sleep comes easy tonight.

At the week's end, now fast friends are making plans, reservations even, to come back this same week next year. Many good-byes are said and addresses exchanged of while children play last minute games until at last their parents bodily force them into the car. They take off down the dirt road, hands waving furiously out the back windows. A moment of quiet. But it's not long before more autos and vans begin barreling down the lane, heads craning to take in the sights. Another week at Averill's Flathead Lake Lodge begins.

At 5:30, most bathing suits are drying on patios and everyone is dressed (casually) and heading over to the Saddle Sore (for some, this is no joke) Saloon.

ROAST GOOSE WITH BLUEBERRY CHUTNEY

Geese are usually available during the holiday season, otherwise you may need to special order one. If you have a wild goose, it will be much leaner than a farm raised goose, and both should be roasted only if young. Geese are also trickier to carve than turkeys.

1 domestic goose, about 10 to 13 pounds, trimmed
carrots, celery, onions, roughly cut up for roasting
2 lbs. fresh or frozen blueberries
2 diced apples
2 cloves chopped garlic
1 cinnamon stick
1 small piece grated ginger
1 tablespoon brown sugar
2 diced mangoes
2 tablespoons raspberry vinegar

1. Trim any excess fat from the goose and rinse it well. Prick goose with fork all over to help fat drain while roasting. Season with salt, pepper and garlic, preferably one day before roasting.

2. Place goose in large roasting pan on bed of cut up onions, carrots and celery. Roast at 350 degrees for about 3 hours or until a meat thermometer (put deep into breast) reads 180 degrees. Let rest 20 minutes covered by aluminum foil before serving.

3. While goose is roasting, place blueberries, apples, garlic, cinnamon, ginger, sugar, mangoes and vinegar in a medium saucepan and simmer for 15 minutes. Serve with slices of roast goose.

Serves 6.

BRAISED PHEASANT IN CHAMPAGNE SAUCE

Pheasants are fairly unusual fare in the U. S., but they can often be found in specialty markets or ordered by your supermarket. Most are between 1 and 3 pounds, with 1 pheasant serving two people. At Flathead Lake Lodge, the pheasant is served with pearl onions and sautéed mushrooms.

4 boned pheasants, boned and cut into serving pieces (save the bones)
½ cup olive oil
1 rough cut carrot
1 rough cut onion
½ bunch celery, rough cut
3 bay leaves
1 tablespoon whole black peppercorns
1 tablespoon tomato paste
1 cup champagne
¼ cup heavy cream
1 cup flour seasoned with salt and pepper
salt, pepper, and garlic to taste

1. In a large, heavy pot warm ¾ cup olive oil over high heat.

2. Dip pheasant pieces seasoned flour to cover on both sides. Shake off excess.

3. Sauté until golden on both sides in hot oil. Remove from pan and set aside.

4. Add leftover pheasant bones and sauté until brown. Add the roughly chopped vegetables and sauté until lightly brown.

5. Add tomato paste, bay leaves, peppercorns, champagne, water and pheasants. Simmer 45 minutes over low heat.

6. Remove pheasants from sauce and strain sauce through mesh strainer. If sauce needs thickening, make a roux by mixing 2 tablespoons soft butter with 2 tablespoons flour. Whisk roux into sauce and simmer until thickened. Add the cream. Adjust seasoning with salt and pepper.

7. Serve immediately or pheasants can be reheated in their sauce later.

Serves 8.

FLATHEAD LAKE BARBECUE TURKEY

This turkey is great for a crowd and a new approach from the typical turkey and stuffing.

1 10-pound turkey, thawed and trimmed
2 tablespoons liquid smoke
2 tablespoons chili powder
1 tablespoon salt
1 tablespoon black pepper
½ cup brown sugar
1 tablespoon garlic powder
1 tablespoon Cajun seasoning

1. Place turkey in a large roasting pan. Mix all seasoning together and rub on inside and outside of bird. Wrap tightly and marinate overnight.

2. Roast turkey at 325 degrees for 4 hours, breast side up, basting often with pan juices or melted butter. Check the turkey for doneness at 3½ hours. If pricked at the thickest part of the thigh, the juices should run clear, not pink.

3. When done, remove from oven and let rest, covered by foil, for about 15–20 minutes. Carve and serve with Cajun stuffing.

Serves 8.

CAJUN TURKEY STUFFING

Stuffing with a little bite. Increase the Cajun seasoning if you like things piquant (like a sticker in your tongue).

8 cups diced bread
1 lb. breakfast sausage
1 medium onion, diced
4 ribs celery, diced
1 red bell pepper, diced
1 green pepper, diced
1 tablespoon chili powder
3 cups chicken stock
3 eggs, slightly beaten
2 teaspoons garlic powder
2 teaspoons Cajun seasoning
1 tablespoon brown sugar
salt, pepper, worcestershire sauce to taste

1. Sauté the sausage in a large Dutch oven. Drain the fat.

2. Add the vegetables to sausage; sauté until tender.

3. Add the chicken stock and seasoning; boil for 10 minutes.

4. Add the bread cubes and mix well.

5. Add the eggs and mix well.

6. Place stuffing in a greased baking dish. Bake at 375 degrees for 1 hour.

Serves 8.

Seal Cove Inn

MOSS BEACH, CALIFORNIA

On a prime patch of property on the Pacific northwest, surrounded by parkland and just a half hour south of San Francisco, Seal Cove is a haven of comfort, beauty and taste.

Having traveled now for two years with *Great Country Inns,* I have a pretty well defined sense of what pleases me most about the best. I know what I like, and don't like, and what I'd include if I were opening an inn. Great Britain's Sir Bernard Ashley wrote, "As the Laura Ashley business has grown worldwide, it has taken me on countless trips to far-flung countries, to stay in numerous hotels and inns. It has made me want to create an hotel which fulfills my ideal of the perfect place to go and stay."

Karen Brown Herbert must have tapped into Sir Bernard's karma. She and husband Rick Herbert have indeed created what is to my mind, the perfect place to go and spend my time. And stay a while longer. It is the inn-traveler's inn.

But this perfection was no accident, nor guesswork or supposition. Karen Brown has traveled long days and weeks for her travel books called the Karen Brown Travel Series (twelve in print) that you see today in your local bookstore. While she and Rick still publish these very popular travel guides to accommodations all over the world, they decided that for the sake of their two children they would join the ranks of innkeepers themselves.

DESIGNER PASSION

Designed from the ground up on a prime patch of property on the Pacific Northwest, surrounded by parkland and just a half-hour south of San Francisco, Seal

Cove is a haven of comfort, beauty and taste. The gabled and multi-chimneyed lines of the graceful house resemble a sand colored stucco French chateau. The front drive is pebbled with cream colored stones, the inn surrounded by graceful wildflower gardens. Teak benches are settled in nooks just off graveled paths for quiet moments of enjoyment.

Step into the "dream inn" world of Karen Brown. To the right is the desk where you will be warmly welcomed. Before you is the living room. Warm antique tables glow in the sunlight. Large deep sofas pose in front of that marble fireplace, with an enormous wildflower arrangement, books and glossy magazines stacked on the pine table just before a glowing fire. The room is punctuated by Karen's collection of antique English, American and Swiss clocks found on her travels as well as her treasured watercolors of California landscapes. Arched doors to the right lead to a dining room filled with dark mahogany tables and chairs. Both rooms are illuminated by sets of French doors that let in the dazzling California sunshine. Beyond the inn are more wildflower gardens and a stone terrace. I can see someone just across the gardens strolling along a path leading to a grove of towering Cypress trees. What a wonderful hike it must be. Must try that later.

UPSTAIRS, DOWNSTAIRS

But my room awaits. Perhaps you'll stay in the Garden Room, just a few steps from the beginning of that very path. Done in garden greens and pinks, it features a queen sized antique iron bed, a grandfather clock that marks time noiselessly (Battery operated so as not to disturb your sleep. As Rick says, "You can't have ticking clocks in rooms where people expect to sleep.") wicker chairs with down cushions before the fireplace and chintz framed French doors that open onto a sunny terrace looking out over the gardens and Cypress bluffs.

But I pad quietly up the large staircase past the huge multi-paned picture window, past the lavender and pink Rotè Rose Room (named after Karen's favorite Swiss inn), and the Carl Larsson Room (decorated with Larsson's children's book prints) to the Ascot Room where I'll be staying.

Done in greens and burgundies with equestrian prints, I immediately open the balcony door to let in the fresh salt air. Wonderful. Looking around I see Seal Cove thoughtfully remembers the accompaniments that travelers desire. The corner fireplace (all rooms have them) is ready to be lit. Deep easy chairs face it for my reading or lounging pleasure. A complimentary bottle of California chardonnay, sodas and mineral water are in a tiny refrigerator just for me, hidden discreetly in the armoire, as is the television. The phone is bedside. The bathrooms have hair dryers (these should be in all inns- they're too bulky to pack), towel warmers (Karen grew to love them in Europe) stocked with generous towels (skimpy towels are awful) and fragrant toiletries. Somebody cares about me and my happiness.

The largest and most eye-popping room at Seal Cove is the Fitzgerald Room, named after the man who was responsible for preserving the incredible marine park adjacent to the inn. The canopied king sized bed is draped with cafe au lait and cream fabric, gathered at the corners. Those soothing colors also adorn the sofa. An ornate antique Austrian clock sits quietly on the mantle by a double set of French doors that open onto Juliette balconies, with views of the Cypress bluffs and the ocean beyond. The bathroom is a fantasy, with an incredible jacuzzi tub that begs for a bottle of champagne. Begging won't be required, however, Seal Cove is always prepared for spur of the moment romantics.

Beyond the inn are more wildflower gardens and a stone terrace. I can see someone just across the gardens strolling along a path leading to a grove of towering Cypress trees.

GRACIOUS COUNTRY INNS

MY FAVORITE PASTIME

As The Seal Cove Inn doesn't serve dinner, you are free to explore and expand your culinary experiences up and down the shoreline. One of Rick and Karen's favorites is just a stroll down the cypress bluffs, a lovely walk overlooking the Pacific to the Moss Beach Distillery. This lively restaurant hangs on the coastal rocks, serving up an unbeatable view, good times and fresh Pacific seafood.

8:00 AM: Rick quietly places a tray with an insulated carafe of fresh coffee by my door (along with the morning newspaper). What a pleasure to find it waiting when I awake, feeling good to my soul as I sit before an early morning fire, a cool breeze drifting off the ocean through the open doors.

The Seal Cove breakfast specialty is Gran Marnier French Toast, served with orange butter (that I could eat by the spoonful), warm maple syrup and plump little sausages, it is rich and it is good. A full pre-set breakfast menu is served in the main dining room. But, you might prefer the continental one in the privacy of your room.

This lively restaurant hangs on the coastal rocks, serving up an unbeatable view, good times and fresh Pacific seafood.

OF ROASTING PITS AND PISTOL SHRIMP

After breakfast, plan on making time for some of the many sights and sounds to experience in the area. Perhaps start with the Fitzgerald Marine Park, which is just a walk down the bluff. I head out in that direction and in a few minutes, I'm on the path that leads through a grove of towering Cypress trees. The view from Moss Beach out over the blue Pacific is breathtaking.

Before long I'm stepping gently through the site of an ancient gathering place for early Native American hunters. White flakes in the dirt are actually pieces of mollusk shells that were fashioned into jewelry or tools. Archaeologists have also dug up stone tools, roasting pits and porpoise bones left behind by those weary travelers 1,500 years ago. I dare say, they were not the beneficiaries of Rick Herbert's merciful coffee deliveries.

The Fitzgerald Marine Reserve was founded in 1969 to protect an entire community of fragile sealife that lives here in the tidepools. Well over 100,000 people visit this incredible reserve yearly hoping to spot starfish, hermit crabs, anemones, seals, sponges and even octopus. A large area covered with smooth cobble rocks is known as the "octopus garden," where one or two can usually be found gracefully waving their eight tentacles during a low tide visit. You can also find the Strongylocentrotus purpuratus (really) otherwise know as the purple sea urchin. Or, spy his cousin the sand dollar.

I gently turn over a rock to see what's underneath (you never know), and hear a loud popping sound from the mud below. One of the Reserve's green-jacketed volunteer guides who lead tours and answer questions, tells me the noise is made by a burrowing pistol shrimp with its thumb-like "trigger claw" designed to scare away predators and subdue prey. (Pick one up and you may become prey – expect a sharp sting.) I carefully replace the rock as I found it, a park rule, and escape with all my fingers intact.

CAPPUCCINO AND CHARDONNAY

Just six miles to the south of Moss Beach is Half Moon Bay, a trendy little California community chock full of art galleries, eclectic shops, espresso stands and restaurants, where you could easily browse the day away in cappuccino-sipping pleasure. Of course, there's San Francisco to the north. One of the world's most beautiful and entertaining cities is a half hour up the Cabrillo Highway placing the Golden Gate Bridge, Chinatown and fantastic museums within easy grasp.

Late in the afternoon, guests are gathering around a blazing fireplace in Seal Cove's Great-room. Everyone is discussing dinner plans and devouring a killer hot spinach cheese compote served on San Francisco sourdough bread. Karen has yet another intriguing suggestion for dinner in Half Moon Bay.

For the moment I simply want to relax and enjoy. My glass of wine and I escape out the French doors to the terrace. I can hear the ocean below and the Pacific sunset is a glowing golden orange. I take a sip of California chardonnay, and feel a profound appreciation for all the pleasures that Seal Cove has managed to combine in one place.

HOT SPINACH DIP

This yummy appetizer is served in the late afternoons in Seal Cove's lovely living room as guests gather for a glass of wine. This makes a large amount, enough for 15–20 people. So have a party!

6 packages frozen chopped spinach, defrosted
*   and drained of all liquid*
2 boxes of dry Knorr Vegetable Soup Mix
1 can of finely chopped water chestnuts
½ cup brie cheese, cubed
½ cup sour cream
½ cup mayonnaise
¼ cup grated Parmesan cheese
1 to 2 loaves of sourdough French bread

1. In a large mixing bowl stir together the dry soup, the sour cream and mayonnaise and then add the water chestnuts, spinach and lastly, the cheese until all is thoroughly and evenly mixed.

2. Spoon spinach mixture into a large, decorative baking dish and bake covered in a traditional oven at 350 degrees for approximately 30 minutes. Check after 30 minutes, stirring to make sure it is thoroughly heated with cheese melted.

3. Sprinkle with Parmesan cheese and continue to bake uncovered for another 5 to 10 minutes or until Parmesan cheese is toasted.

4. Serve with thick slices of sourdough French bread hot from the oven.

Serves 15–20 as an appetizer.

Microwave directions: Heat the spinach dip in a dish covered with plastic wrap for 5 minutes on high. Check after 5 minutes, stir to make sure it is thoroughly heated, sprinkle with Parmesan cheese and then heat uncovered for an additional 2 minutes.

GRAND MARNIER FRENCH TOAST WITH ORANGE BUTTER

This is a sumptuous staple at Seal Cove. The orange butter keeps well and is delicious on pancakes, waffles or biscuits.

12 pieces of Texas bread or 1"-thick slices of
*   French bread*
6 eggs
2 cups whole milk or (better yet!) half & half
½ cup Grand Marnier
½ cup orange juice
2 oranges cut in thin slices for garnish
zest from one orange rind (note use the juice
*   from orange for 1/4 juice listed above)*
½ cup butter
1 cup powdered sugar

1. Beat until egg yolks are thoroughly blended in a large bowl with the milk, ¼ cup of the Grand Marnier and ¼ cup of the orange juice.

2. Generously soak the individual pieces of bread (two slices per person) in the egg and milk mixture.

3. Heat a skillet thoroughly over a medium to low heat. Spray the heated skillet with Pam.

4. Place soaked bread slices in skillet and cook each side one to two minutes or until golden brown.

5. Serve the French toast on a plate garnished with a slice of orange, each piece of toast topped with a teaspoon of orange butter and a dusting of powdered sugar. Serve with warm syrup.

Makes 6 servings.

To make the orange butter: Heat butter in the microwave until melted. Stir in ¼ cup Grand Marnier, orange zest, ¼ cup orange juice. Slowly add the powdered sugar and stir until well mixed and a paste consistency.

NOTE: Orange butter can be made ahead of time. Refrigerate until needed.

The Shelburne Inn

SEAVIEW, WASHINGTON

With the time and tenacity to follow the trail of the great explorers Lewis and Clark, you would end up on one of the most beautiful pieces of coastline in the continental United States. Stretching 28 miles, it's the longest continuous beach in this country. Fortunately, we don't have to be so intrepid just to visit the Long Beach Peninsula in Washington State's southwest corner, just ready for succulent seafood, spectacular scenery and a stay at an inn that's been making explorers feel welcome since 1896.

The Shelburne Inn looks like the Victorian home of an old ship captain – green shingled with gables, leaded stained glass windows, cream colored woodwork, and casual gardens overflowing with a riotous mix of flowers. In days gone by, Portlanders traveled up the Columbia River, transferred to the Clamshell Railroad, and stumbled off the train praying for cool sea breezes and just-from-the-water Willapa Bay oysters, both of which are still in demand today, though the Clamshell Railroad is no more.

ALTARS, OAK AND ART NOVEAU

You'll be in good hands once you enter the front door. David Campiche and Laurie Anderson met when Laurie's car became stuck in the sand and, well, you can guess the rest. The happily married entity has been operating the inn since 1978, and is justifiably proud of the renovations and furnishings which they have added to this West Coast delight.

The Shelburne Inn looks like the Victorian home of an old ship captain.

The front lobby is warm and comfy, with a large wood-burning fireplace facing the perfect sofa for relaxing with a good book. The front desk is a church altar rescued from demolition. A nearby table is set with coffee and tea from early morning through the day and into the night for those who must have their coffee upon arising or upon arriving late at night. To one side of the spacious room are several large oak tables, the scene of gourmet breakfasts. Art nouveau stained-glass windows, four feet tall and rescued from a church about to be razed in England, were purchased sight unseen after a phone call from a friend. "We knew we'd find a place for them somehow," laughed Laurie, who created just the right touches for all the right places at Shelburne.

The inn has been expanded several times over the years. It now offers seventeen uniquely decorated rooms. Filled with antiques, each has a private bath, many with claw footed tubs. Suite # 9 has a large brass bed covered by a colorful patchwork quilt. French doors open on to a charming sitting room with a carved oak settee, matching chairs and a carved oak secretary. Number 9 also has its own private entrance to the outside, up a flight of stairs from the side garden, where you may enjoy your morning coffee.

Number17 is perhaps the most romantic suite, filled with a large mahogany armoire, loveseat and a huge carved mahogany bed. All are antiques found on a European furniture search. A private deck opens onto the side garden. Known as the anniversary/honeymoon suite, guests of this room have the option of breakfast served in bed.

JUMP START YOUR DAY

Arise early in the morning, not difficult if you're still on East Coast time, and take a short stroll to the beach. A path in the sand leads you through a grove of evergreens. Here everything looks fresh and vivid. A spider web strung across a tree sparkles as though freshly covered with diamonds. Over the dune, the brilliant blue Pacific explodes before you. Your only company are the seagulls and sandpipers who tirelessly run back and forth before the waves with their perfectly timed dance.

Over the dune, the brilliant blue Pacific explodes before you. Your only company are the seagulls and sandpipers.

Back at the Shelburne, David has been working even before you awoke, preparing what may be the most eye-popping breakfast you'll ever eat. A crisp corn, bacon and spinach frittata. French toast stuffed with ricotta cheese, cranberries, apples, and walnuts flamed in brandy and topped with cranberry syrup. Crepes stuffed with scrambled eggs, smoked salmon, red onions and fresh spinach. All are accompanied by fresh fruit, juice and homemade pastries. Get the idea about breakfast at the Shelburne? Better plan to work it off before the day's end.

Just down the Pacific Highway in Ilwaco is the Cape Disappointment Historical District. But you'll be anything but disappointed. Explore Fort Canby which once guarded the mouth of the Columbia River, and is now a state park. Bunkers and batteries are still in place along the rock bluffs, and the view of where the Columbia River meets the Pacific is breathtakingly soulful. Take a picnic (The Shelburne Inn restaurant, The Shoalwater, will pack a glorious one), and sit on the bluff by the old lighthouse for the best sights. The lighthouse used to help guide ships through this peril-filled pass known as the "graveyard of the Pacific."

After lunch, don't miss Leadbetter Point. A 1800-acre wildlife refuge at the tip end of the peninsula, this is where those Lewis and Clark qualities are summoned forth. There are no roads into Leadbetter, only foot traffic on the three trails, one of which leads west about a mile and one-half to the dunes and the beach. The others go north for about four miles to the tip of the peninsula, through Lodgepole pines and willows, until you're in mostly dune grass, then into the dunes themselves. Home to deer, coyote and elk, Leadbetter is a birdwatcher's paradise, with scores of shore birds. In the wet winter season, bring hip boots and raingear. This is a hike for the adventurous!

Out on Long Island in Willapa Bay is an even more fascinating spot called the Ancient Cedar Grove. Its 274 acres have never been cut, a rare opportunity to witness a virgin forest of red cedars that sprouted four thousand years ago. As you pad quietly down the soft, spongy path, you'll pass through other groves that haven't been spared the axe. You'll view gigantic cedar stumps cut at the turn of the century, some fifteen feet high and fifteen thick, reminders of how quickly a giant can be felled, and how long it takes for one to grow back. You can get to Long Island only by boat; information can be obtained from the Willapa Bay Wildlife Refuge, (206) 484-3482.

SALMON 'TIL YOU SIGH

As you'll be eating a daring amount of salmon in this area, you might as well see where they begin their accommodating, yet fruitful life. Sea Resources Salmon Hatchery is in Chinook, just down the road a piece. Founded in 1885 as the state's first facility of its kind, they now hatch four million eggs annually. That's a lot of fillet. They are more than happy to give you a free tour between 9 and 5.

The Shoalwater Restaurant is considered one of the top eateries on the peninsula. The Shoalwater does salmon in boundless variety, the spring-run Chinook salmon being a special delicacy. But don't forget this also oyster country. The Willapa Bay is a bountiful source of the blessed bivalves, harvesting about 650,000 gallons a year (the largest harvest in its history – one million gallons in 1947).

After dinner, draw a pint of the local favorite on tap in the Shelburne's pub.

The Shoalwater folks must stay up nights thinking of new and fanciful ways to prepare these creatures. Dinner could be oysters poached in garlic, lime juice, pepper and white wine or oysters with a bit of sauce mignonette or, oysters gently panfried and served with a spicy mayonnaise or, a creamy oyster stew with shallots, leeks and chives or, believe it or not, oysters baked with single-malt whiskey.

But if oysters are not for you (more's the pity), you'll not feel left out. Besides the salmon, you may feast on Dungeness Crab, razor clams (nearly plate-size), fresh Columbia River sturgeon with a green peppercorn and hazelnut demiglace, saffron fettuccine with seafood and smoked meats or roast duck with a blackberry-orange sauce. The Shoalwater has an impressive wine list to match anything you order, with quite a few half-bottles of excellent wines. Bless them.

After dinner, draw a pint of the local favorite on tap in the Shelburne's pub. And then perhaps a walk down mainstreet through the nearby shops and amusements of Long Beach, but the pull of the water will eventually be too strong. Go on, roll up those trouser legs, take off the shoes, and stroll with someone special over the dunes until you hear the roar of the Pacific. Take a deep breath of sea air and feel free to sigh once more.

FRESH FENNEL AND MINT SALSA

This delightful and unusual salsa is quite easy to prepare, and is terrific on pan fried oysters or frittatas. The mint and fennel give it a fascinating and fresh taste, and the three different colored peppers make it beautiful as well.

3 large ripe tomatoes, chopped medium fine
1 small red onion, chopped fine
½ yellow pepper, chopped medium fine
½ red pepper, chopped medium fine
½ green pepper, chopped medium fine
2 tablespoons finely chopped fresh fennel leaf
3 tablespoons chopped fresh mint
3 tablespoons tomato sauce
¼ cup red wine
4 tablespoons red wine vinegar
4 tablespoons olive oil
1 teaspoon sugar
½ tablespoon Tabasco sauce
½ teaspoon cayenne pepper

Mix all these ingredients in any order you feel like. This recipe will keep beautifully for several days.

SALMON POTATO CAKES

This recipe combines two of my favorite foods—potatoes and salmon. To make same day preparation easier, cook the salmon and potatoes the day before. This is a "wow" brunch dish.

½ cup yellow onion, chopped
1½ tablespoons butter
4 large potatoes, cooked peeled, drained and mashed
2½ lb. salmon fillet, baked, skin and bones removed
⅓ cup heavy cream
3 tablespoons melted butter
¼ teaspoon mace

¼ teaspoon nutmeg
¾ teaspoon salt
½ teaspoon fresh ground pepper
1 egg, slightly beaten
2 tablespoons fresh dill, chopped
1½ cups fresh bread crumbs, seasoned with salt, pepper, paprika, and cayenne pepper
2 tablespoons butter for reheating

1. Sauté onion in butter until tender.
2. In a large bowl, add sautéed onions, mashed potatoes, salmon, heavy cream, melted butter, mace, nutmeg, salt, pepper, egg and dill. Mix all ingredients together well.
3. Form 4-inch patties by hand and dip each side in the seasoned bread crumbs and refrigerate until ready for use. (Can be done one day ahead.)
4. Melt 2 tablespoons butter over medium heat in a sauté pan, and place patties in it until heated through, turning once. Serve with a poached egg and Hollandaise sauce, if you like.

Makes 6 servings.

SHELBURNE PANFRIED OYSTERS

In the opinion of the innkeepers, there is nothing—and I mean nothing—better than the first seasonal oyster about seven days after the first fall/winter frost. The fact that we tourists insist on devouring them in the hot season isn't surprising. That simply happens to be what is available. A mediocre oyster is better than no oyster. But the true oyster gourmand, according to innkeeper David Campiche, is as patient as the great blue heron. So beginning in late fall or early winter, Shelburne guests are treated to a morning breakfast of various oyster dishes, but this is the simple favorite. The herbaceous breading compliments the bivalve in mysterious ways indeed. David generally sautés no more than one dozen oysters at a time in 1/4 cup olive oil. He then wipes the pan with a paper towel, and starts again!

2 cups cornmeal
2 cups white flour
1 tablespoon turmeric
1 teaspoon curry powder
2 teaspoons fresh cracked pepper
1 teaspoon dried whole dill weed

1 teaspoon cayenne pepper, or Cajun spices
salt to taste
½ teaspoon each fennel seed, white pepper, and
    coriander seed cracked in a peppermill or
    mortar and pestle
¼ cup olive oil per dozen oysters for sautéing
2 dozen fresh shucked oysters

1. Bread the oysters in the flour/herb mixture.
2. Sauté oysters over medium heat in olive oil until golden brown on both sides, about two to three minutes per side.
3. Transfer to warm plate and garnish with homemade salsa and fresh fennel.

Serves 4.

SZECHUAN STYLE EGG PANCAKES WITH WILD MUSHROOMS, GINGER, AND GARLIC

David and Laurie thought this exotic egg creation might be a bit too much for some folks in the morning, but it's turned out to be one of their most popular dishes. The trick, they say, is to prepare the hot oil several days in advance to let the flavors expand.

When you're ready to do the eggs, do them three at a time. Also, divide the other ingredients to use for four servings.

12 eggs total, beaten 3 at a time
¼ cup heavy cream
salt to taste
½ cup wild mushrooms, preferably chanterelles,
    chopped
½ cup scallions, cut on the diagonal in one inch
    pieces
½ cup Parmesan cheese, grated
1 recipe Chinese Hot Oil (below)

1. Beat 3 eggs with 1 tablespoon of the heavy cream and salt to taste. Set aside.
2. On high heat add 1 tablespoon Chinese Hot Oil in an 8-inch non-stick skillet. Add the garlic and ginger and sauté until golden.

3. Add 2 tablespoons mushrooms. Once they are tender, fold in the eggs.
4. Add 2 tablespoons scallions and 2 tablespoons Parmesan to eggs and push into the eggs until they're covered. Reduce heat to medium.
5. As eggs begin to harden, bring in the edges several times until most of the liquid is firm, then flip the cake. Heat second side just until eggs are golden brown.
6. Lay on a warmed plate, garnish with salsa, crème fraiche, flowers or herbs.

Serves 4.

CHINESE HOT OIL

1 cup olive oil
10 Chinese red peppers
1 head garlic, peeled and chopped
1 tablespoon fresh ginger, peeled and
    chopped

Combine all the ingredients and save at room temperature in a covered jar. Refrigerated, this oil will keep indefinitely. Try using it on grilled meats, fish or vegetables.

Timberhill Ranch

CAZADERO, CALIFORNIA

The drive to this place is spectacular, hair-raising, actually. Up coastal Highway 1 north of San Francisco along the rugged Sonoma coastline, I stop at Goat Rock where the Russian River feeds into the Pacific Ocean. Hundreds of seals laze about, fat and happy in the sunshine. They have no reservations, nowhere they have to be. But I do. So after a moment's enjoyment off I go, winding higher and higher, developing a particular fondness for the sturdy guard rails that curve around the hairpin turns.

I turn off onto a long leafy country lane passing by farms and ranches, then onto another road even smaller and enclosed by trees. The road to nowhere. Have I made a wrong turn? No, there's the wooden sign, Timberhill Ranch, member of Relais and Chateaux. Made it.

Pulling up to the main lodge, I'm met by two fat white geese, heads high in the air, who observe me with some interest. Inside is a large, gracious room, a stone fireplace blazing a welcome and flanked by two cream colored sofas. Tables of magazines for browsing sit beside vases of flowers providing pure pleasure "You made it," smiles Barbara, one of the four co-owners of Timberhill who each take personal responsibility for making sure you have an enchanting stay. "Have a seat by the fire and we'll get you settled in." Sigh. That sounds good.

"Have a seat by the fire and we'll get you settled in." Sigh. That sounds good.

RELIEF AND RELAX

If you come looking for excitement, nightlife or frenetic activity, you're in the wrong place. But if luxury, respite and privacy set in 80 secluded acres sound attractive, this sybaritic oasis dispenses them in generous proportions.

Fifteen private cottages are scattered, barely noticeable, about the property. They could have easily built 30 given the space, but then guests wouldn't have that blissful sense of having their own little cottage in the woods. Cedar paneling inside provides its wonderful fragrance. The baths are huge, with double sinks so you don't have to share. English toiletries and thick, fluffy towels and robes are for your personal pleasure. The queen-sized bed is covered with a handmade quilt made by local artisans, and there are teddy bears on the bed. The tiled fireplace is ready for the strike of a match from matches that have *my* name on them. Comfortable chairs are set before the fireplace so I may soak in the warmth. Children's blocks on the mantle spell out "Welcome." Underneath the hearth is a supply of firewood, but when you leave the room, invisible hands will have relaid it by the time you return.

A deck outside my glass doors offers lovely views of the pines and redwoods. An umbrella is propped on the front porch in case of sudden Sonoma showers. Fresh flowers, a filled ice bucket, books and magazines, and a small refrigerator stocked with refreshment help you feel right at home. These Timberhill folks don't forget anything.

ADVENTUROUS CUISINE

Enough gaping at the cottage. Cleverly arriving in time for one of Timberhill's renowned six-course dinners, I freshen up. A murderous storm hits; rain falls in buckets from the heavens. And the electricity disappears. Yikes. The fireplace provides light. There are candles. So, undaunted and hungry, I finish getting dressed (but not dressed up – it's casual), grab the handy flashlight and umbrella to find my way against the odds along the gravel path to the dining room. I'm somehow childishly excited by the adventurous absence of electric power.

The mouth-watering menu reflects that Timberhill is in the midst of a region rich with fresh vegetables, seafood, fruits and world famous wines with a kitchen that respects them all. Accolades and awards are nothing new here in this candle-lit (it would be anyway even if the lights weren't out), picture-windowed dining room that at present is cooking on emergency generator power.

The first of six courses (they change daily) might be tender steamed mussels with white wine and herb broth or baked Brie and baguette with grapefruit and onion marmalade. Then the soup: purée of sweet potato and orange, shrimp bisque or Southwestern tortilla. Now salad. Mixed greens with Gravanstein apples, grapes and poppy seed dressing or local young lettuces with garlic roasted walnuts, tomatoes and Stilton dressing. About now you need an intermezzo. It comes as a small dish of apricot, pineapple-coconut, or mango sorbet. Just enough. For your entree, might you consider fresh Dungeness crab cakes with red pepper mayonnaise? Or, perhaps the Reichardt Farms duckling with a red wine and currant chutney glaze? Or, medallions of beef tenderloin with wasabi cream? Now you're talking. A tray of unctuous desserts glistening with chocolate, raspberries and hazelnuts appears. For once in my life, I can't. Really.

By now the rain is just a gentle shower, and the smell of redwoods and smoke curling out of fireplaces is intoxicating on the walk back to my cedar cabin. It's late, I'm tired, and the bed turned down is just too inviting to resist. I drift off to sleep, the crimson embers glowing in the fireplace, and sleepily I notice the little blocks on the man-

The tiled fireplace is ready for the strike of a match from matches that have my name on them.

tle now say "good night" and the bears seem to be waving at me from across the room. This is a most romantic pla.........

After a peaceful night's sleep, I'm up early with time for a pre-breakfast walk. Pulling on some jeans and a jacket (mornings are nippy), out I go. The sun has burned off most of the morning fog; the night showers have disappeared. The freshness of the air reminds me of a line from Bemelman's *Madelaine and the Gypsies,* "The storm is gone, the world is new. This is the castle of Fontainbleu, all this, dear children belongs to you!" It's Timberhill, of course, but for the time being, the feeling is one of a private estate that is yours alone. Seeing no other soul on my stroll, I enjoy the solitude, the daffodils blooming and the birds rejoicing in the sunshine. The tennis courts look lonely this early hour but what a dream setting, perched on a hill overlooking the distant mountains. Heading up the lane by the main lodge, I arrive at the barn where the animals are kept. Some of the cutest you've ever seen, too. Guests love the miniature horses, geese, llamas, pot-bellied pig, and little pygmy goats. Frostie is a 33-inch tall stallion who can proudly pull two guests around the pond in his cart.

The path meanders by the pond, where two of the geese honk their welcome as they take an early morning dip. Ooops, it's almost time for breakfast, the one I requested for 8:00 AM. My heavens, it's on time, too. Barbara is bouncing down the trail in the oversized golf cart, loaded with a tray of goodies. What a tremendous thing, really, breakfast in your cottage. The fireplace blazing, or in warmer weather, al fresco on the deck. The joy and luxury of it never leaves me.

The pastry chef who must have a very light touch and a reliable alarm clock, makes scones and croissants fresh every morning. Crusty, tender, warm, altogether delectable. The deep dark coffee is poured from a "you-won't-run-out" carafe, fresh squeezed orange juice and the morning paper. It's so tempting to crawl back under the quilt, and you can if you want. There's no schedule here. As Tarran McDaid, another owner, points out, "That's why people come here, for romance. We designed it to provide relaxation and a stress-free environment."

IF ONE MUST MOVE

But, you're in the middle of some of the most beautiful countryside anywhere. Salt Point State Park is adjacent to Timberhill, with 6,000 acres of Bishop pines, redwoods, bay laurel trees and huckleberry bushes and numerous hiking trails crisscrossing the property. The Stump Beach Trail leads down to the water's edge where observing sealife in tidepools is second only to observing sealife via scuba and snorkeling.

Early summer provides a decent chance of spotting the gray whale. So after Timberhill packs a picnic lunch I'm off to Sentinel Rock in Fish Mill Cove at the foot of Timberhill's bluff. To get there you drive down a winding dirt road that had been a stagecoach route at the turn of the century, past second growth redwoods and lush ferns carpeting the sides of water soaked gulches until you reach the ocean. The wind is setting up a steady blow on the half-mile hike to reach Sentinel Rock's wooden viewing platform. The view that can at times be foggy is gorgeous today. The Pacific is extremely blue but very choppy with whitecaps that make spotting a whale difficult. No problem. I turn my total attention to the turkey sandwich on homemade bread, marinated mushroom salad, fruit tart and brie cheese in my basket. Whale watching takes a backseat to Timberhill food.

Late afternoon, back at the ranch, is a perfect time for a swim in the heated pool or a jacuzzi soak overlooking the countryside. I choose the latter as the air chills with the setting sun. The bubbles relax my body; my mind wanders to the pies I saw cooling earlier in the kitchen, a picture perfect pastry called "Summersnear pie," made with local plums, pears and apples. Dessert won't get by me tonight.

It's Timberhill, of course, but for the time being, the feeling is one of a private estate that is yours alone.

CHARBROILED SWORDFISH CHOP WITH BLACK BEAN AND CORN RELISH

Simplicity itself, the relish is a colorful accompanist to the swordfish. If you don't have time to soak and cook beans, black beans also come canned. Just rinse them first and proceed with recipe.

6 6-oz. center cut swordfish steaks 1½ inch
    thick
1 tablespoon olive oil
1 tablespoon fresh garlic minced
salt and pepper to taste
1 cup black beans washed and soaked overnight
2 cooked ears sweet corn cut off the cob into kernels
2 scallions sliced
1 red bell pepper chopped fine

1. Boil the beans in fresh water until al dente, approximately 1 hour with a little salt and cumin, drain and cool. (*Can be done a day or two earlier.*)

2. Mix the beans, corn, peppers, and scallions together and toss with enough olive oil to lightly coat. Stir in salt and crushed garlic a little at a time to taste. (*Can be done several hours ahead.*)

3. Marinate the swordfish for at least hour in the olive oil, garlic, and salt and pepper.

4. Grill the fish over hot coals about 3 to 4 minutes per side until done, making crisscross grill marks on both sides. Remove and set aside on a platter. Serve with black bean relish.

Serves 6.

BLACK BEAN SOUP

Just a note about the sugar in this recipe. It is used to balance out the flavor of the red wine and vinegar, so it requires your own taste buds to do some work in finding your own balance of sweetness.

2 lbs. black beans
1 tablespoon salt
½ cup red wine
¼ cup red wine vinegar
¼ cup + 2 tablespoons olive oil
1 medium red onion chopped
1 medium green bell pepper chopped
3 cloves garlic, minced
¼ to ½ cup fresh cilantro chopped
Sugar—¼ cup or less
1 tablespoon cumin
Salt and black pepper

1. Soak beans in cold water overnight. Pick through for any small stones or foreign matter.

2. Drain beans and place in large pot and cover with 20 cups of fresh cold unsalted water. Bring to a boil. Turn down to simmer and cook until the beans are soft (about 1½ hours).

3. When the beans are done, take out about 3 cups of beans with liquid and purée in blender. Pour the purée back into the soup pot and add 1 tablespoon salt.

4. Add the wine, vinegar, ¼ cup olive oil, sugar to taste (start with a small amount) and cumin.

5. Sauté the onion, garlic and green pepper with 2 tablespoons olive oil until just soft. Add to soup. Cook slowly until soup thickens to desired consistency. Add salt & pepper to taste.

6. Mix in the fresh chopped cilantro, and check for all seasonings and serve.

Serves 8.

PERSIMMON PUDDING

Persimmons are usually available at some supermarkets and specialty stores in the fall. Their unusual flavor make an distinctive Thanksgiving dessert. I used to walk by an old persimmon tree every day going to school. I've never forgotten that taste.

6 very ripe persimmons
½ cup unsalted melted butter
¾ teaspoon grated nutmeg
1½ cups unbleached all-purpose flour
2 eggs
1 teaspoon vanilla extract
1 teaspoon baking soda
1 cup light brown sugar
2 teaspoons ground cinnamon
½ teaspoon salt
1 cup light cream

1. Halve and scoop out the meat from the persimmons, discarding any seeds. Purée in a food processor or blend until smooth. Set aside.

2. In a large mixing bowl, combine the remaining ingredients with the reserved purée, stirring just enough to mix and moisten flour.

3. Pour into an oiled 9-inch round oven-proof dish and cover with a fitted lid or foil. Make a water bath with hot water in a pan large enough to hold the dish. Water should reach halfway up the sides of the dish.

4. Bring the water to a boil on top of the stove, reduce to a simmer and cover both pots with foil. Steam until set, about 2½ hours. You can also steam the pudding in the oven at 350 degrees.

5. Serve with orange flavored crème anglaise or whipped cream lightly sweetened with 1–2 tablespoons of an orange liqueur.

Serves 12.

STRAWBERRY MILLE FEUILLE

This dessert makes a spectacular presentation and looks lovely on a dessert table.

1 sheet frozen puff pastry dough
3 cups whipping cream
2 pints strawberries – Set 12 beauties aside for
*   decoration, stem and quarter the rest.*
½ cup confectioners sugar
1 teaspoon vanilla
½ cup currant jelly
Mint leaves

1. Chill mixing bowl and beater. Preheat oven to 375 degrees.

2. Let puff pastry dough sit at room temperature until it is pliable.

3. Roll the dough out about one third again of its original size on a lightly floured surface. Brush off extra flour and put on a baking sheet lined with parchment paper. Pierce the entire surface with a fork.

4. Bake about 18 minutes, or until rich golden brown. Let cool.

5. Handle pastry very carefully as it will be quite fragile. With a serrated knife, slice horizontally into three oblong pieces of equal size.

6. Whip the cream and confectioners sugar together until it begins to hold shape. Add the vanilla and continue beating just until stiff.

7. Take ⅓ of the cream mixture and mix with the berries you have quartered. Lay one sheet of puff pastry on a serving platter and top with berries and cream.

8. Top with a second layer of pastry and smooth edges with a flat pastry blade or knife. Take second ⅓ of the cream and spread over second pastry layer, smoothing edges once again.

9. Top with final pastry layer and line whole berries down the center. Spoon the jelly that has been melted in a microwave oven or over low heat and cooled slightly over the berries.

10. Take the remainder of the cream and put in a pastry bag with a decorative tip. Pipe alongside the berries.

Serves 8.

TIMBERHILL COULIBIAC

Wonderful as a starter or entree, depending on the portion size. The cool cucumber sauce is the perfect foil for the warm coulibiac. A Timberhill classic.

8 ounce salmon filet cut into ½-inch strips
2 lbs. filet of sole
2 shallots chopped
2 eggs
1 teaspoon dill
Salt and pepper to taste
1 10×15-inch sheet puff pastry

1. Place ½ of the sole in food processor with salt, pepper, dill, 1 egg, shallots and half of the cream. Process until smooth. Remove and repeat with the rest of the ingredients.

2. Lightly dust the puff pastry with flour and roll it out until it is half as thick as when you started.

3. Spoon half of the sole mixture down the center of the puff pastry dough evenly. Place the strips of salmon end to end down the center of the sole. Cover with the remaining sole mixture to encase the salmon.

4. Dampen the edges of the puff pastry and wrap up the fish mixture.

5. Place on a baking sheet seam side down and brush with egg wash. Bake for approximately 25 minutes in a 350 degree oven or until the pastry is golden brown. Cool for 10 minutes to allow the mousse to set.

6. Slice into 1-inch slices. Serve warm with cucumber dill sauce.

Serves 6-8.

CUCUMBER DILL SAUCE

1 cucumber, peeled, seeded and sliced
2 cups sour cream
2 shallots chopped
1 teaspoon fresh chopped dill
Salt and pepper to taste

Mix all the ingredients and serve.
(Can be made in advance.)
Makes 3 cups.

MIDWEST

Iroquois Hotel on the Beach

MAKINAC ISLAND, MICHIGAN

If you want to take a trip that truly transports you to another era, away from the noisy, gaseous, honking realm of the combustion engine, try Makinac Island (we say it Macki-naw, rhymes with saw). The constant, steady clip-clop of horses hooves as they pull carriages and dray-carts up and down Main Street are more than just local color. That's how you get around. Those confangled driving machines were banned from this island – located at the northern tip of the Michigan peninsula – at the turn of the century by some brilliant city fathers, and mothers no doubt. Their descendants have wisely never seen the need to change things.

AN ISLE APART

But that's only part of this adventure. There is no bridge to the island. So you arrive by boat, just as they did in the 18th century, when the island's natural harbor was quite a prize for the British soldiers who moved here from the mainland during the Revolutionary War. Where the military goes, so too will families and merchants. They naturally settled along the harbor, now part of Makinac Island's "downtown."

Tourists began to enjoy the charms of Makinac Island in the late 1800s, brought by passenger steamers, which continued to sail the Great Lakes through the 1970s. Ferry service began in 1878 with the Arnold and Coats Company running supplies and a few passengers for lumber and fish camps. The Arnold Transit Company is still around and

You arrive by boat, just as they did in the 18th century, when the island's natural harbor was quite a prize for the British soldiers who moved here.

along with Shepler's Ferry and the Star Line has trips departing every half hour in the summer to and from St. Ignace and Mackinac City. Don't worry about the luggage or the car— your bags are loaded on board, your car will be safely stored on the mainland.

Once you've arrived at the docks, your bags will be taken by an Iroquois Hotel porter leading a horse drawn cart. Go on ahead, you'll see your bags shortly. Take a left down Main Street, jostling with fudgies (notorious day tourists who buy a pound of fudge and return to the mainland), residents, sightseers, and carriages everywhere being pulled by overgrown brown and white horses that are crossbreeds of Clydesdale, Belgian, Percheron and Standards. They're huge, lumbering and gentle as a bay breeze. Just down a block or two, with a splendid view of the Straits of Mackinac, is a rambling, white Victorian house, originally built as a private residence, that's been providing hospitality and respite for paying guests since 1904.

The Iroquois Hotel on the Beach has a large lattice work front porch perfect for sipping a cool beverage while watching the puffy clouds float by on an idyllic Mackinac day. Manicured, immaculate flower beds curve around the inn with riotous reds, yellows, purples, and whites in summer bloom. Through the double door entrance is a small lobby and front desk, where you're immediately greeted. Off to the left is a round cupola common room, filled with white wicker chairs and sofas, floral fabrics, and flooded with brilliant sunlight from the circle of windows. A lovely place to rest for a moment, but would you like to see your room now?

Each room has been individually decorated with a definite feminine touch. All have wallpapers and fabrics in summer and sea colors. Room #305 is a third floor suite, with pale blue and white stripes on the walls, and an entire bank of windows overlooking the lawn, the lighthouse and water just beyond. The cathedral ceiling is marbleized with white beams stretching across. Floral curtains frame the many windows, and the same fabric covers the sofa and chairs. Blissfully serene.

Upstairs are two of my favorite rooms. One of several tower suites is a pink and celery-green corner room surrounded by windows that curve around a turret sitting area that overlooks the harbor on all sides. From your chaise lounge, you can harbor gaze and daydream for hours.

Or room #318. The immediate impression upon entering is that it floats over the water. The room is done all in robin's egg blues, and being a third floor corner room, it appears to jut out over the harbor. Only by approaching the windows will you see the rich green grass and weathered docks below. Two queen sized beds and a cozy sitting area make it a harbor-side haven.

The bed linens have been especially selected for each room. No standard white sheets. Pastels, stripes and prints are selected specially for each room, a touch that gives you a unique feeling no matter how many times you return.

Why all the attention to detail? The Iroquois has been owned by the McIntire family since 1954 and is run by daughter Mary McIntire. The business of this 47-room inn is personal, for you and them. All accommodations are reviewed annually and there is constant redecoration underfoot in the off-season because the McIntires love this place. Their attention shows in so many ways. The staff will bend-over backwards to make you feel at home, help with carriage tours, bicycle rentals or dinner reservations. Just ask and thou shall be served with a genuine smile.

The Iroquois Hotel on the Beach has a large lattice work front porch perfect for sipping a cool beverage while watching the puffy clouds float by on an idyllic Mackinac day.

AS THEY DID BACK THEN

In the morning, the sun sneaks through the tiny cracks in the white lacquered shutters at your windows. Looks like a good day to explore the island. A light tapping comes at the door. No more procrastinating, gotta move–breakfast has arrived (also served in the dining room). A waitress dressed out in crisp yellow cottons brings a tray bearing banana bread or hot blueberry muffins, a bowl of fresh fruit and berries, hot coffee and fresh-squeezed orange juice on fine china with pastel embroidered linens. Room service breakfast may be ordered the night before with a card you hang on your doorknob. You can also place a next day order for a "moveable feast" on the same card. Choose from prime rib, turkey or ham sandwiches or fried chicken, plus chips and dessert. Hey, that's lunch for your bicycle tour.

Bicycles rented at the Iroquois have handy baskets for carrying things like lunches. This is the best way to see the island. It will take about 45 minutes to an hour to tour the eight mile road that follows the shore all the way around. And, it's a flat easy ride. Safety tips for cyclers: Horses have the right-of way. Give them plenty of room. On narrow roads, give way for carriages and emergency vehicles. Oh yes, and don't attempt to grab a carriage for a "free ride." It could cost you in more ways than one.

The views away from the hustle and bustle of Main Street Mackinac are gorgeous. Green lawns with flocks of geese nibbling dinner, pristine white churches, long colorful flower beds. Breezes blow in from the water, and several pebble beaches are perfect for a picnic. You'll pass by Arch Rock, a natural limestone formation that stops most people on the road. You can climb up for a better view without too much effort.

Another easy way to get about on the island is, of course, the horse. Around 600 horses are stabled in the summertime for hauling freight, taxis and carriage tours, plus saddle horses. Mackinac Island Carriage Tours (the world's largest horse and buggy livery) depart from the center of town. It's best to call and reserve a seat, or check in early with them and shop until tour time.

Make sure your tour goes up along the West Bluff. Not only is the view spectacular, so are the houses you'll find. Wealthy families from Chicago and other Midwest cities picked this remote spot as that perfect place for a summer residence. While some of these Victorian structures are cottages, some are 30 room mansions, with horse stables and servants quarters. And they had a sense of humor, too. One of the big homes was built by a meat packing tycoon, and is called "Hog Haven."

It will take about 45 minutes to an hour to tour the eight mile road that follows the shore all the way around. And, it's a flat easy ride.

There are two golf courses on the island. The Jewel belongs to the Grand Hotel, and the Wawashkamo Golf Club, built in 1898, is one of the few remaining natural terrain "links" courses in the country. When you play golf at Wawashkamo, you're also on the site of an American/British skirmish in 1814. Both courses are open to the public.

There's a lot of history to absorb on the island, having been under French, British and then American rule. Extensively restored, Fort Mackinac is really a living museum. Authentically dressed soldiers present live demonstrations of Springfield rifles and canon firings, to make vivid their descriptions of the rigorous life of an 19th century soldier. Great for kids and adults.

Shopping will, of course, be a part of your visit. Main Street is packed with charming shops of all kinds. They offer everything – antiques, art, jewelry, baskets, you name it. But you'll notice that about every fourth store or so is a fudge shop. Big plate glass windows offer views of huge copper kettles and pounds of the sugary treat being cooled on 4 foot square marble slabs. Chocolate, double chocolate, maple vanilla, even cranberry fudge tempt you all along the shopping route. They've been making it here for more than 100 years, so the recipes have stood the test of time.

EVENING PROSPECTS

By evening you're ready for a cool drink on the emerald green lawn of the Iroquois that stretches to the sea wall. Sit back and watch huge freighters pass through the Straits of Makinac in the distant mist. Relaxing enough so one's thoughts can turn to dinner possibilities.

The Iroquois has one of the finest dining experiences of the island in The Carriage House. Located on the waterside of the inn, the view is incomparable, and so is the food. You might start with barbecued shrimp and miniature buttermilk biscuits or Northern Michigan smoked whitefish, and perhaps chilled garden vegetable gazpacho. Then on to piquant roast chicken with olives and potatoes, Iroquois Lake Superior broiled whitefish, or a grilled veal chop with Creole mustard butter and four peppercorn sauce. Polish that off with the famous Iroquois fudge ice cream puff, macadamia coconut cake or peanut butter pie with nut crumb crust, and you know you've dined sufficient, thank you.

On to piquant roast chicken with olives and potatoes, Iroquois Lake Superior broiled whitefish, or a grilled veal chop.

IROQUOIS LEMON MERINGUE PIE

1 pre-baked fluted 10-inch pie shell
4 cups hot water
2 cups sugar
1 cup cornstarch
1 teaspoon salt
8 egg yolks
1 cup lemon juice
4 tablespoons butter

1. Blend cornstarch and sugar in 3 quart saucepan. Add hot water, cook stirring over high heat until thickened and clear. Remove from heat.

2. Beat egg yolks in a large mixing bowl and add hot cornstarch mixture slowly just until doubled in volume.

3. Add yolk mixture back into cornstarch mixture, return to heat and cook until it comes back to a boil, about 1 minute.

4. Remove from heat and strain into bowl. Add lemon juice and butter, stir until blended, cover and chill filling.

5. When chilled pour into prepared pie shell.

FOR MERINGUE:

8 egg whites
½ cup sugar
1 teaspoon cream of tartar
1 teaspoon vanilla

1. Whip egg whites until frothy with completely clean mixing bow and beaters (a touch of oil will cause them not to whip); add vanilla and cream of tartar.

2. Whip until soft peaks form.

3. Gradually add sugar and whip until stiff peaks form and sugar is thoroughly dissolved.

4. Top chilled pie. Bake at 350 degrees for 20 to 30 minutes. Cool.

IROQUOIS FETTUCCINE ALFREDO WITH MORELS

Unless you have a secret forest source for morel mushrooms they can be awfully hard to find in supermarkets and expensive if you do. Other wild mushrooms like chanterelles or shiitakes could be substituted.

1 stick unsalted butter
1 cup heavy cream
2 tablespoons cognac
1¼ lbs. fresh morels, rinsed, drained, and patted
    dry, or ¼ lb. dried
1 lb. fettuccine, fresh or dried
½ cup freshly grated Parmesan

1. In a skillet melt 2 tablespoons of the butter over moderately low heat.

2. Add cream, cognac, salt and pepper to taste, and bring mixture to boil.

3. Add morels, simmer covered for ten minutes and keep mixture warm.

4. Cook the two types of fettuccine in boiling salted water for 3 minutes or until al dente according to directions and type of pasta.

5. Drain pasta.

6. In a large skillet melt the remaining 6 tablespoons of butter. Add pasta, the morel mixture, ½ cup of Parmesan and pepper to taste and toss well.

7. Serve pasta on heated plates with additional Parmesan.

Serves 6 to 8 as an appetizer.

CHOCOLATE BREAD PUDDING

Always a bread pudding fan, chocolate combines two of my loves. Make sure all the bread is soaked with the chocolate mixture before baking. Add more cream if necessary.

1¼ cup heavy cream
½ cup plus 2 tablespoons sugar
10 ounces finely chopped semi-sweet chocolate
6 egg yolks
5 ounces butter, room temp., cut into small
    pieces

6 egg whites
5 tablespoons sugar
1 tablespoon vanilla

2½ cups, ¼ inch diced white bread

1. Bring sugar and cream to boil, remove from heat.
2. Add chopped chocolate stirring until completely blended.
3. Add yolks one at a time beating well after each.
4. Stir in butter until melted.
5. Whip egg whites until soft peaks form. Add sugar when just starting to turn white, add vanilla and whip until stiff.
6. Gently fold in the chocolate mixture. Pour over prepared bread in buttered 9×11-inch pan. Gently squeeze chocolate mixture into bread with hands until completely mixed. Let sit for 30 minutes or so to absorb all the mixture. Add more cream if too dry.
7. Bake in a 350 degree oven in a hot water bath (halfway up sides of pan) 45 minutes. Let cool slightly.
8. Cut into wedges, or cubes loosely piled together together. Serve warm or room temperature in a small pool of *Orange Rum Custard Sauce*.
    Serves 12.

IROQUOIS ORANGE RUM CUSTARD SAUCE

2 cups heavy whipping cream
2 teaspoons grated orange peel
2 tablespoons sugar

1. Bring cream, sugar, orange peel to boil. Cover and let stand for 20 minutes. Meanwhile:

8 egg yolks
2 tablespoons sugar
1–2 tablespoons dark rum

2. With a whip blend yolks, and add sugar slowly.
3. Add warm orange cream. Cook in top of double boiler over simmering water, stirring constantly with rubber spatula until it coats the back of spatula.
4. Remove from heat and strain into a small bowl set in a larger bowl with ice water, stir until completely cooled. Place plastic wrap on top of custard to prevent skin from forming. Chill.
5. When ready to serve add dark rum and blend until smooth. Serve with chocolate bread pudding .

BLUEBERRY LEMON MUFFINS

Blueberry muffins get my vote any time of year but the lemon peel adds a unique zing to these. I think you'll like them.

2¾ cups flour
½ cup sugar
1½ tablespoons baking powder
1 teaspoon salt
1⅛ cups milk
⅔ cup oil
2 eggs
1½ cup blueberries
2 tablespoons sugar
1 tablespoon grated lemon peel

1. Blend dry ingredients together.
2. Blend eggs and oil together, and add milk.
3. Combine egg mixture into dry ingredients just until barely mixed.
4. Mix 2 tablespoons sugar and lemon peel to blueberries and mix. Fold into muffin batter.
5. Equally divide batter between greased muffin cups. Brush lightly with melted butter and sprinkle lightly with granulated sugar.
6. Bake at 400 degrees, 15–20 minutes.
    Makes 1 dozen muffins.

Stafford's Bay View Inn
PETOSKEY, MICHIGAN

Rocking back and forth on the front porch of Stafford's Bay View Inn with the cool breezes of Little Traverse Bay blowing in, you'll experience what guests have been feeling on this same veranda for over a century. A blissful sense of peace and contentment, a realization that these simple moments of pleasure are what life is all about. A modest epiphany, if you will.

But this prime stretch of coastline along Lake Michigan's eastern bank has been cherished for much longer than a century. The Ottawa Indians from the Northern Huron area appreciated its charms back in the 16th century, as did the fur traders in the 1700s, and the lumbermen after them who cleared the land making way for the railroad barons. They in turn decided that the natural beauty of Petoskey must be shared with many, not to mention making themselves a tidy profit in the bargain. So began the railroads that hauled in trainloads of folks seeking cool summer air and relief from their allergies.

FROM STEEL AND LUMBER

Thirteen hotels were built. One of them became Stafford's Bay View Inn (then called the Woodland Avenue House), which opened to guests in 1887 and is now the oldest continuously operating hotel in Michigan. Wagons would be sent to the train station every Saturday to collect guests, many of whom would idle away the entire summer. An ad in the Bay View Assembly Herald read:

So began the railroads that hauled in trainloads of folks seeking cool summer air and relief from their allergies.

"A first-class boarding house with hotel accommodations. Finely located one block from the upper RR station, commanding a fine view of the bay. Season rates: Board and room $5 to $8."

Well it's still first class, and the view of the bay is still magnificent. Inflation has hiked the prices. Just a bit.

If you study some of the early pictures of the Bay View you'll see it remains a three-story white clapboard Victorian, with a green Mansard roof, turret and wrap-around porch that is a magnet for those searching for a moment's breezy, quiet respite by the water.

Like any Victorian inn, this one has been changed and expanded many times. When it first opened there were fifty tiny rooms, none with private bath. Pampered sojourners began to expect a bit more as time passed. So Stafford "Duff" Smith, desk clerk in 1957 and owner since 1961, completely renovated the inn, enlarging rooms and adding baths so that the inn "grew" to 35 rooms, all with private bath.

COMFY AND COZY

Stepping inside Stafford's Bay View Inn is stepping into another era. The Smith family has re-established Victoriana while sidestepping the pitfall of being too fussy. The lobby is warmed by a wood stove that vents into an oak and tile mantle. The fires that often burn there usually draw the outstretched hands of smiling guests. Stuffed sofas and chairs make lingering even more likely.

Off to the left is Roselawn Porch dining room overlooking Little Traverse Bay. Green carpet, snow white lacy iron chairs pulled up to pink clothed tables combine for an informal yet romantic setting. Breakfast, lunch and dinner are usually served here, or in the Howard or Staffordshire dining rooms for more formal affairs.

Across the lobby is a sunroom with deep blue walls, white wicker furniture with fat, bunchy cushions, brilliant red floral Clarence House chintz curtains framing numerous windows. Streaks of sunlight make this a terrific room for reading, morning coffee, sewing and the lace-making, knitting and counted cross-stitch classes held here.

When Stafford completed his renovation, the Bay View was as cozy and charming as ever. The floors still creak and the odd here-and-there nooks still make you feel as though you're visiting with family. Accommodations today range from the Primrose Cottage rooms, which are modest and quaint with cottage-style furnishings and quilts to the more opulent Forget-Me-Not suites.

Suite #7. A rocking chair and buttery yellow sofa cuddle up to the fireplace in the sitting room. On the other side of the French doors that divide the parlor from the bedroom, there's a four poster, lace and macrame-canopy bed. And, a jacuzzi in the bathroom.

Room #44. I love the fountain-like faucet that gushes water into the bathtub, and the sink handpainted with spring flowers. A forest green sitting room with an oak-mantled fireplace is just outside, and the antique bed is also carved oak topped with an Amish quilt. By your bedside every night, you'll find a plate of homebaked chocolate chip cookies, and not just any recipe. The inn held a contest to find the "Best Chocolate Chip Cookie in Petoskey." The winner was none other than Stafford's chef.

No matter which room you choose, large or small, you may be visited in the night. Oh, not to fret, they're friendly ghosts – with names yet, Nancy Higgins and Mr. Howard. Just a few floor squeaks as they pass through, looking for breakfast no doubt.

And who could blame them, breakfast is not a ghostly repast at Stafford's Bay View. Get ready for country dishes such as fresh baked malted waffles with three fruit toppings and apple smoked bacon, or consider the 3-oz. tenderloin broiled and present-

The Smith family has re-established Victoriana while sidestepping the pitfall of being too fussy.

ed with farm fresh eggs and country fried potatoes. Even more interesting is the lean turkey hash, made with breast of turkey, potatoes, onions, rutabagas, parsnips, carrots and brussel sprouts and served with poached eggs and Dijon Hollandaise. But the inn is renowned for its Sunday buffet. For 15 years Stafford & Co. been packing them in at the Bay View with the famous sticky buns, waffles, haunches of ham, sausages, Eggs Benedict, hash browns and the traditional tomato pudding ("It's gotta' be there," says Stafford), to name a few of the 30-some dishes that you'll face. Stafford himself usually makes an appearance, resplendent in his white chef's outfit to carve a roast beast or two.

GEOLOGY, GEOGRAPHY AND JAM

After breakfast stroll down to the edge of Little Traverse Bay. Pristine and the deepest midnight blue, you can still find smooth thumb-sized Petoskey stones at the water's edge. What the heck is that? It seems that some 350 million years back, this area was a tropical ocean covered by coral at the ocean's floor. As the ocean evaporated the coral died, one can only hope painlessly. Fossilized coral = Petoskey stones.

Hop on one of the inn's bikes and head for the Petoskey Historical Museum, formerly a railroad depot. Inside, one can be witness to much of the history of this area; stories of the Ottawa tribe, the rugged fur traders of the 1700s, not to mention remarkable hand-sized Petoskey stones. Colorful exhibits make this a stop of interest for both children and adults.

Then take a trip into the downtown historical Gaslight District. Big baskets of red geraniums hang from the gas lampposts and the streets are chock-a-block with shopping possibilities of all kinds. The general store is a gourmet's delight full of exotic foods and wines. Books, clothing, fly fishing equipment, wind chimes, more Petoskey stones, candles, French earthenware and indigenous Michiganian stuff await your browsing pleasure.

Just down Lake Street is American Spoon Foods, a Michigan concern that creates jams, jellies and other items exclusively from Northern Michigan fruit. Most delicious of all, there is a tasting bar, where you can sample all the wares before you buy. Cherry gooseberry chutney, pumpkin butter, wild blueberry preserves, smokey catsup, fruit barbecue sauces, dried Michigan cherries and blueberries with no preservatives or artifical colors, crunchy trail mix with those same dried fruits and almonds, and simply the best peach preserves you'll ever taste are all there. American Spoon also mail-orders just about anywhere, so that taste of Michigan need never be missed.

Summer visitors can enjoy the benefits of one of America's last summer Chitauqua programs. Based on the original in New York State, Chitauqua is a combination of religious, artistic and recreational programs. Lectures, concerts, recitals and vespers, not so different from the Chitauqua of a century ago, are still held in the Bay View Association, an historical community founded along with the Bay View Inn in 1887.

Swimming, sailing on the Great Lakes, hiking, mountain biking, golf, tennis and scenic drives are all available if you wish. The Bay View staff will make arrangements for you.

If you happen upon this corner of Michigan in winter, it will be...white. Petoskey averages 180 inches of snowfall in winter, and they put it to good use. Cross-country ski right from the Bay View's front door. Stafford says that the Bay View and The Perry Hotel (also owned by the Smith family) are about the only accommodations open in the winter and not too many folks are about, so you are free to ski down the quiet streets as well as in the forest. Or perhaps you could pile into a horse drawn sleigh and listen to the jingle of the horse bells as you snuggle under several lap robes. Downhill skiing is also available.

Just down Lake Street is American Spoon Foods, a Michigan concern that creates jams, jellies and other items exclusively from Northern Michigan fruit.

A TOUCH OF WHITEFISH

Back at the inn, feverish dinner preparations have begun. The goal of the kitchen staff is to create country food with a modern gourmet touch. Fresh Michigan whitefish with morel mushroom sauce and asparagus in herb butter, whitefish piccata, and whitefish broiled and served with citrus butter and remoulade sauce bear testimony to Stafford's belief that you can't prepare fresh Michigan whitefish too many ways. But things other than whitefish abound on the menu, such as smoked whitefish sausage (all right, a touch of whitefish), straw and hay pasta with pecan-basil marinara, cold cherry soup, cherry-pepper steak (two medallions of tenderloin seared and served with a port wine demi-glace laced with dried tart cherries), or sautéed pork tenderloin with apple-pear chutney. Then if you dare, a "finale dolce" from the pastry tray. Don't listen to Stafford. He'll encourage you shamelessly.

After a bayside dinner, sunset park awaits, a white picket fenced bluff overlooking Little Traverse Bay. You may feed the flocks of pigeons who await the dispersal of bread or seed on the green lawn, while you behold the bright oranges and purples of Michigan's "million dollar sunset."

Then if you dare, a "finale dolce" from the pastry tray. Don't listen to Stafford. He'll encourage you shamelessly.

GREAT LAKES CHOWDER

This fish stew is based on Michigan whitefish. Trout or halibut could substitute, and salmon could stand in for the walleye.

1¼ lbs. whitefish, diced, skinned and boned
½ lb. walleye, diced, skinned and boned
¼ lb. smoked whitefish
2 leeks, cleaned of grit and sliced thin, white part only
1 large onion, diced medium
2½ oz. smoked bacon, diced medium
1 stick butter
8 cups water
5 cups cream
½ cup flour
1½ lbs. potatoes, diced and cooked
1 oz. clam base (a concentrated paste available at most stores)
1 bay leaf
Old Bay, white pepper, coriander, flour, thyme and salt to taste

1. Bring the walleye and whitefish to a boil in water.
2. Remove fish when done and cool.
3. Add the cream to fish broth.
4. Sauté bacon, butter, leeks and onions in a separate skillet. When leeks and onions are translucent, add flour to pan until combined.
5. Combine bacon-flour mixture to fish stock mixture allowing it to cook a few minutes until thickened.
6. Add potatoes and fish, heat gently and season with salt and pepper
   Makes 1 gallon.

ZUCCHINI BREAD

This moist bread is good for snacks, teatime or breakfast. As this recipe makes two loaves, keep in mind it freezes well too. Or send the other one to me.

1 cup salad oil
2 cups sugar
1 oz. vanilla
3 eggs
1 teaspoon salt
1 teaspoon baking soda
1 teaspoon baking powder
4 cups flour
2 small zucchini, grated
½ cup carrots, grated
1 14-oz. can crushed pineapple, drained
1 cup walnuts, chopped

1. Mix well sugar, eggs, oil and vanilla.
2. Add zucchini, carrots and drained pineapple.
3. Sift dry ingredients together and add to zucchini-sugar mixture. Fold in chopped walnuts.
4. Grease two loaf pans and divide batter between them. Bake at 350 degrees for 50 minutes to 1 hour, until golden and firm in middle.
   Makes 2 loaves.

STAFFORD'S TOMATO PUDDING

The inn always cooks the pudding a day ahead and reheats on second day to serve. It tastes even better.

12 oz. fresh tomatoes, diced
¼ cup brown sugar
2 cups bread cubes, dried and cut into 1" squares
½ cup celery, diced
½ cup onion, diced
2 tablespoons butter
fresh basil, thyme, chopped garlic, salt and pepper to taste

1. Place tomatoes in a mixing bowl and set aside.
2. Sauté celery and onions in butter until tender, then add to tomatoes along with sugar and bread cubes. Mix well.
3. Season with garlic, salt and pepper to taste.
4. Place in casserole dish and bake at 350 degrees for 30-45 minutes.
   Serves 6.

BLACK CHERRY SOUP

Although this soup is served as a cool summer starter at Stafford's Bay View, it would also make a terrific dessert soup. Feel free to use other fruits such as blueberries, strawberries or peaches.

1 cup pitted tart cherries (if canned, drain)
1 cup pitted sweet cherries (if canned, drain)
½ cup sun-dried cherries (save a few for for
  garnish)
1½ cup cherry yogurt
1 cup sour cream
1 cup heavy whipping cream
1 cup milk
sugar and brandy to taste

  1. Place tart and sweet cherries in food processor and purée. Set aside and add dry cherries.
  2. Place yogurt, sour cream, whipping cream and milk in a large mixing bowl and mix thoroughly. Add cherry mixture, sugar and brandy to taste. Chill several hours or overnight. Garnish servings with extra dried cherries.
  Serves 8.

STAFFORD'S CHICKEN SALAD

A big favorite at the inn, Stafford's goes through 8–12 gallons every other day. This salad is distinguished by dried Michigan cherries and almonds.

2½ lbs. boneless chicken breasts, boiled and
  cooled
¼ cup green onions sliced on the bias
¼ cup red onion, diced small
¼ cup sliced almonds
¼ cup celery, diced small
½ cup dried cherries
mayonnaise

  1. Mix all ingredients together and bind with mayonnaise to your taste.
  Serves 6 to 8.

SUN-DRIED TOMATO SPREAD

If you have dried tomatoes that are not packed in oil, reconstitute with hot water and toss in olive oil with herbs.

1½ lbs. cream cheese
½ cup sun-dried tomatoes, packed in oil
2 green onions, sliced thinly

  1. Rehydrate tomatoes in hot water until softened (if not already packed in oil), then soak in olive oil with basil, oregano, marjoram, thyme and bay leaves. (Save the oil for salad dressings.)
  2. In a food processor, chop drained tomatoes and green onions. Combine with cream cheese
  3. Serve with crackers or French bread toast.
  Makes 1 quart

The White Gull Inn

FISH CREEK, WISCONSIN

If you've never been to Wisconsin, specifically Door County, you're in for a treat, especially if you love shoreline views. There are more than 250 miles of shoreline in a county that has more state parks and more lighthouses than any county in the United States. Add lush cherry orchards, towering limestone cliffs, and picturesque villages that curve along the water and you have one gorgeous piece of countryside by the shore.

Heading up the eastern Wisconsin peninsula with Lake Michigan on one side and Green bay on the other, you'll pass Sturgeon Bay ship canal. Branch off onto Hwy. 42 past Horseshoe Bay and Egg Harbor. You'll soon come to the little town of Fish Creek and The White Gull Inn, which has been operating continuously since 1896.

CREATED FOR HEALTH AND COMFORT

A three story white clapboard with black shutters, The White Gull virtually radiates warmth and hospitality, with a double storied front porch stretching across the entire front of the inn. Peonies, ornamental cabbages, hanging baskets of begonias beckon you inside, where you're greeted by a paneled lobby. An old fashioned front desk is where you check in and the gift shop where you may buy the most wonderful homemade granola and sweet lavender soaps. A cozy sitting area with stuffed chairs and sofas grouped around a stone fireplace invites you linger for a moment. This is a good place to learn some of the fascinating history of The White Gull Inn.

A cozy sitting area with stuffed chairs and sofas grouped around a stone fireplace invites you linger for a moment.

It began when the inn and cottages around it were built by German born Dr. Herman Welcker, who fell in love with the tiny village of Fish Creek. Part of the buildings were dismantled in Marinette, Wisconsin and actually slid across the frozen waters of Green Bay during the winter. He filled the rooms with fine walnut and marble furniture shipped in from Cincinnati.

According to Anna Thorp, a Fish Creek historian, Dr. Welcker was quite the health enthusiast, modeling his program for guests on European health spas with lots of exercise, hearty meals, cultural activities, and rest. Says Thorpe, "A two hour silent period was followed and strictly enforced. Herr Doktor strode through the cottages and hallways shaking a small handbell, calling 'Ruhe, ruhe!' (Quiet, quiet!)."

Andy and Jan Coulson, who bought the inn in 1972, went through the formidable task of renovating The White Gull, which had fallen into a sad state of disrepair. Jan redecorated with lovely fabrics and wallpapers, and looked for period antiques to go with ones still at the inn from Dr. Welcker's time. Hard work? Yep, but over 20 years later, innkeeping is in their blood, and you won't find more charming or hospitable hosts. They don't enforce Herr Doktor's quiet time today, but they make sure that guests are so comfortable, they just may find that afternoon nap irresistible.

The rooms and cottages are all named after the special women in Dr. Welcker's life. The Henriette (his wife) is a white frame cottage behind the inn, surrounded by flower beds and tall trees. There's a screened porch for enjoying the cool nights, and a living room with a fireplace just in case the night is a bit cool. Inside are English pine antiques, a camelback loveseat covered in a cherry print sits in the corner with a twig swan resting just behind on the windowsill. A separate room contains the four poster bed, pine armoire, with chintz swags at the windows.

Room C in the Cliff House is a favorite of romantics and honeymooners. A beautiful walnut sleigh bed made by a local furniture craftsman is tucked under the eaves. You have your own private balcony that offers a tree view in summer, and a view of the limestone bluffs in the other seasons.

The most loved room at The White Gull is in the main inn, room #1. Its private entrance, one of the original woodburning fireplaces, Waverly fabrics, a brass four poster bed, and English antiques make it most charming.

But no matter where you sleep, don't miss breakfast at The White Gull dining room generously and forgivingly served from 7:30 to noon, for late risers. A warm, paneled room with a large riverstone fireplace, and windows that overlook the back terrace, it is a charmed setting for a country breakfast. If pancakes are your favorite, you'll be in heaven – the chef changes them every day; peach walnut, blueberry, cherry, apple, pecan, granola and buckwheat. Or you could begin the day with Door County cherry-stuffed French toast, the chefs's own blend of homemade corned beef hash with beef brisket, grated baked potato and onions. Don't miss the granola (you can also take some home), mixed and baked in The White Gull ovens to crunchy goodness, served with fresh fruit and milk. Or choose the Swedish limpa bread made with brown sugar, caraway and anise, white and rye flour.

THE DAY

Now you're in fine form to explore. One of those numerous Door County state parks is in your back yard. Some consider the Peninsula State Park the jewel of Wisconsin's state park system. There are miles of quiet roadways and trails perfect for biking through the dappled forest. The Backroad Bicycle Route is a 100-mile ride on both sides of the peninsula that winds along scenic coastal towns and countryside. Maps area available at the Door County Chamber of Commerce (414) 743-4456.

They don't enforce Herr Doktor's quiet time today, but they make sure that guests are so comfortable, they just may find that afternoon nap irresistible.

You may want to bait your hook while you're here. Walleye, small mouth bass, giant northern pike, lake trout and salmon are netted at different times of the year within a fish-fertile 30 mile radius on both sides of the peninsula. And if you happen to visit in the winter, don't forget ice fishing. There are occasionally hundreds of hardy fishermen on the ice tundra in their frail ice shanties, fishing for huge schools of perch.

On a sunny, summer day, there is no better way to enjoy the beauty of the Fish Creek coast than to take a sail from the Boat House of Fish Creek, where many local launches are docked. Slicing through these blue waters protected from the sometimes wild and unpredictable winds of Green Bay is a great way to witness the splendor of 200 ft. tall limestone bluffs and the famous Eagle Bluff Lighthouse.

Don't forget to save a couple of hours to simply drive or bike around the Door County area admiring the cherry and apple orchards, roadside stands bursting with fresh fruit, jams and pies or, perhaps browse through some of the many crafts and art galleries that dot Fish Creek.

But as much as fishing, swimming, sailing and cycling are a big part of the Fish Creek area, so are the gentler arts. The Peninsula Players, set in a garden overlooking Green Bay, is the oldest summer theater in America. Come early to catch the sunset. Then, there's the Peninsula Music Festival in Ephraim which brings symphonic joy to sweet summer days. The American Folklore Theater breathes life into America's past introducing you to lively folk tales and ballads. Music, dance, and theater combine with the works of potters and painters to complete the arts scene.

THE SEASONS

Most visitors come to The White Gull Inn during the spring, summer or autumn for obvious reasons. Winter is their "quiet season." As Andy points out, "It gets pretty darn cold here in Wisconsin, December through March." But Door County is pretty in white, and the inn puts together special winter packages for those who like cross-country skiing, as there are many miles of trails in Peninsula State Park. Add ice fishing, ice skating, snowmobiling or even a horse-drawn sleigh ride to pat that winter holiday into a snowball. After the winter fish boils (a bit more on this later), folk music concerts are held once a month in the dining room. As soon as Andy laid eyes on the room, he thought it perfect for '60s style folk concert. "Unfortunately in the '70s, not many people were listening to folk music," he explains. Not so anymore and the concert series is now going into its second decade. For people who don't eat fish (What, no boiled fish?), the inn has introduced a very popular series of pre-concert ethnic dinners. Reservations for both concerts and dinners are recommended.

ALL YEAR ROUND

By now you'll be feeling those hunger pangs. Back to The White Gull for dinner. If it's not "fish boil" night, the chef will be offering rosemary rack of lamb, roast pheasant with a raspberry vinaigrette, shrimp and artichoke romano, or asparagus and brie cheese-stuffed chicken breast with a creamed brandy cider sauce. Aaaaaaahhhh.

But if it is one of several fish boil nights every week, dress down for a unique culinary experience. By evening the air turns crisp as folks begin to congregate on the flagstone terrace behind the main inn. As the equipment for the fish boil is set up, doubtful first-timers begin to talk among themselves.

Misgivings abound. ("Ever been to one of these before?") But not to worry. Not only is this evening completely memorable and fishy fun, Russ Ostrand, the master boiler, is also a consummate chef. How a man can take whitefish, potatoes and salt

Walleye, small mouth bass, giant northern pike, lake trout and salmon are netted at different times of the year within a fish-fertile 30 mile radius.

How a man can take whitefish, potatoes and salt blasted over a kerosene stoked fire and turn it into fine food is beyond me.

blasted over a kerosene stoked fire and turn it into fine food is beyond me. But, he does it. This is an event you'll take home and talk about.

I would be remiss if I did not mention that The White Gull has its own cookbook, to satisfy the many requests of happy customers. They graciously allowed me to reprint some of their favorites from that book. You may purchase a copy, plus terrific granola (they sell close to 1,000 pounds a year), homemade hot fudge, and cherry preserves by mail order through the address at the end of this chapter.

After dinner, put on a sweater, and stroll a block down the street to a little green park with a stone wall overlooking Green Bay. Children play at the water's edge, laughing and throwing pebbles into the water. Couples hold hands and talk softly, but all are waiting for the same thing. A glorious, golden-orange sunset.

WHITE GULL FISH BOIL

The moment you set foot in Door County, you'll hear of the traditional outdoor fish boil. Part local history, part flaming entertainment, part great eatin', this ritual feast has been performed at The White Gull for the past 25 years by the dean of the "master boilers," Russ Ostrand.

How did the fish boil get started? Russ answers that he remembers churches doing them to raise money when he was a child. "People came from miles around to taste the local fish, potatoes and Door County cherry pie. I figure they boiled it because how else could you cook fish for such a large group?"

When Russ adds the salt, one pound for every two gallons of water, it usually shocks the crowd. "Is that salt?" someone gasps. "Oh, just a pinch," Russ deadpans. He goes on to explain that the salt doesn't make the fish salty, but raises the specific gravity of the water. "Kind of makes it like the ocean and everything wants to float. All the fish oils that we don't want to eat rise to the surface. When the fish and potatoes are done, (the potatoes, after 30 minutes of boiling, the fish added for the last nine minutes) I throw on a small amount of kerosene."

Russ knows that kerosene doesn't sound too appealing and stresses it goes on the fire only. The big flareup causes an overboil. When the water in the top half of the pot boils over the edge, it takes the oils with it..

The guests now respect him – totally. Russ tosses on the kerosene, the fire shoots toward the sky, and everyone takes a picture (you will too). Russ and his assistant ease a pole through the nets of fish and potatoes, lifting them to a nearby tray.

Served inside with the fish and potatoes are cole slaw, rye bread, Wisconsin beer and Door County cherry pie, without which, it wouldn't be a fish boil.

12 small red potatoes
8 quarts water
2 cups salt
12 whitefish steaks, cut 2 inches thick
melted butter
lemon wedges

While the White Gull cooks the fish outside over a wood fire, this recipe can be done at home on the kitchen stove with a 5 gallon pot. If your pot does not have a removable basket or net, you can use a cheesecloth bag to hold the potatoes and one for the fish, or drain the food in the sink using a colander. To expand this recipe add 1 cup of salt for each additional gallon of water.

1. Wash the potatoes and cut a small slice from each end for flavor penetration. Bring the water in the pot to a boil; keep it boiling as much as possible throughout the recipe.

2. Add the potatoes and one-half the salt; cook 20 minutes. Check doneness with a fork.

3. When potatoes are almost done, add whitefish with the remaining salt. Cook about 8-10 minutes, until fish are firm, but begin to pull away from the bone when lifted with a fork. (Don't attempt the kerosene routine at home, simply skim the oils from the surface with a spoon while the fish is cooking.)

4. Lift cooked potatoes and fish from the water; drain all in the sink in colander.

5. Serve fish and potatoes on a large platter garnished with lemon wedges and dishes of melted butter.

Serves 4 generously.

WHITE GULL DOOR COUNTY CHERRY PIE

The traditional dessert at the White Gull after the famous fish boil is homemade cherry pie, made the bountiful cherries of Door County. While a great ending for that unusual menu, I've never been known to turn down this cherry pie after any meal.

1½ cups sifted flour
¾ teaspoon salt
½ cup lard
4 tablespoon ice water
5 cups fresh red tart cherries, pitted
2 teaspoons Kirsch or 2 drops almond extract
1 teaspoon grated lemon rind
1 cup sugar
⅛ teaspoon salt
4 tablespoons flour
1 tablespoon butter

1. With a pastry blender cut ¼ cup lard or butter into 1½ cups flour mixed with ¾ teaspoon salt to obtain a coarse meal consistency. Add remaining ¼ cup lard and cut again with pastry blender. Sprinkle dough with ice water, mixing lightly with a fork until it holds together. Wrap in plastic wrap and chill for 1 hour.

2. Line a 9-inch pie pan with the rolled out pastry, saving 1/3 of the dough for the lattice top crust.

3. In a separate bowl, mix cherries, kirsch or almond flavoring, and lemon rind together. Combine the 4 tablespoons flour, sugar and 1/8 teaspoon salt, and mix with the cherries. Pour filling into dough-lined pie pan. Dot with the butter and cover with lattice work crust.

4. Bake at 450 degrees for 10 minutes, then reduce heat to 350 degrees and bake 30 minutes longer until golden brown.

Makes 1 pie.

WHITE GULL GINGERBREAD PANCAKES

If you're really feeling fanciful, or have a sick family member who needs a special breakfast treat, make these dark, yummy pancakes using a gingerbread man cookie mold. Make sure you spray it with oil first!

1¼ cups flour
3 tablespoons sugar
1 tablespoon baking powder
1½ teaspoon baking soda
½ teaspoon salt
2 eggs
1 teaspoon dry ground ginger
1 cup buttermilk
2 tablespoons melted butter
½ cup molasses

1. Combine dry ingredients thoroughly in a large bowl.

2. In a separate bowl, mix eggs and buttermilk. Pour wet mixture into dry ingredients and stir just until smooth.

3. Add melted butter and molasses to batter and stir to combine.

4. Heat a skillet or griddle lightly coated with vegetable oil over medium heat. Pour batter to make 4-inch cakes. Flip pancakes when bubbles appear on surface, and bottom side is well browned.

5. Serve with maple syrup.

Yields 12 4-inch pancakes.

MID-ATLANTIC

The Inn at Perry Cabin

ST. MICHAELS, MARYLAND

Living in Baltimore, I have visited what is called the Eastern Shore (of the Chesapeake Bay) many times. It is one of the most flavorful parts of the state, literally and figuratively. Watermen tong and dredge for briny oysters. And, blue crustaceans are what crabbers hope to find when they pull their wire traps up from the bay depths. Huge flat farms line the roads as do produce stands overflowing with red Maryland tomatoes and truckloads of Silver Queen corn (the only edible kind). Occasional flocks of ducks or geese fly by in formation, circle and land in a plowed under field pecking at the leftovers.

The historic little town of St. Michaels is right on the water of the Miles River, near where the river empties into the Chesapeake. I've toured there frequently and finally paid a visit to the rambling white Colonial mansion I've admired from the road so often. The four-star and four-diamond Inn at Perry Cabin is just outside the town proper, set on twenty-five green and perfectly manicured acres on the banks of Fogg Cove.

Turn down the long entrance drive shaded by leafy trees. Through the front door there is no check-in, per se. You are greeted by a staff member who has been expecting you. "Welcome to Perry Cabin. Did you have a nice drive?" We travel down a hall past several parlors, each different, each a fugue of English wallpapers and polished chintzes.

The four-star and four-diamond Inn at Perry Cabin is just outside the town proper, set on twenty-five green and perfectly manicured acres on the banks of Fogg Cove.

THE BRITISH RETURN TO THE EASTERN SHORE

This is no accident of course. This interior decorator's dream house is owned by Sir Bernard Ashley, head of the worldwide Laura Ashley empire based in Great Britain. Every fabric and wallpaper, and many accessories are from the extensive Ashley collection. Several parlors are filled with polished British antiques, plush down filled chairs and sofas, oil paintings and handcolored prints, corner cupboards filled with Sir Bernard's personal glass collection, bouquets of fresh flowers and baskets of fresh fruit. I resist the desire to touch all the shining surfaces as we walk along, discussing the history of the place. My gracious guide continues, "The main part of the house was built in 1820 by Samuel Hambleton, a shipmate of Commodore Oliver Hazard Perry during the war of 1812. B.A., that's what we call Sir Bernard, bought it in 1989." A riverside manor on genteel grounds amidst an historic setting – it's easy to see why Sir Bernard thought this the perfect spot for his first American inn. (Keswick Hall is also an Ashley property and featured in another section of this book.)

We arrive. Room #24 is one of forty-one accommodations and it's a resplendent retreat of pinks and greens. A scalloped canopy tops a carved pine four poster bed. Two down stuffed chairs and a loveseat sit in a bright bay of windows that overlook the water. The fat, bunchy balloon curtains must have used a luxuriant amount of yardage, but after all, this is Laura Ashley territory. An antique writing desk at the side is set with Perry Cabin stationary for letter writing and the armoire across the room hides the television. The bathroom is stocked with thick towels for my bath, a towel warmer for my sensitive nature, soft terry robes for my leisure and Ashley toiletries for the pure luxury of it all. #24 has its own entrance to the outside lawns and gardens, for my privacy.

Master suite #32 is a two room Ashley extravaganza in muted russet tones and dark forest green. The sitting room is filled with English antiques and prints on the walls, the bedroom features a half canopied bed with an antique "fainting sofa" at the foot. Open the French doors to your private balcony overlooking the green lawns and the waterfront. Baskets of fresh fruit and mineral water are always provided.

Four gigantic white columns grace the classic facade of the inn. This is a perfect spot to enjoy breakfast in warm weather or a glass of wine in the late afternoons. Walking down to the little pier, I catch a ride down river (or up river) aboard the sloop John D to St. Michaels. It's an easy stroll but going by boat is not only more fun, it's much more in the spirit of the town.

DUCKS AND DECOYS THAT SAVED A TOWN

Stop first at the Maritime Museum. Don't miss the red roofed lighthouse at the water's edge. This treasure of maritime life and history was jump-started in 1965 by volunteers who realized with alarm that some of the traditions of the Chesapeake were rapidly disappearing and needed to be preserved. What started as a small effort now covers 18 acres. In nine buildings are housed one of the largest existing collections of waterfowl decoys, a fleet of typical baycraft – like skipjacks, bugeyes and crab dredgers, and a monstrous firearm called a "punt gun." It took several men to hold, but one shot would fell thirty to fifty ducks. The jewel of the museum is the Hooper Strait Lighthouse, built in 1879 and moved here in 1966. Set up as though occupied by the lighthouse keeper, one can get a sense of his austere and lonely life here in his round house.

Just behind the museum campus is the St. Michaels marina, filled with bobbing sailboats whose owners and occupants are either lolling in the sunshine or have jumped aboard dinghies for shore to eat lunch at one of the crab houses surrounding the water. Until you've sat down to a mound of steaming blue crabs, covered with Old Bay spices

The bathroom is stocked with thick towels for my bath, a towel warmer for my sensitive nature, soft terry robes for my leisure and Ashley toiletries for the pure luxury of it all.

and eaten Maryland style (tables covered with brown paper, a small knife and wooden mallet in hand, and a pitcher of cold beer at your elbow) you haven't lived life to the fullest. Roll up you sleeves and dig in.

Main street St. Michaels is a strolling browser's delight, with loads of Victorian storefronts filled with antiques, sailing togs for that proper "Eastern Shore" look and candy stores with rich chocolates shaped like crabs and oysters.

In 1813, just a year after Perry Cabin was built, the British sailed up the Chesapeake with the ill intent of bombarding St. Michaels, busy shipyards. Always on their toes, the clever townspeople hung lanterns at the tips of ships masts and in the tops of trees. It worked like a charm. The Brits thought the town was on a bluff and aimed their canons up and over the town. Only one house took a shot, now named quite rightly the "cannonball house." St. Michaels still proudly calls itself "the town that fooled the British." All except Sir Bernard.

St. Michaels still proudly calls itself "the town that fooled the British." All except Sir Bernard.

From St. Michaels, it's an easy drive to the picturesque towns of Easton or Oxford (take the little Oxford ferry). The inn can also arrange golf, horseback riding, charter boat fishing, yachting or duck and goose hunting. The life of owning a country estate is at your fingertips.

RESTORATION, INSPIRATION AND TEA

If you get back to Perry Cabin in the late afternoon, a British tea will be set up in one of the parlors. Fresh baked scones, clotted cream, jams and pots of hot tea are laid out with gleaming fine china and silver to provide a bit of afternoon restoration. Thus refreshed, you may take part in a game of croquet on the lawn, a walk by the water or perhaps a swim in the heated indoor pool. A steam room and sauna are also available with towel and toiletry stocked dressing rooms poolside.

Sir Bernard Ashley stated his philosophy for a good hotel like this, "In the hotel, I want a certain peace. I want to wear what I like and sleep when I like, and if there are to be excitements, let them arrive at the dining table." I'm feeling those sentiments as I walk to dinner. All the parlors and halls are now softly lit by candles. This must certainly be the perfect English country house.

The dining room views the water and its fading last rays of light. A fire burns cheerfully in the fireplace, warming my back as I peruse the menu. To start. Lobster in puff pastry with spinach and chives? Or salad of duck breast with red onion and pear? No, the Parma ham, baby lettuces and melon are just what I want.

Now the main course. Let's see, grilled tenderloin of beef with shiitake mushrooms and mashed potatoes? Papillote of rockfish steamed in white wine and vegetables? Or, a roasted fillet of marinated lamb with herb jus and dauphinois potatoes? That's the one.

Dessert. The choices become more difficult still. Poached pear with maple pecan ice cream and butterscotch sauce. Trio of chocolate with coffee sauce. Coeur a la crème with fresh berry coulis. The pear and ice cream, definitely.

After a dinner sublime, I float back through the candlelight to my turned down bed. All draperies have been drawn. The only effort required is crawling between the covers. My eyes fall on the homemade chocolate cookies at bedside. But I just can't, and drift away.

KIPPERS TO RUN UNDER THE BRIDGE

Just like Sir Bernard would have wished, I sleep when I want. Unfortunately, I long ago lost that delicious ability to sleep endlessly in the morning. So now, I'm up at

7:00 AM, looking for coffee. A smiling waitress delivers it on a silver tray to my room. Dressing and taking my coffee (and one of the cookies) outside, I wander down to the pier. A small family of mallards are quacking about and a light mist hangs over the water. Otherwise all is quiet. Soon I shall have to return home, but not before breakfast.

This inn believes that while dinner is an event, breakfast is equally important, as it's the last meal guests have here before they depart for home. It must go well. And it does. The day is too pretty not to eat on the terrace. Fresh squeezed orange juice arrives quickly with more coffee. Petit pain, blueberry muffins and buttery croissants follow hot in a basket, along with a dish of yogurt with fresh strawberries and blueberries. I could choose grilled Loch Fyne kippers or a smoked salmon omelette with salmon caviar. But a fat, crisp Belgian waffle with hot maple syrup is placed before me and the world is a happy place, at least in my corner.

Too soon I drive back down the long shady drive, toward the Chesapeake Bay Bridge that will return me to my side of Maryland, the Western Shore. As many times as I have seen St. Michaels, I realize how good it is to occasionally see old friends from new vantage points.

Breakfast is equally important, as it's the last meal guests have here before they depart for home.

La Colombe d'Or
HOUSTON, TEXAS

Murals on the walls of the penthouse suite

Inn at Starlight Lake
STARLIGHT, PENNSYLVANIA

Aerial lakefront

Photo: George Gardner

Overlooking the
St. Lawrence River...

La Pinsonniere
CAP-A-L'AIGLE, QUEBEC

Breakfast in chamber #211

A thatched retreat...

Little Palm Island
LITTLE TORCH KEY, FLORIDA

Balmy dining al fresco...

Courtyard fountain...

Courtyard dining...

Maison de Ville
NEW ORLEANS, LOUISIANA

The Bistro...

Right on Fleming Street...

The Marquesa Hotel

KEY WEST, FLORIDA

Trompe l'oeill dining...

*Courtyard and pool
at evening...*

Adirondack classic...

The Point

SARANAC LAKE, NEW YORK

The boathouse...

The wood nymph suite with handmade bough bed...

RiverSong
ESTES PARK, COLORADO

Riverstone jacuzzi and fireplace

The inn from the cypress bluffs…

Seal Cove Inn

MOSS BEACH, CALIFORNIA

The garden room…

On the Pacific highway…

The Shelburne Inn

SEAVIEW, WASHINGTON

Breakfast time in the dining room…

Sooke Harbour at low tide

Sooke Harbour House

SOOKE, BRITISH COLUMBIA

Ictholocist room...

Room #1...

Victorian style…

Stafford's Bay View Inn
PETOSKEY, MICHIGAN

Fireplaces and rockers…

Traverse Bay dining…

A summer paradise

Stein Eriksen
PARK CITY, UTAH

A winter wonderland...

A cozy fire...

Hangin' out under the palovede trees...

Tanque Verde Guest Ranch

TUSCON, ARIZONA

Riding through the seguaros...

to breakfast...

The pool and main lodge...

Timberhill Ranch
CAZADERO, CALIFORNIA

California countryside

Cozy cabins

Winter holidays...

The White Barn Inn

KENNEBUNKPORT, MAINE

The 5-star White Barn Restaurant

Period bedchambers

*Dinner by
the fire...*

The White Gull Inn

FISH CREEK, WISCONSIN

*Porches, clapboard
and shutters*

GLAZED LAMBS SHANK WITH A CASSEROLE OF WELSH LEEK, POTATO AND THYME

(SERVED WITH SEASONAL VEGETABLES AND SUN DRIED TOMATO SAUCE)

This is simply one of the best lamb recipes I've ever tasted. Everyone at the table had the same dish. We all just looked at each other with that "Yep, it's incredible" look.

4 lambs shanks, trimmed of fat and sinew
1 tablespoon tomato purée
1 8-oz. jar sun dried tomatoes – packed in oil
10 cloves of garlic, peeled
parsley stalks
4 tablespoons sherry vinegar
3 tablespoons honey
3 tablespoons tarragon vinegar
6 pints of chicken stock and water mixed
1 oz. flour
1 teaspoon chopped fresh thyme leaves
1 clove garlic
freshly ground pepper and salt

1. Place the trimmed lamb shanks in a Dutch oven, just cover with water and chicken stock. Add the tomato purée, the sun-dried tomatoes, the sherry vinegar, parsley stalks and garlic. Bring to simmer and braise in the oven at 400 degrees for approximately 2 hours, until the meat is tender.

2 large carrots
1 kohlrabi
2 beetroot
2 zucchini
1 parsnip
2½ lbs. peeled potatoes
3 medium sized leeks, cleaned, sliced horizontally

2. Clean and wash the leeks, slice into circles. Peel potatoes and carrots along with swede, kohlrabi and beet-root and cut into neat cubes. Blanch in boiling salted water for 5 minutes and drain.

3. Remove the lamb shanks from their broth; brush with the warmed honey and tarragon vinegar and roast in 400 degree oven until golden.

4. Strain the sauce, add a few more sun-dried tomatoes and reduce the liquid until the sauce is thick enough to coat a spoon. Keep warm.

5. Pre-heat a frying pan and pour in two tablespoons of oil, add the sliced leeks and vegetables and sauté just until done. Season and sprinkle with the chopped thyme.

6. Place the glazed lambs shanks on heated plates, garnish with the vegetables. Pour on a little of the sauce and serve the remaining in a sauce boat. Garnish with fresh herbs.

Serves four.

TOMATO SOUP SCENTED WITH ORANGE

A beautiful red soup when tomatoes are ripe and plentiful, with a delightful fragrance of orange. And with no milk or cream, it's quite low-fat.

1 large onion
2 carrots
2 cloves of garlic
1 leek
1 bunch of celery
8 ripe plum tomatoes
1 teaspoon sugar
1 bay leaf
6 tablespoons tomato purée
peeled zest from two oranges
2 tablespoons flour
2 cups stock (vegetable or chicken)
salt and pepper
2 tablespoons olive oil

1. Peel and cut the vegetables into small cubes. Put them in a large saucepan, cook gently in the olive oil until onions are soft, adding a drop of water to moisten.
2. Add the tomatoes cut into to small pieces and cook until softened. Mix in the tomato purée, sugar and orange zest.
3. Stir in the flour and add the stock. Bring to a simmer and add bay leaf.
4. After 1 hour strain through a sieve. (Do not push the vegetables through the sieve, as the tomato flavor will be impeded by that of the vegetables.)
5. Season the soup with salt and pepper.
Serves four.

BREAST OF CHICKEN ON ROASTED NICOISE VEGETABLES

Colorful and flavorful, this dish is simple to prepare. I like adding capers to the finished vegetables.

4 boneless breasts of chicken
12 shallots
3 medium sized zucchini, cubed
3 medium sized squash, cubed
1 red pepper, cubed
1 yellow pepper. cubed
1 green pepper. cubed
2 cloves of garlic, chopped
5 plum tomatoes, skinned cut into quarters and
    seeded
6 stuffed green olives
½ tsp. sugar
salt, freshly ground black pepper
6 Tablespoons olive oil
6 basil leaves, shredded at the last moment

1. Skin the breasts of chicken and pound until approximately ½ inch in thickness.
2. Spoon the olive oil into a high-sided saucepan. Add the peeled shallots and a ½ cup of water to moisten.
3. In a separate frying pan, cook the zucchini and squash cubes in olive oil. Season with salt and pepper. After 2 minutes, remove from the pan and drain. Add the cubed peppers to the shallots and continue to cook for another 2–3 minutes. Then add the squash and zucchini, season with salt, pepper, sugar and chopped garlic.

4. Blanch, peel and seed the tomatoes. Chop the flesh into large pieces. Then place on a large roasting tray, along with the partially cooked vegetables too. Sprinkle on the chopped olive and roast for a further 10 minutes at 400 degrees.
5. Re–season if necessary, and add the shredded basil. Grill the chicken breast just until done and slice on top of the vegetables, divided onto four warmed plates. The dish is good served with new potatoes cooked in olive oil.
Serves 4.

The Inn at Starlight Lake

STARLIGHT, PENNSYLVANIA

There is some mysterious joy found in a place undiscovered by mainstream tourists. Particularly so if that region is also tranquil, beautiful and inviting. The upper Delaware River Valley in northeast Pennsylvania is all those things. Here in this valley at the end of a long leafy country lane is the inn that you hope to find. Not flashy or opulent, never. Perched at the side of a mountain-pure lake are three-stories of forest green shingles and white trim is a quintessential country stopover, The Inn at Starlight Lake.

I walk out onto the lakeside dock and sit for a moment in one of the classic Adirondack chairs. The hillside across the lake is blazing with an autumn palette of reds, oranges and yellows. Caught it on just the right weekend. (That's what people thought last weekend too, no doubt.)

HOOTCH HISTORY

Inside, the cast-iron wood stove (its water jacket provides hot water baseboard heat) gives off a welcome warmth to the folks basking and reading at its glowing front. A grand piano waits to provide entertainment. There are plenty of good over-stuffed chairs and ottomans, antique oak tables holding baskets of dried flowers, in the corner a broad stone fireplace extending up through the ceiling. Old-fashioned prints hang on the walls, gentle light gleaming from beaded and fringed Tiffany parlor lamps.

In the next room a long auburn-colored red oak bar seems to hold every spirit distilled in the civilized world. While the liquor license was granted in 1963 and the bar added in '75, this remote hostelry was a source of "hootch" during the days of Prohibition. While the bootleg source is unknown, or at least unspoken of, to this day, it was understood throughout these parts that a hospitable nip or two could be obtained. As owner Judy McMahon laughs, "Guests also brought their own, so there was always a good chance a party would be going on." A fine heritage that bespeaks of good times and mellow evenings.

1909 was the year that The Inn at Starlight Lake first opened to city-weary travelers. By train they flocked from New York, Philly and New Jersey. With trunks packed for summer-long stays, guests reveled in the surroundings of meadowland farms and green forests. The little village of Starlight had its own store, creamery, church, school, tannery and blacksmith shop. It's not much bigger today. The inn became so popular and overpopulated that men and boys were at times plunked out of the hotel onto tent platforms, making room for the gentler sex who remained inside. Those tents became cottages in the '20s, a clay tennis court was to be installed, the dining room enlarged and a front porch running the length of the building was added.

Judy and Jack McMahon, professional "big apple" actors and singers (who met in an off-broadway production of "John Brown's Body"), purchased the inn in 1974. Moving from the footlights to a rural inn is not as strange a transition as it might sound. Judy nods in agreement when Jack says, "Let's face it. When you're an innkeeper, you're always 'on'. Acting skills come in mighty handy sometimes." They are a delightful couple, both skilled raconteurs who spin witty tales through the evening.

GRANDMA'S HOUSE

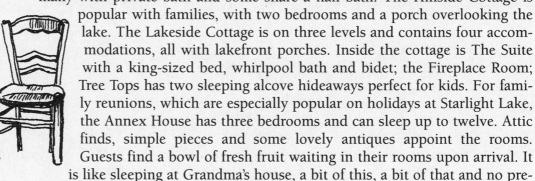

The inn is composed of five structures. The main house has fourteen bedrooms, many with private bath and some share a hall bath. The Hillside Cottage is popular with families, with two bedrooms and a porch overlooking the lake. The Lakeside Cottage is on three levels and contains four accommodations, all with lakefront porches. Inside the cottage is The Suite with a king-sized bed, whirlpool bath and bidet; the Fireplace Room; Tree Tops has two sleeping alcove hideaways perfect for kids. For family reunions, which are especially popular on holidays at Starlight Lake, the Annex House has three bedrooms and can sleep up to twelve. Attic finds, simple pieces and some lovely antiques appoint the rooms. Guests find a bowl of fresh fruit waiting in their rooms upon arrival. It is like sleeping at Grandma's house, a bit of this, a bit of that and no pretensions of grandeur. Here in Wayne County, PA, it's perfect.

After a night of soothing country silence, I'm awakened by birds. I'm also ravenous. Bounding into clothes to head downstairs (the stairs squeak just right), you can't help but notice some of the charming touches of the past. Old fashioned white push button light switches with hammered repousse copper switchplates. One shows a little girl tiptoeing upstairs with a candle, one has a woman admiring her reflection at her dressing table. Charming. These, as well as lovely hammered copper light fixtures and chandeliers, some with mica paneling, were hand-fashioned in the '20s by a local craftsman named Fred Fitfield and remain a tribute to his artistry.

The main dining room overlooks Starlight Lake, as does the solarium dining area, fashioned from enclosing part of the front porch. Bedecked with plants and hanging baskets, it makes a lovely breakfast area for good and sensible dishes that begin the day: buckwheat-blueberry pancakes, homemade granola, cheese and mushroom omelettes, or lox and bagels. The coffee is always fresh ground.

AT AND AT 'EM

Then jump onto one of the inn's bicycles for quiet ride down the country lanes bounded with old stone dry walls. If you want a real tour, the McMahons will give you a scenic route to follow. At the dock are canoes, rowboats and sailboats for your lake-top pleasure. No motorboats are allowed on Starlight Lake, so the water is not only clean, it's blissfully silent.

The water slide also sits noiseless now, but in the warm summer months it's the preferred way for kids, whooping and giggling, to get from dock to water. A shallow play area close to the sun deck allows the littlest ones to enjoy the water with tiny feet on the ground.

Play shuffleboard or tennis on the outside courts. Ping-pong or pool in the gameroom. But one of the most enticing pastimes is to walk. Trails and roads through meadows and forests are just right for spirited family hikes or romantic strolls for two. These same trails provide winter's entertainment as well.

"When we bought the inn," Judy muses, "We knew it would have to be open year round. And since we're surrounded by old logging and quarrying trails, for heaven's sake why not use them?" The McMahons began one of the first "touring centers" for Nordic skiing, better known today as cross-country. The trail begins right outside the front door. That's convenience. Skiers then cross the lake which freezes two and three feet deep in winter (this big ice cube also makes a spectacular outdoor skating rink), to fifteen miles of marked, groomed and tracked trails that snake across fields and through the woods to the village of Starlight. The outer perimeter of trails climbs a ridge and leads skiers along breathtaking ledges. At the far end, an intimidating climb called "Yes-U-Can" rewards your efforts with farmland panoramas. Downhill skiing is within driving distance.

Winter or summer, this corner of PA is fertile plowing for antique lovers. Just five miles down the road is the old river town of Hancock, NY, just over the state line at the headwaters of the Delaware River. You'll find local crafts and antique shops worthy of poking through. And in the pretty little town of Deposit some fifteen miles north more shops in historic clapboard and stone houses that date from the 18th and 19th centuries.

Don't forget fly fishing. The Delaware River is just fine for shad and trout fish. Outfitters, guides, and instruction are all available. Just tell the McMahons what you want.

I'M HUNGRY

Appetites are large whether you've been skiing or swimming. Dinner at the Starlight is viewed with great anticipation as everything from breads to pastas to ice creams are made totally from scratch. Chicken liver pâté, homemade pasta with pesto sauce and trout locally smoked in applewood with sour cream and horseradish may begin the meal. Then you might choose from a dish as simple and good as golden roast chicken with buttermilk mashed potatoes or as unusual as pork Jaegerschnitzel sautéed with pickles and mustard. Or somewhere in between with shrimp, lobster and scallops in garlic or alfredo sauce served over pasta. The homemade ice creams will be hard to resist, so order the made-that-day vanilla with the fresh sour cream apple pie. Can I lick the ice cream paddle?

After dinner, Jack rounds up his sated guests and announces that, being a weekend night, it is movie night. Pulling a movie projector down out of the game room ceiling (quite an ingenious contraption) he asks our pleasure. A dedicated movie buff, his collection includes classics such as "The Third Man," "Night at the Opera," "Little

Trails and roads through meadows and forests are just right for spirited family hikes or romantic strolls for two.

Foxes," "My Man Godfrey," and "Western Union." Beaming his approval, we select "Naughty Marietta" starring Jeanette MacDonald and Nelson Eddy.

Christmas ushers in more family gatherings, special holiday menus and yuletide dramas. After guests carol around the piano, Judy, the director, hands out scripts and assigns parts for Dicken's "A Christmas Carol." While the role of Scrooge is much sought after, perhaps the most important job is that of sound effects specialist. "The clock striking the hour, clanging of chains, wind, footsteps and doors banging shut. Think about it. "Noises are crucial in this production," points out Ms. Director. Jack can, with his experience and resonant tones, play any part not snapped up by would-be thespians. And so ends a snowy holiday night at the Inn at Starlight Lake. Guests gathered around a fireplace of glowing embers, laughing at and applauding each other's dramatic efforts. "Merry Christmas, Cratchit, and you too, Tiny Tim." God bless us every one.

Christmas ushers in more family gatherings, special holiday menus and yuletide dramas.

GRACIOUS COUNTRY INNS

STARLIGHT LAKE PECAN PIE

Pecan pie is a homey favorite with almost everyone.

1½ cups pecans
9" crust
1 lb. dark brown sugar
¼ cup flour
½ teaspoon salt
½ cup milk
1½ teaspoon vanilla extract
3 eggs, beaten
½ cup melted butter

1. Blend sugar, flour and salt.
2. Add the milk, vanilla and melted butter.
3. Add beaten eggs last. Mix only until blended.
4. Place foil around crust so it won't get too brown. Pour in brown sugar filling. Add pecans.
5. Bake 45 minutes to 1 hour at 400 degrees until firm. Let cool before serving.

PORK JAEGERSCHNITZEL

An unusual German recipe but one that is a long time favorite of Starlight guests. Eating is appreciating.

1½ lb. boneless pork loin (or 4 thick cutlets)
½ cup flour
1½ cups heavy cream
1 egg
1½ cups seasoned bread crumbs
1¾ cups brown sauce
2 Polish dill pickles, chopped fine
2 teaspoons dijon/country mustard

1. Butterfly the individual cutlets. This method slices the cutlet almost in two, but retains a "hinge" so that when spread out, it looks somewhat like a butterfly. Pound it with a heavy cleaver or mallet to flatten.
2. Use following breading procedure:
   (a) Flour the cutlets.
   (b) Dip cutlets in a mixture of beaten egg and heavy cream.
   (c) Dip cutlets then in bread crumbs.
3. In a heated sauté pan, cook cutlets over medium heat in 2 tablespoons butter about. 5 minutes on each side until cooked through. Remove from pan and keep warm.
4. Add remainder of ingredients. Simmer for one minute.
5. Place cutlet on plate, sauce on top. Garnish with fresh herbs.
   Serves 4.

STARLIGHT DINNER ROLLS

Regular all-purpose may be substituted here but take note that it will not have the elasticity of hi-gluten bread flour and will take longer to rise. Flour for making bread is now available in most all supermarkets under many brand names.

3¼ cups hi-gluten flour (such as bread flour)
4 oz. unsalted butter, melted
1 tablespoon sugar
1 teaspoon salt
2 teaspoons dry yeast
1⅛ cup milk
1 egg yolk
1 whole egg

1. Warm milk in separate pan.
2. In mixing bowl, add the yeast, butter, yolk, sugar, salt and milk.
3. Add enough of the flour to make a soft dough. Mix and knead until it bounces back when touched with a finger.
4. Let rise to twice the size in an oiled bowl put in a warm place. (also oil the top of the bread and cover bowl with plastic wrap.)
5. Cut into golf-ball-size pieces, form into pretzel shapes. Let rise again until twice the size. Then baste with beaten egg. Bake on a greased baking sheet(s) in 350 degree oven 15–20 minutes until golden brown.

Makes about 2 dozen.

SOUR CREAM APPLE PIE

Apples and sour cream are topped with a wonderful brown sugar mixture in this country and family favorite.

TOPPING:

⅔ cup brown sugar
⅔ cup flour
2 teaspoon cinnamon
¼ cup soft butter

Mix all ingredients well in separate bowl.

FILLING:

4 tablespoons flour
¼ teaspoon salt
1⅓ cup sugar
2 eggs
2 cups sour cream
1 teaspoon vanilla extract
½ teaspoon nutmeg
6 medium apples, peeled and shredded

1. Mix all filling ingredients together.
2. Place filling in a deep dish 10" pie shell.
3. Bake for approximately 40–45 minutes till firm at 375 degrees.
4. Then place sugar topping on pie. Bake 5 minutes longer at same temperature until golden. Serve with vanilla ice cream.

Makes 1 pie.

Keswick Hall

KESWICK, VIRGINIA

If you've ever journeyed through the heart of Virginia, Charlottesville in particular, then you know how splendid it is. Full of history, wealth, exclusive country estates, rolling countryside with picturesque fox hunts, this is fine country living at its apogee. Thomas Jefferson retired here to Albemarle County after forty-five years of public service and described his homeland as "the Eden of the United States." And for a time, Virginia squire living can be yours at Keswick Hall.

BURNED AND REBORN, THEN REBORN ONCE MORE

Keswick has its own fascinating history. On this beautiful acreage stood Broad Oak, an antebellum mansion that was burned during the Civil War. On that spot followed the Italian styled Villa Crawford built in 1912. The next chapter reveals a 1940s country club twice the site of the Virginia State Open. Turn the page, a peeling mansion fallen on hard times. When Sir Bernard Ashley, the magnate of the Laura Ashley empire, saw Keswick, he believed it perfect for a Virginia country house hotel in the English tradition and immediately purchased it from bankruptcy. What that means to the rest of us is one perfectly gorgeous, elegantly decorated inn with everything imaginable to offer its guests. It's an interesting twist that works: British correctness blended with Southern hospitality.

Turning in the front gate and down a shaded, leafy drive you will come upon Keswick Hall on your left. A creamy yellow three story mansion accented with gables and

When Sir Bernard Ashley, the magnate of the Laura Ashley empire, saw Keswick, he believed it perfect for a Virginia country house hotel in the English tradition.

chimneys and dark Rockingham green trim, it is impressive. Someone is always watching for you or has an uncanny sense of timing. Whether it's your first time through the door or the fifteenth, a uniformed staffer welcomes you with a smile and friendly salutations.

You enter the Great Hall, a grand room floored with 250 year old handmade terra cotta tiles from three different French chateaux. Oriental rugs cushion the halls. Capacious persimmon colored sofas flank a marble fireplace and mantle. A square coffee table almost big enough to nap on separates them, covered with glossy English periodicals such as *Country Life*. Historic paintings from Sir Bernard's European homes adorn the walls; marble busts, carved antiques, downy tapestry pillows add elegance sans stuffiness.

That's an important point. In a place so immaculately decorated, it is easy to feel as if one is in a museum. "Pretty, don't touch." "Watch out for the vase." "No, don't sit there." But, Sir Bernard wants you to feel as if you're an honored guest in his home. Ever obliging, I happily fling myself on the sofa and crunch on one of many polished apples stacked in a lovely Chinese bowl.

Across the back of the villa stretches an enormous terrace of marble, from which you have the most splendid view of the rolling Virginia countryside. The immaculate flower beds are bordered by dwarf English boxwoods and holly. English lavender, blue salvia, purple and white pansies, and blue aegeratum add accents of color, white cascading petunias spill over the sides of large stone urns.

Sir Bernard (B.A. to his staff) keeps a close eye on his properties and drops in from time to time to see that things are running smoothly. He happened to be on one of those "look-sees" while I was there. A charming and delightfully informal man, he admits that the place was "a bit of a wreck" when he purchased it. Not one to leave decisions to others, Sir Bernard has personally overseen every purchase and decision at Keswick, from dessert spoons to fabrics.

MORE LIKE BUTTER THAN BUTTER

The Crawford Lounge is an original part of the house, furnished with butter-yellow velvet sofas trimmed in 5-inch bullion fringe, genteelly faded gold brocade chairs and needlepoint pillows with walls in shades of saffron yellow. The room is a reproduction of one at the Ashley home in Brussels, and the heavy yellow silk draperies came from that house. Silver picture frames are grouped on polished antique tables. The frames surround pretty black and white photos of girls in Ashley frocks, snapped by B.A. himself. "My daughters," he says proudly. "I used them for models in the cottage industry days of Laura Ashley." A proper English tea is served in these graceful sitting rooms each afternoon, with homemade scones (the recipe follows), clotted cream, jam and lemon curd (ditto) washed down by pots of hot English tea served on silver trays.

B.A. toured me to the wine red snooker room. The mahogany snooker table hung with yards of plush red fringe looks very much like a pool table. But the game isn't. Sir Bernard tried to explain the idea to me, something about the red balls and the non-red balls, but I'm not a very good snooker pupil. If you want to play, maybe Sir Bernard will drop in and supervise your lesson.

ODE TO LAURA

There are forty-eight bedrooms at Keswick. Each is different and they range from the smaller house rooms to the largest master suites with dining or sitting room plus private terrace or balcony overlooking the mountains or the golf course. All are decorated in sumptuous Laura Ashley fabrics and wallpapers, and furnished with English and American antiques. I had no inkling Laura Ashley designed so many pat-

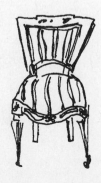

terns, but many lines are manufactured specifically for other countries that we Yanks might never see, except in an Ashley mecca such as this. Many of the patterns that adorn Keswick are from the designer lines only available through interior decorators.

I am ensconced in state room #48, done in a Swedish theme. The wallpaper is an unfamiliar but lovely silvery gray and white stripe. A sofa and chair are upholstered in an equally cool-toned white on white pattern, and a dark honey colored antique dressing table, which I dearly love, is set with silver brushes and hand-mirror. An immense walnut armoire, shipped from Europe in twenty pieces and reassembled in the room covers most of one wall, and the mahogany four poster bed is covered in pure cotton softness. The bathroom is a shining white marble temple with an enormous bathtub set in, loads of Keswick's own toiletries, fluffy white towels on a towel warmer, and roomy terry robes.

I wait for my breakfast in the morning dining room overlooking the golf course and gardens. Freshly squeezed orange and grapefruit juice, country style yogurt with banana- mango jam, a three-pepper and tomato frittata, traditional English mixed grill and Scottish smoked kippers all sound tempting. But the old fashioned oatcakes with maple syrup and *whipped cream* are as indulgent as I feel. No undue lingering for there's far too much to occupy my time. One last gulp of coffee and I'm off.

DOING IS BELIEVING

The Keswick Club is a private, members-only golf and leisure club. But a Keswick guest has privileges for which the members pay dearly. The 18 hole golf course was designed by Arnold Palmer himself, difficult enough to challenge professionals yet enjoyable for the duffer, as well. The perfectly groomed emerald fairways wind through tall oaks, mountain streams and small lakes. The first tee sits right behind Keswick Hall. Also yours at the club pavilion are an indoor-outdoor pool, outdoor jacuzzi, exercise rooms and tennis courts.

Just across from the main entrance to Keswick is the Keswick Hunt Club. Many mornings you might see the members unloading muscled, shining horses from trailers. The riders are dressed in their fitted red hunt jackets, black boots and white riding breeches. And remember, if you stop by to admire the baying hounds waving their tails, they are just that – hounds. Not *dogs*. Never, ever dogs. As the hunt master says, "Every hound is a dog, but not every dog is a hound."

Old fashioned oatcakes with maple syrup and whipped cream are as indulgent as I feel.

LEAVING ROYALTY TO FIND MONTICELLO

Just a few minutes away is Thomas Jefferson's fabled home, Monticello. If you only tour one attraction, this is it. Jefferson designed this classical red brick home himself, taking forty years to complete. It's crowned with a white octagonal dome and filled with many original furnishings and ingenious Jeffersonian inventions. The gardens, vineyards and orchards have been carefully recreated, and the tour is a fascinating glimpse into the life of a true renaissance man. Interestingly, when he retired from the presidency in 1809, Jefferson's estate and finances were in terrible condition, and he turned his considerable energies to correcting those situations. However, he viewed this homecoming challenge with joy when he revealingly wrote, "Never did a prisoner released from his chains feel such relief as I shall on shaking off the shackles of power." Monticello is inspirational, don't miss it.

Not too far away from Monticello is The University of Virginia. Founded by Jefferson, he regarded it as one of his greatest achievements, and when you see it you will too. Jefferson drew up the curriculum, hired the faculty, selected the books for the library and drew the plans for the buildings. It opened in 1825 with forty students. I wandered around the beautiful campus for some while before I found the wide green courtyard called "the lawn." At one end is the Rotunda, patterned after the Roman Pantheon with six tall white columns and circular design, one of the most memorable buildings I've ever seen.

The estate of fifth president James Monroe is also in Albemarle, as he moved there to be near his good friend Jefferson. Ash Lawn-Highland creates the atmosphere of a working farm, with spinning and weaving demonstrations, and special events throughout the summer.

If you desire something more on the adventurous side, day and overnight trips canoeing and tubing on the James River are available. Various outfitters provide all equipment and transportation you'll need. Keswick Hall can help arrange such a strenuous outing, *and* will schedule you for a therapeutic massage at the Pavilion upon your return.

Wine enthusiasts will enjoy tastings at the Jefferson Vineyards, where Thomas set out the first vineyards in the colony or, at Montdomaine Cellars just south of Monticello. Montdomaine produces varietal wines such as chardonnay, cabernet and merlot. And, you're invited to bring a picnic and tour the winery.

MORE BUTTER AND OTHER DELIGHTS

But, now it's time to walk from the Great Hall, where you've been enjoying canapés and conversation, down the thickly carpeted stairs with wrought iron handrails. Through a chamber of white sofas around a roaring fireplace, you pause here for a pleasant moment to admire the softly lighted cabinets full of pretty china. Soon you're seated for dinner at a table of the starched white napery and elegant settings. Put your fingertips together carefully, purse your lips and give the menu serious consideration. It deserves no less.

The kitchen and chef specialize in "belle epoque" cuisine. Imaginatively conceived and brilliantly executed, this will be a meal you will not soon forget. Starters of grilled tuna on white bean salad with basil oil, chilled melon soup scented with ginger, and lasagna of smoked salmon and spinach beckon. Not to be ignored are the Virginia striped bass with artichokes, tomatoes, olives and brown caper butter, or tournedo of beef glazed with Stilton. But, my finger moves slowly down this tempting list to pause at the "Oxford John" lamb steak accompanied by bubble and squeak, Keswick style. That's the one. Finish up with a selection of English and French cheeses or passion fruit crème brûlèe, coffee and migardises (little sweets). Mr. Jefferson would approve.

If you desire something more on the adventurous side, day and overnight trips canoeing and tubing on the James River are available.

GRACIOUS COUNTRY INNS

SAUTÉ OF SNAPPER WITH ARTICHOKES, TOMATOES, OLIVES AND BROWN CAPER BUTTER

This dish is easy and quick to prepare, and you can add diced zucchini or eggplant to the vegetable mix. If you don't have red onions, use yellow ones. The dish will still have plenty of colors from the tomatoes, herbs and olives.

2 boneless snapper fillets
1 medium Idaho potato, peeled and cut into
   medium dice
½ medium red onion, diced
2 cloves garlic, minced
4 artichoke bottoms, quartered
2 tablespoons of chopped mixed herbs (parsley,
   basil, cilantro, chervil, rosemary or chives)
2 tablespoons olive oil
8 pitted green olives, quartered
tomato concasse from 2 large tomatoes (instructions below)
2 tablespoons capers
2 tablespoons butter
1 tablespoon parsley
juice of 1 lemon
salt and pepper

1. For concasse, peel and seed the tomatoes. For easy peeling, plunge tomatoes in boiling water for 10 seconds and refresh in ice water. Remove skins, quarter and dice the meat.
2. Sauté the potato in olive oil till golden brown.
3. Add onion and garlic and cook until translucent.
4. Add olives, tomato concasse, artichoke bottoms and chopped herbs. Toss, season to taste and keep warm.
5. Sauté the snapper in a non-stick oven-proof pan with olive oil. Cook until golden on both sides. Finish cooking for about 5–7 minutes in a 350 degree oven.
6. Place half of vegetable mixture in middle of warm plate. Place a fillet of snapper on top.
7. Over high heat, cook butter till it burns, quickly add capers, parsley and lemon juice. Pour over fish. Serve immediately.
   Serves two.

KESWICK SCONES

You can add lemon or orange zest, raisins or currents, nutmeg, ginger or cinnamon to these scones. They are served every day at Keswick for afternoon tea.

1 lb. pastry flour
1 lb. butter
3½ tablespoons baking powder
½ teaspoon salt
3 oz. sugar
2 cups cream

1. Mix all dry ingredients together.
2. Rub butter into dry ingredients with fingers till flour resembles the texture of cornmeal.
3. Add cream and mix just till it barely holds together. Chill 1 hour (or overnight).
4. Knead the dough only what is necessary to hold it together. Roll to a thickness of a ½" and cut into circles.
5. Bake at 425 degrees for 15 minutes until lightly golden.
6. Serve with whipped cream, jam or lemon curd.
   Makes 25 scones.

KESWICK LEMON CURD

This lemony jam is good with pound cake or with scones (if truth be told, I have been known to eat a spoonful right from the jar). Lemon curd can be kept refrigerated for several weeks unopened. I have a friend from Britain who makes lemon curd at Christmas in big batches and gives dressed up jars of it as gifts. My friend has always told me lemon curd is "dead-easy" to make. She's right. Maybe I'll give away a few jars this year.

2 lb. sugar
9 oz. butter
5 lemons
5 eggs, lightly beaten

1. Zest the lemons by grating just the bright yellow skin (not the white underneath) on the smallest size of a grater.
2. Juice the lemons.
3. Bring lemon juice, zest, butter and sugar to a boil. Let cool.

4. Add the eggs, whisking . Bring to a boil over medium heat whisking constantly to keep from burning, and continue to boil, whisking, for one minute.

5. Remove from heat, cool and jar in sterilized jars. Refrigerate.

Makes about 1 quart.

KESWICK SORREL AND GARLIC SOUP

While this delicious soup may be made in advance, the sorrel must always be added at the last moment to maintain the most vibrant color.

Coarsely chop:

1 large onion
1 white part of leek
6 cloves of garlic
2 large potatoes
1 bunch of sorrel
1 tablespoon butter
2 cups heavy cream
6 cups chicken stock
salt and freshly ground white pepper to taste

1. Sauté the garlic, onions and leek in a large saucepan or soup pot with butter over medium heat till translucent.

2. Add chicken stock and potatoes, bring to a boil and turn down to a simmer for 20 minutes.

3. Add heavy cream and simmer gently for 20 more minutes. Do not boil.

4. Place soup in blender and add sorrel. Blend till smooth and frothy.

5. Adjust seasoning with salt and pepper. Serve immediately.

Serves six.

CANADA

The Aerie

MALAHAT, BRITISH COLUMBIA

T he Bahamas, 1984. Two native Austrians are baking in the tropical zone, there by fate and profession. Leo is executive chef for the too wealthy and far too famous in glamorous, glittering resorts, and Maria in charge of her own luxury resort. Enough. The Schusters decided the time had come to run their own place. Lake Tahoe, Colorado, even New Zealand had been considered, anywhere with a change of seasons and cooler weather. At the last minute, friends twisted their tanned arms to make them watch home vacation videos of British Columbia. No one knows how well they were shot, but the decision was made. Vancouver Island it would be.

VISIONARY

Leo and Maria jetted there immediately, staring at aerial photos until their eyes popped out. Finally, the spot. It was on Malahat Mountain, about 30 minutes north of Victoria, part of which is an old healing and burial site for the Malahat Indians. The Schusters, decked out in their Bahamas whites, stumbled through the bush and underbrush on the property and climbed trees to get a sense of the view overlooking the long curving waters of Finlayson's Arm, which leads to Saanich Inlet and the waters between Canada and Washington state. There were no roads, no electricity, no semblance of civilization. But, it looked like home. It took Leo and Maria two years of cajoling and begging to convince the owner to sell them this property. It was worth the wait.

There were no roads, no electricity, no semblance of civilization. But, it looked like home.

LUXURY FOR LOVERS

By definition, aerie means an eagle's nest or a house built on a high place. But what started out to be a small guest house is now the Schusters' castle on a mountain. Opened in 1991, Leo designed The Aerie as a white Mediterranean villa. Gables, cupolas, balconies and red tile roofs adorn the exotic fantasy structure overlooking the inlet below. "We think the climate is very similar to that of Lake Lugano in northern Italy, so we decided on Mediterranean for the architecture," says the blonde Maria with her charming Austrian accent.

Maria and Leo want The Aerie to be synonymous with escape and relaxation. "A place to have the chance to be romantic," proclaims Maria passionately, "Everyone is so busy today. People have too little time for each other. Here there are no phones and no TVs on purpose, so that there are no interruptions." She tells the story of a couple, married for 25 years, that came for one night. No phones, no television. "They almost went crazy," Maria laughs, "I was sure they would check out the next day. But one day became five. They cried when they left, saying it was their first honeymoon in 25 years."

And the Honeymoon Suite would certainly inspire that brand of, well...passion. Italian in design, with zebra sofas, columns, a king size bed with a white Dior duvet, the room sports a jacuzzi set in a bay window with a view of the inlet below like that from an airplane. Right by the tub is a fireplace to warm up the waters and the bedroom on the other side as well. This is fantasy you can touch.

Eight new luxury suites were added in 1993, each 900 square feet in size. Open the door to one and you'll understand better Maria's definition of luxury. A grand foyer leads to the multiple levels of the suite. Right in front of you is a jacuzzi, big enough for four and ensconced between four gold columns, that looks down upon the waters of Finlayson's Arm. Up the steps is the peach colored bedroom with a king sized canopy bed designed and made here at The Aerie, draped with delicate cream colored lace. In the sunken living room are the fireplace, wet bar, alcoves with shelves of books and Italian design furniture. Each suite has a covered, private patio looking down the inlet. While one could become a hermit in such sumptuous rooms, don't miss Leo's breakfast.

Maria and Leo want The Aerie to be synonymous with escape and relaxation.

Breakfast is served in the dining room. Gently scrambled eggs are crossed with three perfect green chive blades and rosy smoked salmon, their colors intensified against the stark black china. Consider some delicate fresh blueberry crepes or just-from-the-oven, crusty croissants. A plate of fruit appears, looking as though Renoir stepped into the kitchen for a moment, with a bounty of ripe watermelon, strawberries, raspberries and oranges. I grow wistful just thinking of an Aerie breakfast.

IN THE DOING

Don't linger too long, the day awaits. You may want to arrange an early tee-off at one of the most gorgeous golf courses in British Columbia. The new 12 million dollar Olympic Golf Course in Victoria has 12 lakes, 20 acres of wildflowers, and at the end of one fairway, a spectacular 60-foot waterfall tumbles off a rock wall. The Aerie can arrange the details that nature hasn't covered.

The quarry-turned-paradise of Buchart Gardens, with fifty-five acres of flowers and seventy-five acres of trees and streams, attracts 750,000 admirers every year. Fifty-five professional gardeners indefatigably re-plant the beds four or five times a year. At the bottom of the old rock quarry, fountains spring up hundreds of feet into the air in intricate patterns, with elaborately arranged flower beds setting the stage. Gardeners will adore this place.

And only 25 minutes south of The Aerie is the quaint town of Victoria. The charming streets are lined with lushly planted hanging baskets, shops and restaurants of every description, but the waterfront is the real draw. Huge ferries disembark passengers from Washington and Vancouver, and cute little water taxis dart off for little trips across the harbor. The Empress Hotel and the Parliament Building are good stops.

The Royal British Columbia Museum was created in 1886 by citizens concerned over masses of greedy collectors hauling off Indian art and artifacts. It has been dedicated to preserving Native American antiquities ever since. Though the woolly mammoth died out 12,000 years ago it has been re-created here, in all its hairiness. From exhibit to exhibit you may trace the area's time-line with a walk on turn-of-the-century streets or a visit to the cramped quarters of Captain Vancouver aboard the H.M.S. Discovery or, a richly carved native ceremonial longhouse.

Across the Victoria harbor at the Ocean Pacific Resort is a full service spa, where you should treat yourself to a variety of beauty indulgences. Scrubs, facials or a marine-mineralized-algae-body wrap, they have it all plus a terrific view. Feel free to have a cocktail as the lights come on across the harbor in downtown Victoria.

Mid to late October is the time of year in B.C. when the salmon swim up the Saanich Inlet into Finlayson's Arm and continue into nearby Goldstream River, yearning to pass along their progeny. Quite often the spawning salmon are hungrily pursued by seals who have no feeling for pregnant fish save gluttony. The seals are, in turn, ardently followed by Orca whales who believe the seals to be tasty morsels. The chances of an inlet whale sighting this season are excellent and according to Maria, the sight of millions of salmon filling the Goldstream River is unforgettable.

IN THE DINING

Speaking of salmon, dinner at The Aerie is an elegant event that happily requires no effort on your part. After a full day of gadding about here and there, you may not feel like getting all gussied up for dinner. That's fine. While some diners will be dressed up, many won't. As Maria says, "We want people to feel at home here. While the dining room looks formal, we aren't. So enjoy."

On the wall is the framed Chaine des Rotisseurs striped ribbon and medal of the exclusive worldwide club that has pronounced Leo Schuster a master chef. You're in the creative culinary hands of a man whose credo is fresh, fresh, fresh. Having cooked in exotic locales worldwide, local vegetables, fruits, seafood, and herbs from his own garden are the passion of Chef Schuster now quietly practicing his artistry on Malahat Mountain. His menus, which change two or three times weekly, are classic, elegant and exquisitely presented.

Relax and take a look at the large selection of British Columbian wines. Americans don't see B.C. wines very often because the Canadians wisely gobble them up. Buttery chardonnays, rich merlots and flinty pinot blancs are regional specialties.

Now the menu. You might begin the meal with a "bouquet" of enormous tiger prawns with a mild horseradish cream, a perfectly seasoned venison pâté, or cool, smooth asparagus vichyssoise. Entrees may include basil-crusted veal with shiitake mushroom sauce, grilled ahi tuna with pineapple-melon vinaigrette and lime butter, or almond-crusted pheasant with lingonberries and chanterelles. Maria will come around to urge you on to further indiscretions with an unctuous blueberry crème brûlèe or tiramisu with fresh B.C. raspberries.

After dinner, I recommend a trip to the rooftop deck, perhaps for a dip in the heated indoor pool or rooftop jacuzzi, or simply a romantic stroll by the water gardens. After all, it's an Aerie evening. If you stumble across a more pleasant spot on earth, let me know.

Quite often the spawning salmon are hungrily pursued by seals who have no feeling for pregnant fish save gluttony.

AERIE CORN AND WILD RICE FRITTERS

⅓ cup kernels of fresh corn
⅓ cup wild rice, cooked
2 tablespoons red pepper, diced finely
1 tablespoons shallots, diced finely
1 teaspoon fresh thyme, chopped
2 strips bacon, sliced
salt and black pepper to taste
1 tablespoon butter

1. In a medium skillet, fry bacon over moderate heat for approximately 1 minute. Add butter, shallots, red pepper, fresh thyme, and seasonings. Toss in pan for another minute.

2. Add corn and wild rice. Mix well. Remove from heat and allow to cool.

BATTER FOR FRITTERS

1 egg
¼ cup whole milk
1 tablespoon sherry wine
⅓ cup flour
1 teaspoon baking powder
pinch of salt

1. Combine dry ingredients in a small mixing bowl.

2. Whisk together the egg, milk, and sherry in another bowl. Stir into dry ingredients. Your batter should be slightly on the thick side. (Add only enough batter to your cooled rice mixture as to bind it together.)

3. In another pan, add 4 tablespoons canola oil. Bring up to medium heat.

4. Spoon in rice mixture and form into rough circles (approximately size of silver dollars). Cook until golden brown and flip.

Allow 2 or 3 per serving. Serve with venison or any roasted meat.

MEDALLIONS OF VENISON WITH SUN-DRIED CHERRY SAUCE

8 3-oz. pieces of venison loin
1 teaspoon fresh thyme, chopped
fresh black pepper and salt to taste

SUN-DRIED CHERRY SAUCE

5 or 6 juniper berries, lightly crushed
1 clove
6 whole black peppercorns
1 small garlic clove, crushed
1 small shallot, cut into several pieces
⅓ cup cranberry juice
⅓ cup apple juice
⅓ cup rich venison stock or beef stock
⅓ cup sun-dried cherries

1. Tie the juniper berries, clove, peppercorns, garlic clove, and shallot in a spice bag. Put the bag in a small sauce pan with the stock and the juices. Bring to a boil and reduce heat to a simmer for 5 minutes.

2. Add the cherries. Simmer another 10 minutes and remove from heat.

3. Remove spice bag and purée the sauce in a blender. Pass through a fine strainer. Keep warm while sautéeing the venison.

   Makes 1 cup.

4. In a larger skillet, sauté venison over moderate to high heat for approximately 45 seconds per side or until medium-rare.

5. Place 2 venison medallions on top of a puddle of sauce. Serve with corn and wild rice fritters. Garnish with extra sun-dried cherries and fresh thyme sprigs.

   Serves four.

AERIE GRILLED BLUE POINT OYSTERS WITH SWEET PEPPERS AND CHIVE BUTTER

12 large fresh oysters (shucked)
1 tablespoon lime juice
fresh ground black pepper (to taste)

1. Mix oysters gently in a bowl with lime juice and black pepper. Let stand.

1 each red and yellow peppers cut into triangles
(approximately 3/4 inch per side)
2 tablespoons virgin olive oil
fresh black pepper (to taste)

2. Toss together and let stand for as long as several hours.

TO MAKE CHIVE BUTTER:

1 Tablespoon. shallots (chopped)
2 oz. white wine
2 oz. fish stock
2 Tablespoon fresh chives (chopped)
3 Tablespoon butter
fresh black pepper

1. Sauté shallots over medium heat. Add white wine and fish stock. Let liquid reduce slightly.
2. Whisk in butter one tablespoon at a time and remove from heat (do not boil or your sauce will separate). Add chives and black pepper. Keep warm.
3. Place oysters on a hot, well-oiled grill. Cook for about 1 minute and turn them. Place peppers on grill also. Cook one more minute.
4. Remove oysters and peppers from grill. Pat them on a paper towel to remove excess oil.
5. Pour a small puddle of the sauce on four warm plates and place three oysters on each puddle, alternating colored peppers between the oysters. Garnish with chive blossoms. Serves four.

BLACKBERRY-MANGO YOGURT FRAPPE

An "Aerie" drink for after exercise or for a brunch.

½ cup blackberries, stemmed
½ cup mango, ripe
½ cup plain low fat yogurt
¼ cup club soda
1 tablespoon fresh lime juice
2 teaspoons sugar

1. Place all ingredients in a blender and blend until smooth and foamy.
2. Serve right away.
Serves 2.

The Inn at Manitou

McKELLAR, ONTARIO

Y ou have stumbled out the door at 7:45 AM for the morning health hike, just as you promised yourself you would. Thank goodness for that 7:30 coffee and the fresh oranges arriving on a wicker tray. Otherwise, you might never have made it.

The morning is cool, feels good, really. Weights in hand, you begin your trek with other industrious souls, thinking of everyone else still snug in bed, enjoying a Canadian sleep-in. Momentarily jealous, the feeling begins to evaporate as the smell of the fir trees, the singing of the birds, and the sparkling ripples off of Lake Manitouwabing clear sleep from the brain. Your staff guide encourages you onward and upward, literally. "Let's get those bodies moving and that blood flowing. Think how good breakfast will taste after this walk!" Ummmmm, that is a helpful thought; breakfast for those who have earned it is extra sweet.

STAY ACTIVE, EAT WELL

And so it is, served on the flagstone terrace at the lodge, black wrought iron tables set with Villeroy and Boch china under a spreading basswood tree. Classical music plays as early risers read their morning newspapers. A cold buffet offers home-made granola, a red, yellow and green mosaic of sliced fruits on a silver tray, melons, a big bowl of unsweetened yogurt, silver-topped carafes of juices, and various muffins, croissants and brioche. Or, you can order eggs any style, fried, scrambled or Benedict, with bacon and sausage. Or, consider a fluffy stack of pancakes with Canadian maple syrup.

That is how days at the Inn at Manitou in Ontario, Canada begin, if you wish. This is a place that offers so many options to guests, the only real difficulty is deciding.

The inn has been named by *Tennis* Magazine as "the number one luxury tennis resort on the planet." Now those are pretty strong words, but one can understand the compliment after being here for a day or two. The surroundings are spectacular, the food is to die for, and the tennis program is the best.

The Inn at Manitou has been operated by Ben and Sheila Wise for over 20 years. They love tennis, have made it their number one priority, and it shows. Ben Wise is firm when he says, "We want people to feel successful when they come here. Not to feel as though they're been pushed around all week by a know-it-all tennis pro. Learn something, improve, of course. But it should be fun, not painful."

The inn has 12 courts (no waiting), and not 1 or 2, but 10 tennis pros, all excellent teachers from around the world. The program is exuberant, joyful and simple. The theory according to Ben Wise: "Why make it difficult when it should be easy?" Guests can choose from several tennis clinics. For example, Different Strokes is back-to-basics work on strokes. Winning Ways focuses on the skills and savvy it takes to win matches. And Tennis Work-Up is for a guest who wants to focus on a specific aspect of their game with a personal trainer who will set up a schedule just for you. Group instruction in the morning is followed by social and tournament play in the afternoon.

But perhaps that much tennis is not really your racquet. How 'bout a spa experience? The Inn at Manitou has a complete health, fitness and beauty program. The spa director guides you in setting up a personal routine that may include a pre-breakfast health walk, a morning or afternoon high or low impact aerobics class, plus use of the exercise room with Lifecycles, Stair Masters and Treadmills.

But the fun part of the spa program is all the treatments: mud wraps, herbal wraps, body polishes, manicures, pedicures, facials, hydrotherapy and of course, my favorite, massage. Swedish, shiatsu, holistic, aromatherapy, reflexology, all members of the massage family are there, waiting to relax those tired, tight muscles aching from too much tennis or too much stress.

TOP WORLD RANKING

Wander over to the main lodge for a glass of iced tea. The building is cedar sided, with teal green trim, and looks very "California." Three flags fly in the breeze, Canadian, United States, and Relais and Chateaux. Once inside, it's not too difficult to comprehend why the five-star Inn at Manitou has the only Gold Shield (highest rating of everything) in Canada from the prestigious French hotel group Relais and Chateaux.

Just through the front doors, four skylights throw squares of sunlight onto the terra cotta tile floors. The front desk is an antique Biedemier dug up in London. In fact, many of the furnishings in the common areas are Ben and Sheila's eclectic and unusual finds from years of travel, one of their passions. A carved screen from Hong Kong, a marble topped table from Paris, an antique Victorian bird-cage from Toronto, a French iron umbrella stand used today for guests' tennis racquets, a three-seated chaperone's chair that permitted no sweet nothings to be whispered unheard, and a framed antique corkscrew collection by the bar.

Just down the hall is the tea room where high tea is served every afternoon at four o'clock complete with scones and clotted cream. The room is all bold marbleized yellows and even brasher reds. "It's different but it works," remarks Ben, as he points out the Moroccan camel saddle framed on the wall, the brass Moroccan tea kettle over by a French antique white marble mantle with a Chinese silkscreen above. Vivid crim-

But the fun part of the spa program is all the treatments: mud wraps, herbal wraps, body polishes, manicures, pedicures, facials, hydrotherapy and of course, my favorite, massage.

son chintz bathes sofas and chairs, with red rugs from Morocco underfoot. Ben reminisces, "We drank a lot of tea bargaining for those."

Flowers are everywhere. Fragrant white lilies rest in an oriental bowl; blood red lilies in a stark black vase, a Chinese vases loaded with pink, ruffly peonies are surely the largest I've ever seen.

All 33 rooms are located away from the lodge, some overlooking Lake Manitouwabing. Most are called deluxe rooms. Deluxe as in cedar cathedral ceilings, log burning fireplaces (always freshly laid), comfy sitting areas, private sundecks, separate dressing rooms, grey marble bathrooms, hair dryers and monogrammed robes. The beds are covered with Swiss cotton duvets.

Take a deluxe room and add an antique marble mantle, a step-down living room, double his-and-her sinks, bathroom skylights and jacuzzi tubs, some with private cedar saunas, and you have the luxury junior suites. All guests find a welcome note and a split of chilled wine when they first arrive.

"We didn't want our rooms to *astound* anybody," explains Ben, "so we did them basically all the same. Our goal was for them to be luxurious, but calm and restful for the guests after a very busy day." And they are, with monochromatic creams, whites, and light woods setting the color scheme.

WHEN YOU HANG UP THE RACQUET

Put on your robe, and take the short walk down the wooden stairs to the lake. The water is almost transparent, very clean and just the right temperature. Drop the robe on one of the padded sun cots on the dock, and lower yourself into into the fresh coolness. Aahhhhh. Floating, you hear the sounds of a few skiers, some happy children playing across the lake, and the lapping of the waves on the shore. This is heaven.

And if you really like the water, just a half-hour drive away at Snug Harbor a wilderness boating adventure awaits you, as do 30,000 islands. The largest concentration of freshwater islands in Canada is right here in the Georgian Bay, once an ancient sea. Kevin Madigan of Canadian Island Holidays operates a small, personalized three- or six-hour tour on his Limestone 24, a sturdy 24-foot boat that takes the waves like butter.

You zip past the Snug Harbor lighthouse, its red roof bright against the blue sky, to a series of seemingly endless rocky islands tossed about the shoreline. This area is a true geological wonder and bird watcher's paradise. Erosion and glacial activity have left these rock formations exposed. Many are crowned with artist-inspiring windblown pines, looking as though they have been riding high speed on a motorcycle for too long. "Georgian Bay gold," a yellow lichen that grows on some of the bare rock outcroppings, is prized by local artisans who use it to dye their hand-knitted sweaters blue, believe it or not. "A lot of people come out here to camp," yells Kevin over the wind and boat noise, "and the unwritten rule is, if someone is already on an island, you have to find another one." No problem; after all, there are 30,000 of them. At many locations folks like to get out and swim from island to island. Many are that close to each other. Kevin might take you to the 3 precious acres of Heron Island, where hundreds of great blue herons nest. Not to get out of course, but just to watch.

If you'd rather see all this beauteous stuff from the air, the inn can arrange for you to be picked up at their dock by a float plane. You're speeding along the water, here comes the shoreline, and then up, up over the trees to the Georgian Bay for a real bird's eye view. These same planes will deliver you to one of several pristine wilderness lakes, where you can spend a half or full day fishing for trout, bass and pickerel. Your expert fishing guide will assist you, and then create an on-shore fish fry with part of the catch if you like. (Let's hope you catch something.)

All guests find a welcome note and a split of chilled wine when they first arrive.

Or you can pick one of the mountain bikes parked just outside the front door of the lodge and trek around some of the bike trails wandering through the property. You can do the same on horseback. The inn is located on 550 acres of private forest in the middle of what Ontarians call "cottage country." wide open wilderness where people naturally gravitate for holidays and exploration.

GOURMET ANYONE?

But don't be late for dinner. Whether it is gourmet night, when the meal is formal French and a coat is required for gentlemen, or bistro night, which is more casual, you'll be knocked out by the food. Celery remoulade with roast goat cheese and pistachios, lobster salad with haricot verts and warm potatoes, or a colorful foie gras and vegetable terrine served on Rosenthal or Bernadeau Limoges china might start your meal. Then move on to a grilled veal tenderloin with prosciutto and Parmesan, Atlantic salmon with potato "scales" and "ravigote" with lobster oil and lavender. For dessert, there are always imported cheeses, and special desserts such as a Carmelite banana terrine or perhaps a perfect warm apple tart. The inn's wine list is well chosen.

Now, how does one plan on shedding a few pounds at the spa or on the court with this extravagant food? One of the chef's biggest challenges in the kitchen was coming up with a menu that was high in flavor but low in calories. He did it, and the Spa Menu was born. You may guilt-free and palate-happy partake of asparagus salad with leek dressing and grape seed oil or gratineed goat cheese and apple, then a smoky grilled veal chop with a ravigote of thyme or roast poulet with a fricassee of mushrooms.

You'll feel better for it, but none of this is mandatory, even if you are on the spa program. You may choose from the regular or spa menu as you please, as do all guests. It's simply available if you wish. Now, how about that pre-breakfast hike in the morning?

Whether it is gourmet night, when the meal is formal French and a coat is required for gentlemen, or bistro night, which is more casual, you'll be knocked out by the food.

MANITOU SHRIMP SAUTÉED WITH HERB BUTTER AND CRISPY POTATOES

Created by the inn's chef, this is a rich dish that makes a great starter or entree. The original dish calls for fresh snails, but as they can be almost impossible to get in many parts of the country, we've substituted shrimp. Canned snails are available in some areas and can be used as well.

20 large shrimp, shelled or 20 canned snails, rinsed and drained
2½ tablespoons butter
1 cup heavy cream
⅓ cup dry white wine
2 cloves garlic
2 shallots
2½ tablespoons pernod
½ bunch chive
½ bunch chervil
½ bunch parsley
½ bunch tarragon
1 baking potato

1. Put the butter in the processor with all the herbs, trimmed and washed, plus 1 shallot and 1 garlic clove. Process until the butter becomes creamy, then add salt and pepper and the pernod. Process until all ingredients are will mixed.

2. Peel and slice the potato very thin like a chip and deep fry them until golden (use 3 per person).

3. Put the remaining shallot chopped with the wine in a sauce pan, put it on the heat and reduce it to half. Then add cream. Boil for 2 minutes.

4. Remove the mixture from the heat and whisk in the herb butter a small piece at a time, whisking well after each addition. Keep warm, but make sure the sauce doesn't boil again or it will separate.

5. Sauté the shrimp in a pan with butter, salt and pepper for about 5-10 minutes, just until done. If using canned snails, sauté in butter until just heated through.

6. Serve 5 shrimp or snails on a plate, add some sauce and 3 potato crisps for each plate, artfully arranged and garnished with fresh chopped herbs.
Serves 4.

FRESH FRUIT TERRINE IN ALMOND CREAM

This layered terrine is a simple recipe using fruits of the season, mixed with exotics like kiwi and mango. A beautiful summer dessert.

¾ cup white granulated sugar
⅔ cup almonds, ground
⅔ cup melted better, cooled
1 cup heavy cream
Grand Marnier
1 pint fresh raspberries
2 fresh kiwis, peeled and sliced
1 fresh mango, peeled and sliced

1. Mix all the fruits gently together in one bowl with Gran Marnier.

2. In another bowl, whip the cream vigorously with the sugar until thick. Add the ground almonds and the melted butter (room temperature).

3. Spread a layer of cream in the terrine.

4. Then on top, add a layer of mixed fruit

5. Repeat with layers of cream and fruit until top is reached with three layers.

6. Refrigerate for 12 hours, and serve carefully sliced with some raspberry sauce or whipped cream.

MANITOU GRATIN FOREZIENNE (POTATO GRATIN)

This dish is a rich classic from the French mountains of Forez. Simple, but oh so good with any meats or fish.

2 lbs. potatoes
1 cup milk
1¼ cup heavy cream
Salt and fresh ground pepper

1. Wash and peel the potatoes. Slice ⅛-inch thick.
2. Dry them in a cloth. Season with salt and pepper
3. Bring the milk to a boil in a deep non-stick sauce pan. Put in the potato slices, one at a time, and cook slowly for 10 minutes.
4. When the potatoes have just about absorbed the milk, add the cream and bring to a boil again. Reduce to simmer.
5. Cover and cook over low heat until tender.
6. Transfer the potatoes gently to a buttered gratin dish and put them under the broiler until golden.

Serves four.

MANITOU FREE-RANGE CHICKEN BREAST IN HAZELNUT CRUNCH WITH WILD MUSHROOMS

This wonderful chicken dish was created especially for the Inn at Manitou. The contrast of the hazelnut crunch and the soft wild mushrooms provides a provocative blend of tastes and textures.

4 boned chicken breasts, free range if possible
1 lb. fresh chanterelle mushrooms
4 tablespoons water
2 tablespoons butter
Flour
2 lbs. leeks, white part only, thinly sliced
1 beaten egg
1 lb. hazelnuts, ground
1¼ cup chicken stock
2 oz. hazelnut oil
Salt and pepper
Juice of a half lemon
4 tablespoons butter

1. Clean and wash the mushrooms and sauté over medium heat with 4 tablespoons water and 2 tablespoons butter for 5 minutes or until soft. Season with salt and pepper; keep warm. (Save the juice.)
2. Cook leek slices in just enough water to cover for 6 minutes. Drain and keep warm.
3. Season the chicken breasts with salt and pepper and bread them on one side only (dip in the flour first, whipped eggs second, and chopped hazelnuts last.)
4. Sauté them in a frying pan in the hazelnut oil – hazelnut side first. Cook until golden on both sides and just cooked through, about 6–8 minutes per side.
5. Reduce the juice of mushrooms with the poultry stock by one-quarter by bringing them to a boil for a 5 minutes.
6. Add leftover hazelnuts, the lemon juice, and whisk in the 4 tablespoons one tablespoon at a time.
7. Put the leeks and mushrooms in the middle of a plate, cover with the chicken breast and pour some sauce on top.

Serves four.

La Pinsonniere

CAP-A-L'AIGLE, CHARLEVOIX
QUEBEC, CANADA

Driving from Quebec City east along the northern bank of the St. Lawrence River, the "Mother of Canada," you motor through towns and villages with names like Boischatel, Les Eboulements and Point-au-Pic. The original highway of fur traders, explorers and colonists hundreds of years ago, the St. Lawrence is even more vast than I imagined, over fifteen miles wide in some places. Signs for fromageries and boulangeries flash past, tempting you to stop. Even cheese and bread seem more exciting in French. And Quebec is as French as you can get without being on the Champs Elysees. People speak French, the signs are in French, TV stations broadcast in French. Don't let that be a hindrance. Enjoy it. That same Quebecois attitude extends to hospitality, good food, good wine, and the appreciation of living the good life. And at La Pinsonniere (which means house of finches) in the little village of Cap-a-l'Aigle, fine living has been distilled to its essence.

Upon arrival you are greeted by a two storied clapboard, turreted building, startling white against the blue sky above and water below, with black shutters at the windows. Built into the side of a steep hill 200 feet above the St. Lawrence River, the two visible levels belie the other three hidden from view at this vantage point.

HONORS, HERITAGE AND HOME

Step into the lobby, where on the wall 10 china plates mark 10 proud years with the prestigious French based Relais and Chateaux. The framed Wine Spectator's Award of Excellence and the AAA 4-Diamond Award tell of hosts who know what they're doing. Hot coffee in fine china cups is set out to perk up bone-tired travelers. A red leather sofa awaits for a moment's relaxation, and the walls are filled with beautiful original paintings. Art is an obvious passion at La Pinsonniere, all the product of Quebec artists, and much of it for sale. For accomplished innkeepers Jean Authier and his daughter Valerie, who are an accomplished and charming team, it is their way of pleasing their guests aesthetically, themselves artistically and local artists financially.

A small bar overlooks the many blues of the St. Lawrence below, as does the living room which has a fireplace much used in the winter. If you step through the French doors onto the terrace, you immediately feel the cool breeze off the water. Set with groupings of padded chairs and tables, this is an imminently pleasant place to share a glass of wine in the afternoon or coffee in the morning.

La Pinsonniere was built as a private home in 1952, and bought by the Authiers in 1978. Jean Authier had a long, successful career in men's clothing and transferred that style and business acumen to creating a haven of refined pleasures. What a job he and his wife Janine, and now daughter Valerie, have done. In her soft French-accented English, Valerie explains, "This has been my home since I was 10. I grew up watching my parents run La Pinsonniere, so it's in my blood, a way of life really."

All 28 rooms have been furnished with comfort in mind. My room, #204, is just down the hall from the lobby; no stairs to climb. With incredible views of the river, it is cozy, light and airy with seashell pink, blue and green wallpaper. Those colors repeat themselves on the fabrics of the curtains and the pine bed canopy. Delicate electrified oil lamps provide soft lighting. A fireplace is laid with a fire-log ready for the strike of your match, and a cool breeze blows through the open windows. My favorite touch is the classical music piped into the room to be enjoyed at the turn of a wall switch.

Room #211 is a spacious room with a king sized brass bed covered with a white lace duvet. A tall cavernous pine armoire seems to expect you to unpack your clothes. The large bath is white marble, with pedestal sinks, a double whirlpool tub and a separate glass shower. But what you'll really love about this room is just a step outside the glass doors. The large semi-private deck stretches before you, with glorious views of the St Lawrence. Wooden rectangular planters are blooming with colorful marigolds and geraniums.

The bay windows of La Pinsonniere's newest luxury room, #315, overlook the fragrant purple lilac blooms in the entrance courtyard. The king-size brass bed is flanked by two milky alabaster lamps. And, the thoughtfulness of designing the fireplace, not on the floor where it can't be seen from the bed, but elevated for enjoyment from every angle will be much appreciated (this is true of most fireplaces at the inn). But this particular fireplace is double-sided, so that you can also enjoy its warmth while luxuriating in the double therapeutic hydromassage whirlpool tub, or, as you step out of your own private cedar sauna. A world class bathroom.

ROOM AND SERVICE

Being a creature who loves the indolence of room service, I request a continental breakfast of fresh, flaky croissants, French coffee and thick cream. I mention this only because at home I feel honor bound to put skim milk in my coffee. So when cream shows up on my breakfast tray, well, I don't feel any guilt at all pouring in a generous

Ten china plates mark 10 proud years with the prestigious French based Relais and Chateaux.

GRACIOUS COUNTRY INNS

dollop. For the croissant, a little white china pot of homemade rhubarb compote is remarkable.

If you eat in the dining room, one floor below the lobby, breakfast is a multi-course meal changing daily, beginning with fresh squeezed juices, a French pastry, followed by a yogurt flan with fresh fruit. The third course might be a salmon quiche or eggs benedict. And, oh joyful moment, a La Pinsonniere breakfast desert – perhaps crepes stuffed with fruit and served with maple syrup.

WHALE AND WALKS

A short drive down the St. Lawrence River is the town of Baie-Sainte-Catherine. This is the closest point to catch a three-hour whale sighting expedition. The Cavalier des Mers and the Cavalier Royal are ships designed specifically for whale watching. Belugas, minkes, and finbacks are the species most likely to rise from the depths, and the guides will help you understand their adaptability to this inland environment. Certain tours will also take you to the Saguenay Wilderness, one of the world's longest fjords. The towering 1,500 foot cliffs of the fjord majestically meet the river and plunge under the water's surface at some points to an icy depth of 750 feet . This unspoiled arctic marine microclimate produces the only belugas you'll find south of the arctic. By the way, don't forget a coat or sweater. It can be bone-chilling on the water, but the ships make a mean cup of hot chocolate.

This unspoiled arctic marine microclimate produces the only belugas you'll find south of the arctic.

For those more inclined toward terra firma, try shoreside whale watching with Saguenay Marine Park naturalists. Plus there's hiking, backpacking and glorious vistas for picnics (which La Pinsonniere's staff will pack upon request).

The finches called me out to play early one morning so I quietly shuffle outside for a morning hike. Down 200-some steps I bounce over hand-hewn logs and handrails leading me through spruce, cedar and birch trees carpeted at their base with tiny periwinkle blue wildflowers. Ignoring the rest benches I finally arrive at a glorious, rugged stretch of coastline that must look the same as when French explorer Jacques Cartier passed this way in 1535. Jean Authier has told me that this river has tides as large as 15 feet at times and the water here, 700 miles inland, is salty. I have to taste it. He's right, of course. A wonderful place to enjoy a quiet picnic or just a moment's solitude, the briny air is at least 10 or 15 degrees cooler here at the water's edge.

In the winter, this area receives over a hundred inches of snowfall each year. Guests flock here for downhill skiing at nearby Mont Grand Fonds, which can be easily arranged by La Pinsonniere. Or 150 kilometers of groomed cross country trails await, with cozy heated huts along the way. Inside you can make your own coffee and eat a gourmet picnic packed by the inn. Of course, there's a bottle of good red wine. Here, luxury graces every day, every season.

Plan on hooking up with a "technical wine tasting" session. You'll be taken to the Authier's formidable 10,000-bottle, cool, dimly lit wine cellar. Moving through a corridor of floor-to-ceiling bottle-to bottle wines of the world, you come to a small room where all you see from wall to wall are the green circles of bottle bottoms and a table covered by white linen. The whole gothic treasure is illuminated by candle light. Five pre-chosen bottles have been opened by the sommelier and soon will be reverently poured into the five crystal glasses before you. Each one is carefully swirled, sniffed, sipped, rolled around the tongue – and finally – swallowed. There will be no spitting in my presence. The sommelier discusses each wine as happily you tastebud your way through the grape quintet. Before you head back upstairs for a swim in the heated indoor pool, a round of tennis or perhaps a scheduled Swedish massage, you're invited to select your own bottle for dinner.

Dinner at La Pinsonniere is a ritual with all the entertainment one could require for a perfect evening. Much thought is put into the selections. You dine. Relax. Enjoy this proper French meal, a leisurely event filled with conversation, laughs, delectable food and exquisite wines in a gracious art filled dining room overlooking the St. Lawrence.

Jean Authier proclaims, "If someone doesn't like something, they should tell us and we'll get them something else. We instruct our waiters, if guests have put down their forks and knives and have not eaten much, they are to remove it and say, 'You didn't care for this, what can we get for you?' Our patrons are our number one priority."

My dinner (at which I rarely put down the knife and fork) begins with sweetbreads and shrimp richly sauced, served in a cunning little copper and brass pot. Then comes a lovely green flecked watercress soup with a swirl of white cream through it. This is followed by a decadent buttery soft Quebec foie gras with baby salad greens. I sigh in happiness. Next a loin of lamb medallions in a savory dark reduction sauce.

Jean sees that I must have something light for dessert; this surfeit of food must show in my eyes. A trio of sorbets – coffee, raspberry and cantaloupe – in a puddle of raspberry sauce. Perfect. And yet here comes the cheese trolley. I intend to say, "No, thank you." But these are no regular cheeses. They are flown from France, made from the unpasteurized milk of cows, sheep and goats, to make cheese taste the way the French know it should. Just a bit of the chevre or a sliver of the sheep's milk cheese? A glass of red wine appears, deep burgundy, and then disappears along with the cheese. I think of nothing save the wonderful flavors in my mouth. The evening has now drifted into that timeless place where the conversation is free flowing and I bear ill will toward no person. This is how dinner should always be.

Enjoy this proper French meal, a leisurely event filled with conversation, laughs, delectable food and exquisite wines

LA PINSONNIERE RABBIT IN SAGE AND WILD MUSHROOM SAUCE

Have all the ingredients chopped and measured out before you begin to cook as rabbit meat dries out if overdone. Many of us here in the U.S. have never eaten rabbit but in France and in Quebec, it is a regular part of the family menu.

1 young rabbit with liver, cut into serving pieces
⅓ cup unsalted butter
5 morel mushrooms sliced
2 shallots, peeled and minced
½ cup dry white wine
2 tablespoons brandy
2 tablespoons chopped fresh sage
1 cup rabbit or chicken stock
½ heavy cream
salt and freshly ground pepper to taste
rabbit liver, if included with rabbit pieces

1. Preheat oven to 325 degrees.
2. Wash rabbit pieces and pat dry. Reserve the liver.
3. About one half hour before serving, melt 3 tablespoons of the butter in a heavy skillet. Over medium heat, sauté the rabbit until partially cooked and beginning to brown. Place the pieces in a lightly oiled 9×13-inch pan. bake for 30 minutes.
4. During the final 10 minutes of baking, heat the morels and shallots gently in the same pan that browned the rabbit . Cook covered over low heat until the shallots are translucent but not browned.
5. Add the wine, brandy and sage. Increase the heat and reduce the sauce to one-third its original volume.
6. Pour in the stock and reduce again to one-third of its volume.
7. Whisk the cream into the wine stock. Remove the skillet from heat and whisk in the remaining butter (cut into small bits) one piece at a time. Season with salt and pepper. Keep the sauce warm but do not boil.
8. Sauté the liver in 1 tablespoon butter until just pink on the inside.
9. To serve, place the rabbit on a heated serving platter, cover with the sauce and garnish with the liver that has been sliced across the grain.

Serves 4.

LA PINSONNIERE FLOATING ISLAND

2 cups milk
2 cups water
3½ oz. sugar
2 vanilla beans

1. In a large saucepan, bring first set of ingredients to a boil. Turn down the heat and allow to simmer.

8 egg whites (save yolks and use in crème anglaise below)
3½ oz. sugar
pinch of salt
fresh raspberries

2. Meanwhile, beat the egg whites with a pinch of salt until soft peaks form. Add sugar and keep beating until peaks are stiff. Using two teaspoons, form the egg white mixture to 8 egg like shapes. Poach in the simmering liquid 3 minutes on each side. Carefully remove egg white "islands" with a strainer and drain on paper towels. Serve "floating" on puddle of crème anglaise sauce below, garnished with fresh raspberries.

Serves 8.

CRÈME ANGLAISE

8 egg yolks
4 oz. sugar
1 quart milk
1 vanilla bean, split

1. Beat the egg yolks in a large saucepan until sticky, about 1 minute. Gradually beat in the sugar.
2. Heat milk with vanilla bean.
3. Slowly beat in the hot vanilla milk by droplets. Cook over moderately low heat until sauce is thick enough to coat a spoon. Do not let the sauce come to a simmer or the egg yolks will curdle. Remove vanilla beans before serving.
4. Serve warm or cool.

Makes 1 quart.

LA PINSONNIERE
SCALLOP SALAD WITH
CANTAL CHEESE

Cantal is a nutty flavored semifirm cheese that is one of the oldest in France. If you cannot find a Cantal, try a good Gruyère instead.

Mixed salad greens such as oak leaf, red leaf or
 Boston lettuce
4 oz. Cantal cheese, shaved or grated
12 sea scallops
2 tablespoons olive oil
2 teaspoons heavy cream
2 chopped shallots
1 tablespoon white wine vinegar

1. Wash and drain lettuce. Pat dry on paper towels. Season greens with a lemon juice vinaigrette. Set aside.
2. Heat olive oil over medium high heat. When the oil is almost smoking, add the scallops and toss for about 3 minutes until brown on the outside but still rare on the inside.
3. Add chopped shallots to the scallops, cook 1 minute and deglaze the pan with the white wine vinegar. Add the cream, reduce over heat for 30 seconds. Remove from heat.
4. Arrange seasoned greens in middle of plate. Sprinkle with cheese shavings. Place warm scallops on top.

Serves 4.

LA PINSONNIERE
CHICKEN STOCK

Any French chef worth his salt believes in making chicken stock from scratch. While I do often use canned stock, there is no comparison to this hearty homemade broth. If you have the time to make this stock, it freezes beautifully for future recipes.

3 onions, chopped
2 minced leeks, white part only
Chopped leaves from 1 bunch celery
2 bay leaves
1 tablespoon whole peppercorns
1 large boiling chicken, including wings and neck
10 cups water

1. Put onions, leeks, celery leaves, bay leaves and peppercorns and chicken into a large soup kettle.
2. Add the water, cover and bring to a boil. Reduce heat and simmer slowly for 2 hours, skimming any fat and scum regularly.
3. Strain and use or let cool, then refrigerate or freeze.

Makes 8 cups.

Sooke Harbour House

SOOKE, VANCOUVER ISLAND, CANADA

Strolling up the crunchy gravel path from Sooke Harbour past lush plantings of nasturtiums and lavender, I pause for a moment, sitting on a teak bench to admire the view. A couple of seals are joyfully playing tag in the blue harbor water. Off in the distance I can see the deeper blue of the Juan de Fuca Strait and the dark purple Olympic Mountains of Washington. Surely there cannot be a place more lovely than this. And indeed, I have never been anywhere more appealing than the Sooke Harbour House, tucked in the southwest corner of Vancouver Island, British Columbia.

Having often heard the claims of friends regarding the incredible beauty of Vancouver Island, I was astonished to find those claims entirely true. Discovered by the Spanish in 1774 and explored by the British in 1792, America actually laid brief claim to the 285 mile long island but surrendered those rights to the British in 1846 by the terms of the Oregon Boundary Treaty. What a loss for the states.

WARMTH AND COMFORT

The climate is surprisingly mild year round, thus the luxuriant growth. Warmed by the Japan current, this part of the island with its southern exposure has the mildest climate in Canada, one almost Mediterranean in nature. Sinclair and Fredrica Phillip take full advantage of that fact. Their hemlock tree grows eight feet a year and the Harbour House has a rosemary plant ten feet tall. Sinclair jokes, "When Texans come

Warmed by the Japan current, this part of the island with its southern exposure has the mildest climate in Canada.

to visit, we tell them it's the biggest in the world and we're entering it in the Guiness Book of Records." Their gardens are not only beautiful, but a study in plant life of the Northwest.

The inn itself is friendly, not at all pretentious, with a white clapboard exterior and expanses of windows overlooking the water. Built in the 1930s, Sooke Harbour House has always been an inn, but when the Phillips first bought it in 1979, it had only five bedrooms, a restaurant, and no gardens. Yet, they still saw the perfect country inn. Says French-born Fredrica, "In France, we always had guests staying with us. We would gather produce, cook good meals and drink the local wine. This is just an extension of our life there. We wanted to create a place where you can relax and feel at ease, like in a French auberge."

They did just that, enlarging the inn to fifteen bedrooms in 1986, all with water views and fireplaces. I know first hand how welcoming Sooke Harbour is, because the evening is etched in my memory. Arriving at almost midnight after an exhausting series of flights, drives, delays and ferries, I trudge directly to my quarters, the Edible Blossom room, in a fog. My desolation is complete. The luggage deposited, I look around. On the first level of the room, the bed is already turned down invitingly but, I summon the strength to stumble the few steps down into the sunken living area. A sofa and chairs lounge before a ready laid fire. One strike of the match, and warm orange flames begin coaxing me to a better state of consciousness. A tray on the sideboard is set with a decanter of port and crystal glasses. Pouring myself a self-pitying measure, I cheer up immensely. Climbing into that soft bed with my port and watching the flames light up this pretty room will always be a fond memory.

But the next morning holds even greater surprises. Having arrived in the dark, I have no idea of the gorgeous view via the glass doors leading to my private terrace. The terrace walls are extended with chest-high plantings of sumptuous yet unfamiliar flowers. Out beyond these stretch the lawn, sloping down to Sooke basin and the harbor. The sky is translucent blue. After a few moments' introspection about how things can unexpectedly turn out so very well, there's a tap at the inside door. I glance at my watch. That's right, I did order breakfast for 8:00.

"Good morning, how did you sleep?" says a smiling woman bearing a tray of delightfully fragrant goodies. "Would you like breakfast here, on the terrace or by the fire?" On the terrace is fine. More than fine. Gently scrambled eggs with smoked salmon and tarragon, ripe red strawberries with fresh mint, fresh squeezed kiwi juice and hot coffee. Kiwi juice? Yes, I'm told the fruit grows on a vine just outside the inn's restaurant. I'll have to see it. Kiwi growing in Canada?

NATURE AND NURTURE

After exhaustive research by Sinclair and gardener Byron Cook, native plants that had largely disappeared were reintroduced. Here in the inn's carefully tended beds, hundreds of varieties of edible flowers and herbs are grown. Early native American food plants are their specialty, such as licorice fern, a root six hundred times sweeter than sugar. And tropical fruits – pineapple, kiwi, guava and passionfruit grow abundantly in this mild climate. I can tell you, the pleasure of a glass of fresh organic kiwi juice in the morning is a revelation.

Inside the main house is a cozy sitting room centered around a large fireplace. The restaurant, which has become justifiably famous in Canada for its inventive cuisine, is also here, overlooking gardens and the harbor. Upstairs is the Blue Heron Room, which indisputably has the best view in the house. With loads of windows, you can enjoy the 180-degree view from your queen-sized bed or from the jacuzzi tub. Just out-

GRACIOUS COUNTRY INNS

We wanted to create a place where you can relax and feel at ease, like a French auberge.

side the glass doors is a large deck overlooking the water, the gardens and the newest section of the inn.

In that extension are most of the inn's accommodations, all of which have a theme and are decorated with that in mind, The Edible Blossom Room, the Herb Garden Room, and their largest and most spectacular, the Victor Newman Longhouse Suite. A noted Kwakiutl native American artist, Newman's carved masks and bright paintings are the perfect foil for the white walls and handmade cedar furniture from local craftsmen. The bed is a beautiful cedar four-poster creation with a delicate curving canopy of cedar above. The fireplace is double sided, opening to the sitting area and to a double jacuzzi tub set in cedar. Inspired and romantic.

Fredrica and Sinclair's aim was to make each room a private cottage for guests, a little home to return to each evening. Thus all have fireplaces, sitting areas and private terraces or balconies overlooking the water for quiet reading or morning coffee.

Sinclair notes that for the first few days guests usually just unwind and do nothing except read, take walks and enjoy the surroundings. But in this invigorating climate, it's not long before they're out exploring the countryside.

EXPLORING

Victoria, the quaint capitol of British Columbia, is twenty-three miles east of the inn and a charming place to spend the day. Called B.C.'s most "English" city, its narrow winding streets are lined with shops, restaurants and harbor promenades with hanging baskets of red geraniums. Worth a stop are the stone legislature buildings and the Empress Hotel. One of the must-see attractions in Victoria is the Royal British Columbia Museum.

Fishing, kayaking, scuba diving and sailing are all popular; even the surfing is good here. Sinclair tells of some South African visitors who spent hours surfing in front of the inn at night. He laughs and shrugs. "They said the surfing was terrific."

For the truly invigorated, the rugged West Coast trail, all seven kilometers of it, waits to be conquered. It takes three to five days to complete. As you might imagine, most of us are not up to such an encounter. But trails through green, unspoiled glades abound for hiking, and many of them lead to isolated beaches whose white pebbles are perfect for picnics. Sinclair will steer you to the best of them.

You might even see an elusive cougar. In the early days people came to Vancouver Island to shoot these abundant and beautiful cats. Pictures exist of smiling, exultant hunters with six to eight foot cougars draped across their backs. While people still come to this island to find cougars (though shy they be), they come with cameras. Everyday sightings of whales, bald eagles, seals, sea lions, hummingbirds, river otters, and waterfowl make this a wildlife watcher's paradise.

Just around the corner from the Sooke Harbour House are Sooke Coastal Explorations. Zipping myself into a full-length fetching red "floater" suit, we blast off. All too frequently the black rubber raft shoots completely out of the water as we crest the waves. (People wanting a smoother ride should avoid the front seats.) On this trip, we miss spotting any of several killer whale "pods" that live in these waters in the summer feasting on salmon. But hundreds of male stellar and California sea lions put on quite a show, barking and lolling about on Race Rocks. On occasion 1,500 sea lions in all their male pulchritude congregate here in late summer and winter between mating seasons, resting up for the next romantic escapade.

One of the most satisfying and accessible walks is just out your terrace door. A long finger of land that points into Sooke basin is called Whiffen Spit. Collect beautifully shaped pebbles and stones, watch the seals play, sit on a driftwood log and simply enjoy the moment.

The bed is a beautiful cedar four-poster creation with a delicate curving canopy of cedar above. The fireplace is double sided, opening to the sitting area and to a double jacuzzi tub set in cedar. Inspired and romantic.

CREATIVELY SPEAKING

In the kitchen, a team of young intense Canadian chefs are preparing what will be a meal you will never forget. Fredrica compares what they do to artistry. "As a painter stands before the canvas with all the colors and makes a painting, so do the chefs stand with the ingredients. That's what a wonderful meal is – a combination of colors, flavors, and textures all put together." Eminently edible art.

Sooke Harbour chefs specialize in the freshest possible regional cuisine and local ingredients, particularly seafood. As Fredrica points out, "Why serve Maine lobster, when we have delectable Dungeness crab caught that morning?" Indeed, you will not eat Maine lobster or Gulf of Mexico shrimp. But you will feast on fresh Pacific oyster and roasted nasturtium tuber soup, cracked Dungeness crab with sundried tomato, sage and garlic mayonnaise, and salads concocted of organic baby garden greens, ox-eye daisies, sheep's sorrel and dandelion greens (all from the house garden) with organic gooseberry dressing. Then move on to carrot pasta and leek terrine with sea urchin sauce, rosemary, garlic and red onion braised rabbit leg and sage roasted loin, or Pacific oysters baked in their shells and wrapped in sea lettuce. Sinclair offers an extensive wine list specializing in wines of the region. Trust his advice. Desserts are equally adventurous and delightful, marionberry custard with white chocolate mousse, lemon thyme ice cream and rhubarb ginger crumble tart with cinnamon-basil ice cream. Or how about chocolate walnut cake with espresso ice cream and lemon balm glaze served in your room by the fire? Now you're talkin'.

Sooke Harbour chefs specialize in the freshest possible regional cuisine and local ingredients, particularly seafood.

SOOKE HARBOUR HOUSE SPRING SALAD WITH AN ORGANIC GOOSEBERRY DRESSING

Sooke Harbour House is famous for its fabulous salads made from exotic ingredients. If you use flowers or greens from your garden or yard, be sure they are edible and have not been chemically sprayed.

Suggested salad greens, herbs and flowers could include lolla rossa, butter crunch, red oak leaf, lamb's lettuce, winter chicories or radicchios of any kind, ox-eye daisies, chickweed, dandelion greens, sheep's sorrel, anise hyssop, fennel, tarragon, pansies, violas, calendula, julienned tulip flowers or English daisies.
2 cups fresh or frozen red English gooseberries
½ cup dry pear or apple cider
⅓ late harvest Riesling
½ teaspoon finely chopped fresh ginger (optional)
1 tablespoon walnut oil, organic refined
2 tablespoons + 2 tablespoons hazelnut oil, preferably organic cold-pressed
1 teaspoon clear fireweed honey or other clear honey
½ cup roasted organic hazelnuts

1. Select ½ cup of the nicest gooseberries and reserve for a garnish.
2. Place remaining 1½ cups gooseberries, cider, wine and ginger into a 1 quart saucepan. Over medium heat, stir while bringing to a boil. Boil for 2 minutes to slightly reduce liquids.
3. Place cooked gooseberries into blender and purée until smooth. Strain into a bowl, pushing liquids through strainer with a small ladle. Discard seeds.
4. Whisk the walnut oil first and then 2 tablespoons of hazelnut oil into the gooseberry purée. Taste. If too tart for your palate, whisk in honey to taste.
   Yields 1 cup of dressing.
5. Wash the salad greens and edible flowers in very cold running water. Put in salad spinner and spin excess water off. Pat dry in a clean towel.
6. Toss with dressing and garnish with reserved gooseberries.
   Makes 4 to 6 small salads.

SOOKE HARBOUR HOUSE LEMON THYME ICE CREAM

Keep this delicately flavored ice cream in the freezer no more than two days, as the lemon thyme flavor will fade.

1 cup whole milk
1 cup whipping cream
⅓ cup and 2 tablespoons lemon thyme sprigs
5 egg yolks
½ cup sugar

1. Place milk, cream and ⅓ cup chopped lemon thyme sprigs in a 1 quart saucepan. Heat over medium heat until scalded. Set aside to steep for 15 minutes.
2. Place the egg yolks and sugar in a stainless steel bowl. Over medium heat or double boiler, whisk the egg yolk-sugar mixture until it is light yellow and somewhat thickened. Remove from heat.
3. In a slow, steady stream, pour the cream mixture into the yolks constantly whisking. When completed, return mixture to heat and using a rubber spatula to scrape the bottom of the pan, cook until the custard is steaming and glossy. To test for doneness lift the spatula out of the custard, draw your finger across it and, if it holds a clean line, custard is cooked.
4. Strain the custard through a fine mesh strainer and cool. Freeze according to the directions of your ice cream maker.
5. At the end of the freezing process, add the remaining 2 tablespoons chopped lemon thyme. Store in the freezer in an airtight container.
   Makes 2½ cups.

SOOKE HARBOUR HOUSE GRAVORING

What an elegant appetizer this is, and it can be made more than a week ahead. Slice and serve with French bread, capers, diced onion and lemon wedges.

1½ lbs. fresh halibut (minimum ¾" and maximum 2½" thick, preferably from the mid-section, skinned)
4 tablespoons sea salt if possible
4 tablespoons sugar
1 bunch fresh fennel, with mainstem removed
8 crushed black peppercorns
1 tablespoon mustard seeds
6 juniper berries, crushed
12 basil leaves, chopped (optional)
2 clusters of fresh lavender flowers, chopped (optional)
fresh fennel fronds
fresh basil tops
lemon or lime slices

1. Sprinkle half of the salt and then the sugar on the bottom of a stainless steel pan or Pyrex dish large enough to hold the fillet. Add half of the fennel sprigs, crushed pepper, mustard seeds, crushed juniper berries, basil and lavender flowers over top.

2. Now place the halibut on top of the spice and salt mixture. Sprinkle the rest of the sugar and then the salt evenly over the fish and then sprinkle the remaining herbs, pepper, berries and flowers on top.

3. Cover loosely with plastic wrap.

4. Place another stainless steel pan or Pyrex pie plate over the prepared halibut and weigh it down with a stack of 10 small plates or perhaps two bricks (15 lbs. or more).

5. Refrigerate from 12 to 16 hours, depending upon the thickness of the fish, until the white-fleshed fish looks translucent or clear and feels firm to the touch. It is important to note that the halibut will become tough and overly salty *if left too long in the brine.*

6. Remove the gravoring of halibut from its brine and gently scrape off herbs and seasonings. (If not using immediately after curing, wrap gravoring in plastic and store it in the refrigerator for up to 10 days.)

7. Slice into paper-thin slices vertically through the filet. Display them attractively on a plate in a circular pattern garnished with fresh fennel fronds, basil sprigs and lemon or lime wedges. Cover and refrigerate until needed.

Serves 8.

Just the Facts

This information is subject to change. Always call ahead to check with inns on rates, open and closed dates, etc.

The Aerie - P.O.B. 108, Malahat, British Columbia, Canada V0R 2L0
604-743-7115 / Fax: 604-743-4766

The Aerie is open from February through December, closed in January. Rates range from $165 to $350 (Canadian dollars) In high season (April 30–October 11), and from $145 to $300 in low season. All prices are double occupancy and include a full breakfast in the dining room, as well as access to pool, sauna, fitness room and tennis court. No pets. All rooms are non-smoking. The Aerie is adult-oriented, but children are accepted. No televisions or telephones in rooms.

How to get there: You may fly into Victoria, which is about 20 miles south of The Aerie. The Aerie is located off Highway 1. Take the Spectacle Lake turnoff near the Malahat summit.

Applewood, An Estate Inn - 13555 Highway 116, Pocket Canyon, California 95446
707-869-9093

Applewood, An Estate Inn is open all year. Room prices range from $115 to $250 a night, single or double occupancy, and include a full breakfast. All rooms have telephones, televisions, and private baths, use of heated pool and jacuzzi.

How To get there: You can fly into San Francisco and rent a car. Applewood is a 2-1/2 hr. drive north on Coastal Hwy. 1, or 1-1/2 hrs. on Hwy. 101, near Gurneville on Route 116. The brochure contains a map.

Blantyre - PO Box 995 Lenox, Massachusetts 01240-0995
413-637-3556 / Fax: 413-637-4282

Blantyre is open May through November. Room rates range from $160 up to $575 a night, double occupancy, including continental breakfast, use of tennis and croquet courts, pool, jacuzzi and sauna. All rooms have television and telephones. Smoking is permitted.

How To get there: You can fly into Albany, New York, 37 miles from Lenox on most major airlines. Blantyre is a four-hour drive from Boston or New York. There is a terrific brochure available from Blantyre on taking a driving tour of the wonderful Berkshires, telling about all the sights available, how to get to them, and how long to allow at each place. Very helpful.

The Boulders - 34631 North Tom Darlington Drive, PO Box 2090, Carefree, Arizona 85377
602-488-9009 / Fax: 602-488-4118

The Boulders is open ten months a year, September through June. Casita rates range from $225 to $450 per night double occupancy with no meals, and from $335 to $550 per couple per night, breakfast and dinner included. All casitas have fireplaces, fully stocked mini-bars and balcony or terrace. Prices depend on the season, high season being Jan. 14 - May 14 and Dec. 23 - Jan. 1. Children are welcome; no pets. The Boulders Club is a members-only country club, but all guests have access to the facilities, including two golf courses & six plexi-paved courts. All golf and tennis charges apply.

How To Get There: Fly into Phoenix Sky Harbor Airport (33 miles away) or Scottsdale Airport for private planes (13 miles away). Call ahead for ground transportation.

C Lazy U Ranch - Box 379 Granby, Colorado 80446
303-887-3344 / Fax: 303-887-3917

The C Lazy U Ranch is open mid-December-March and June-September. Rates average $145 per person, per week in summer, and $130 per person, per night in winter, and include all meals, all on-ranch activities and equipment. Ask about special winter packages and children's discounts.

How to get there: You may fly into Denver, which is a two hour drive from the ranch. Private shuttles can be arranged, but the ranch suggests renting a car for convenience. Two local airports, Granby (VFR) and Kremmling (IFR) can accommodate private jets.

Cedar Grove Mansion - 2300 Washington Street, Vicksburg, Mississippi 39180
1-800-862-1300 / Fax: 601-634-6126

Cedar Grove is open year round. Rates range from $85 to $160 per night, double occupancy, including a full southern breakfast (eat your grits), use of the tennis court, exercise room and a tour of the mansion. Children are accepted. Smoking is allowed in one of the guest rooms and in the dining room. No pets.

How to get there: If you fly into Jackson, Vicksburg is just a half hour drive west on I-20. If you wish to connect Vicksburg with a New Orleans visit, Vicksburg is about 3-1/2 hours north of New Orleans.

The Charlotte Inn - South Summer Street, Edgartown, Massachusetts 02539
508-627-4751

The Charlotte Inn is open all year. Room rates range from $125 to $450 in the off season, and from $250 to $550 in the summer high season, including continental breakfast. Most accommodations have telephone and television, and many have fireplaces. Children over twelve are accepted. Heavy cigarette smoking is discouraged, and pipes and cigars are not allowed in guest rooms.

How to get there: Ferry reservations are required if you are bringing a car onto the island. Those can be had by calling (508) 477-8600. The ferry arrives a 15 minute ride from The Charlotte Inn. You may also fly into the Dukes County Airport on various commuter flights. I highly recommend renting a car to drive around the island.

Averill's Flathead Lake Lodge - Box 248, Bigfork, Montana 59911
406-837-4391 / Fax: 406-837-6977
Averill's Flathead Lake Lodge is open mid-June to early September . Rates for adults are $1,456 per week, $1,092 for teens, $952 for children 6-12, $721 for children 3-5. Rates include all meals and all recreational on-site activities. No TVs or telephones in rooms. Smoking is allowed. No pets.

How to get there: The Kalispell, Montana airport is served by Delta and other regional airlines. Amtrak comes into Whitefish. Pick-up service and rental cars are available.

High Hampton Inn and Country Club - PO Box 338, Cashiers, North Carolina 28717-0338
800-334-2551 or 704-743-2411 / Fax: 704-743-5991
High Hampton Inn and Country Club is open April through mid-November, and for Thanksgiving. Room rates are per person, per day, and include private bath and all meals, and range from $69 to $88, depending on season and location. They also offer golf and tennis packages. Private home rentals run from $184 to $344 per night, no meals included. Green fees are $24 a day, and tennis courts are $5 per person, per hour. No smoking in the dining room. There are no telephones or TVs in rooms. Pet kennels and laundry are available. No tipping and no service charge added to your bill.

How to get there: Transportation services for guests can be arranged to and from the airports at Asheville, North Carolina, and Greenville, South Carolina, and the Amtrak station at Greenville, South Carolina.

The Home Ranch - Box 822, Clark, Colorado 80428
303-879-1780 / Fax: 303-879-1795
The Home Ranch is open June-September and December-March. Room rates range from $375 to $500 per night double occupancy, including three sumptuous meals a day, daily maid service, downhill shuttle service, once a week laundry service, guided hikes into the wilderness, horseback riding (for ages 6 and over), private fishing, riding lessons, evening entertainment, children's programs and heated pool and sauna. The lodge is smoke-free. No pets.

How to get there: Clark, Colorado is located 16 miles from the airport in Steamboat Springs and airport transfers are included in the cost of your stay.

The Inn at Blackberry Farm - 1471 West Millers Cove Road, Walland, Tennessee 37886
615 984-8166 or 1-800-862-7610 / Fax: 615-983-5708
The Inn at Blackberry Farm is open all year. Room rates are from $350-$450 per night, per couple, including a full breakfast, lunch and dinner, and use of all recreational facilities on the farm. Special weekend packages are available. There are no televisions or phones in rooms, but both are discreetly available (as well as VCRs and videos) in most common rooms. Smoking is allowed only on the veranda. Jackets, but not ties, are required at dinner for gentlemen. The inn also has conference facilities to accommodate up to 50 people, with a full compliment of audio-visual equipment, overhead projectors, fax and copy service.

How to get there: The inn is located about 4 miles off U.S. 321 (15 miles east of Maryvale), about 20 minutes from the Knoxville Airport, and 3 miles from the Great Smokey Mt. National Park.

The Inn at Manitou - Summer - McKellar, Ontario, Canada, POG 1CO
416-967-6137 or 705-389-2171 / Fax: 705-389-3818
Winter: Closed - Contact: 251 Davenport Road, Toronto, Ontario, Canada, M5R 1J9
416-967-3466 / Fax: 416-967-6434
The Inn at Manitou is open May through October. Room rates range from $152 to $315 (Canadian dollars) per person, per day, and include breakfast, lunch and dinner. A private 3-bedroom luxury country house rents at $995 Canadian per day, no meals. Ask about packages for tennis, spa, and golf, and wilderness exploration, or yoy may purchase these services n an a la carte basis. All rooms have phones but no television. For guests staying 4 days or longer, free laundry service is available. There are facilities for small business or executive meetings at certain times of the season.

How to get there: The inn is a 2-1/2 hour drive North of Toronto, just east of Parry Sound. Call for specific directions.

The Inn at Perry Cabin - 308 Watkins Lane, St. Michaels, Maryland 21663
410-745-2200 or 800-722-2949 / Fax: 410-745-3348
The Inn at Perry Cabin is open all year. Rates range from $175 to $525 per night double occupancy, including daily newspaper, a full English breakfast and afternoon tea. All rooms have telephones and cable television, individual heating and air conditioning. No pets allowed. Children over ten accepted. Smoking is permitted everywhere but the dining room. Reservations for dinner are strongly advised.

How to get there: The nearest major airport is Baltimore Washington International. Easton airport receives shuttles from BWI and Washington National by Maryland Air. The inn is a two hour drive from Washington or Baltimore, 4-1/2 hours from New York, and 3 hours from Philadelphia.

The Inn at Shelburne Farms - Shelburne, Vermont 05482
802-985-8498 / Fax: 802-985-8498 (same as phone)
The Inn at Shelburne Farms is open mid-May through mid-October. Rooms with shared bath cost from $85 to $140 a night. Rooms with private bath run from $155 to $250, double occupancy, including breakfast. Call or write for a Shelburne calendar of events and program information.

To get there: Burlington, VT has daily direct flights to and from Boston, New York, Chicago, Pittsburgh, Washington Dulles and Philadelphia. From the airport, You'll have a 20 minute drive to Shelburne. To drive, allow five or six hours from New York or Boston. Ask the Shelburne staff for directions.

The Inn at Starlight Lake - PO Box 27, Starlight, Pennsylvania 18461
717-798-2519 or 800-248-2519 / Fax: (717) 798-2672

The Inn at Starlight Lake is open year round. Room rates range from $127 to $200 per night, double occupancy (less for shared bath rooms), depending on the season. The rate includes an allotment of $10 for breakfast and $40 for dinner per couple. Children under seven stay free in parent's room, their food a la carte. Babysitting available. Conference space for up to twenty is available, with special corporate rates. Rates include all on-site recreation: swimming, boating, canoeing, fishing, tennis courts, shuffleboard, and bicycles. Ski rentals are available. Pet kennels are nearby.

How to get there: The inn is about a three hour drive from New York and New Jersey via Rt. 17, and 3-1/2 hours from Philadelphia via I-81. The Inn will send maps on request. The only public transportation is the Shortline Bus from Port Authority Terminal, NYC to Hancock, NY. The inn will pick meet you at the depot upon request. (I can just picture you there.)

Iroquois Hotel - May to Nov. 15. : Box 456, Mackinac Island, Michigan 49757
906-847-3321 or 906-847-6511
Mid-November to May: 2488 Village Drive S.E., Grand Rapids, Michigan 49506
616-247-5675

The Iroquois Hotel on-the-Beach is open mid-May to mid-October. Room rates depend on size, view, and time of year and range from $98 to $325 in high season (mid-June to mid-Sept.), no meals included. Special packages are available for mid-week, and spring and autumn. No pets, but children are welcome.

How to get there: If you come by car, there is frequent ferry service from Mackinac City or St. Ignace, with parking facilities. Commercial airlines fly into Pellston Airport, which is 12 miles South of Mackinac City ferry docks. Mackinac Island has a 3500 foot runway for private or charter aircraft. Plus air taxi service between Pellston, St. Ignace and Mackinac Island airports is offered 24 hours a day.

Keswick Hall - 701 Country Club Drive, Keswick, Virginia 22947
804-979-3440 or 1-800-ASHLEY-1 / Fax: 804-977-4171

Keswick Hall is open all year. Room rates range from $200 to $650, per room, per night and includes a country house full breakfast and traditional English afternoon tea. All Keswick Hall guests have access to golf, leisure and fitness facilities at the Keswick Club, subject to availability, including indoor/outdoor pool, clay tennis courts, spa, saunas and steam rooms.

How to get there: The Charlottesville Airport accommodates commercial commuter flights and is only 15 minutes from Keswick Hall. The Richmond Airport is approximately 1 hour and 15 minutes away from Keswick. Dulles Airport is just over 2 hours away. The inn has specific driving directions from Charlottesville, Richmond and Washington, D.C.

La Colombe d'Or - 3410 Montrose Blvd., Houston, Texas 77006
713-524-7999 / Fax: 713-524-8923

La Colombe d'Or is open all year. Suites range in price from $200 to $275 per night, double occupancy, and $575 per night for the penthouse. Telephones and TVs in all suites. Smoking allowed and children accepted.

How to get there: The inn is located about 5 minutes from the Houston business district and 20 minutes from the airport. Call the inn for specific directions.

La Pinsonniere - 124 St. Raphael, Cap-a-l'Aigle, Charlevoix, Quebec, Canada GOT 1B0
418-665-4431 or 800-387-4431 / Fax: (418) 665-7156

La Pinsonniere is open all year, except for November. The rooms range in price (in Canadian dollars) from $100 to $230 in low season (Nov. - April) and from $120 to $250 in high season (May - Oct.) per night, double occupancy no meals. High season including breakfast and dinner range from $220 to $350. Rates include use of indoor pool, sauna, tennis court, rustic beach, nature trail and wine tastings with commentary. Children welcome. Smoking allowed.

How to get there: If you fly into Quebec City, rent a car and drive Highway 138 east to Cap-a-l'Aigle, about 1-1/2 hours..

Little Palm Island - Rt. 4, Box 1036, Little Torch Key, Florida 33042
1-800-343-8567 or 305-872-2524 / FAX: 305-872-4843

Little Palm Island is open year around. Suites range from $465 per couple per night from Dec. 20 to April 30, and $330–$385 per couple, per night May 1 to Dec. 20. Two meal plans are available. AP includes breakfast, lunch and dinner and is $190 per couple, per day. MAP, including breakfast and dinner only, is $150 per couple, per day. Rates include launch service, daily newspaper, use of pool, sauna, exercise room, wind-surfers and instruction, hobie day sailors, kayaks, canoes, snorkel gear, fishing gear and beach gear. Smoking is allowed and children over twelve are accepted.

How to get there: If you fly into Miami, the staff will be happy to arrange for limousine service, or rent a car and take Florida Turnpike South to its end, then south on U.S. 1 for 120 miles to Little Torch Key and Mile Marker 28. Look for the Little Palm Ferry sign. The trip takes about 3 hours.

If you fly into Key West, limousine service or a van shuttle is available with advance notice. If you drive, take U.S. 1 north 28 miles to Little Torch Key. Turn right into Dolphin Marina to Little Palm's Shore Station.

Maison de Ville - 727 Rue Toulouse, New Orleans, Louisiana 70130
504-561-5858 / Fax: 504-561-5858 or 800-634-1600

Maison de Ville is open all year. Rates range from $145 (double room) to $635 (for a 3-bedroom cottage) in low season (July, August and December). In high season rates run from $175 to $725. All rooms include continental breakfast, butler and concierge service, and port and sherry served in the afternoons. Valet parking is available. Smoking is permitted. Children accepted. No pets.

How to get there: You may fly into the New Orleans International Airport. Rent a car or taxi into New Orleans–about a 25 minute drive. Take I-10 (towards Slidell) into New Orleans (don't take 610 or the Superdome exits). Take the French Quarter exit. Make the left U-turn onto Toulouse street. Maison de Ville is about 3-1/2 blocks down on the left.

The Marquesa Hotel - 600 Fleming Street, Key West, Florida 33040
305-292-1244 / Fax: 305-294-2121

The Marquesa Hotel is open all year. Accommodations range from $120 to $280 per night depending on the season, not including meals. Telephones and TVs in rooms. Smoking is allowed in rooms but not the restaurant. The hotel is centrally air-conditioned and offers the services of a full-time concierge to assist guests with their entertainment plans.

How to get there: Key West is a 30 minute plane trip from Miami (then take a taxi), or 3 &1/2 hours by car, crossing over a 6 mile long bridge, one of the longest of its kind in the world. Parking is available.

The Point, HCR 1, Box 65, Saranac Lake, New York 12983
800-255-3530 or 518-891-5674 / Fax: 518-891-1152

Prices for a night at The Point range from $775 to $1,025, including all meals, unlimited wines and liquors, and all activities. Their policy is to never say no to a guest!

To get there: You can fly into Saranac Lake (via U.S.Air) from Newark, Albany, LaGuardia and Burlington, VT. If you let the staff know in advance, they'll meet you at the airport, or you can rent a car at the airport.

If you drive, The Point can be reached in 6 hours from Manhattan, 3 hours from Montreal, 2 1/2 hours from Burlington, VT, and 3 hours from Albany. **There are no signs to The Point.** Make sure you get detailed instructions from the staff before setting out.

RiverSong Inn - PO Box 1910, Estes Park, Colorado 80517
303-586-4666

RiverSong is open all year. Rates range from $125 to $195, double occupancy, and include a full breakfast. No televisions or telephones in the rooms. No pets; not suitable for young children. No smoking inside.

How to get there: Estes Park is 70 miles from Denver, with no mountain passes to cross and is readily accessible year-round. Let the inn help you pick the most scenic route for each season.

The Seal Cove Inn - 221 Cypress Avenue, Moss Beach, California 94038
415-728-7325 / Fax: 415-728-4116

Seal Cove is open year round, except for a week at Christmas. Rates range from $165 to $250 per night, double occupancy, including a full breakfast, wine and hors d'oeuvres in the afternoon, complimentary wine and drinks in the rooms. All rooms have televisions, VCRs (video library available) and telephones. No smoking. Children accepted. No pets.

How to get there: You may fly into San Francisco and rent a car. Seal Cove is about a half-hour from the airport down the Cabrillo Highway (Highway 1).

The Shelburne Inn - PO Box 250, 4415 Pacific Way, Seaview, Washington 98644
206-642-2442 / Fax: 206-642-8904

The Shelburne Inn is open year round, and has been named one of the "Top 25 inns worldwide" by Conde Nast, and "one of America's Ten Best Country Inns" by Uncle Ben's, Inc. Rooms range from $89 to $160, including a full gourmet breakfast. Special packages are available.

How to get there: Seaview, Washington is right off of Rt. 101, also known as the Pacific Highway, on Route 103. A 6-1/2 drive from Vancouver, 3 hours from Seattle and Portland. The inn has a brochure complete with map directions from all these cities.

Sooke Harbour House - 1528 Whiffen Spit Road, Sooke, British Columbia, Canada V0S 1N0
604-642-3421 / Fax: 604-642-6988

Sooke Harbour House is open all year. Rates are from $195 to $275 (Canadian dollars) for two and includes breakfast and lunch. Ask about their special romance packages. One room is especially designed for the disabled. Telephones and radio, but no television in rooms. Some rooms are non-smoking, as is the restaurant. Children are welcome, and pets by prior arrangement. French is spoken.

How to get there: You may fly into Vancouver, rent a car, then ferry over to Vancouver Island. Ferries also leave from Port Angeles on the Olympic Peninsula of Washington, and from Anacortes, Washington. You can also fly directly into the Victoria airport via Air Alaska. The inn is 23 miles west of Victoria and offers a detailed map.

Stafford's Bay View Inn - 613 Woodland Avenue, Petoskey, Michigan 49770
616-347-2771 / Fax: 616-347-3413

Stafford's Bay View Inn is open mid-May through October and Christmas through March. Accommodations range from $88 to $175, including a full country breakfast. No televisions or telephones in rooms. No pets (a kennel is nearby), but children are welcome. Sixteen of the rooms are non-smoking, as is the dining room.

How to get there: Some major airlines fly into Traverse City. Petoskey and Stafford's Bay View Inn are right on U.S. 31, about 70 miles north of Traverse City, a 90 minute drive.

The Stein Eriksen Lodge - 7700 Stein Way, P.O. Box 3177, Park City, Utah 84060
801-649-3700 or 800-453-1302 / Fax: 801-649-5825

The Stein Eriksen Lodge is open all year. Rates range from $400 to $2000 in the winter and from $135 to $500 in the summer, and include ski-in/ski-out access to Deer Valley lifts, concierge, cable TV, shuttle to Park City, heated outdoor walkways, heated underground parking, service ski equipment lockers, heated outdoor pool, fitness room, sauna, hot tub and massage rooms, In the summer golf, tennis, mountain biking trails, hiking, horseback riding, fishing. Four non-smoking rooms are available, restaurants are non-smoking. Children welcome.

How to get there: If you fly into Salt Lake City International Airport, Park City is a 45 minute drive on I-80 east. The Stein Eriksen is located above Silver Lake Village, at mid-mountain Deer Valley. Lodge has maps. Rental cars are available at the airport. Airport transfers and rental cars are available through the concierge.

Tanque Verde Ranch - 14301 East Speedway, Tucson, Arizona 85748
602-296-6275 or 800-234-3833 / Fax: 602-721-9426

Tanque Verde is open all year. Rates range from $205-$270 (summer) and $270-$380 (winter) per night double occupancy, including three meals a day and all activities on site, including riding, tennis, swimming, nature programs, hikes, use of the spa and exercise room, evening programs and children's program. Children under 4 $15 a day. Smoking is allowed. No pets.

How to get there: If you fly into Tucson, Tanque Verde is a 40 minute car trip. The ranch will pick you up free if you"re staying 4 nights or more, otherwise they charge $15 a trip.

Timberhill Ranch - 35755 Hauser Bridge Road, Cazadero, California 95421
707-847-3258 / Fax: 707-847-3342

Timberhill Ranch is open year round, weekends in January. Rates are $350 per night on weekends, ($325 weeknights) double occupancy, including a six-course dinner and continental breakfast delivered in the morning, and use of all on-site recreational facilities.

No televisions or telephones in rooms. Not appropriate for children. No pets. Smoking restricted to designated areas. Handicap access available. Timberhill can accommodate up to thirty for corporate meetings or gatherings.

How to get there: Timberhill Ranch is 2-1/2 hours north of San Francisco. Call the inn for written driving instructions.

The White Barn Inn - P.O. Box 560 C, Beach Street, Kennebunkport, Maine 04046
207-967-2321 / Fax: 207-967-1100

The White Barn Inn is open all year. Rates range from $130 to $295 in season, double occupancy, including a bountiful continental breakfast, daily afternoon tea and use of the touring bicycles. On most weekends they require a two-night stay. Restaurant is closed January and 1st week of February. Conference facilities available. No pets. Older children accepted. Smoking only at the bar.

How to get there: You may fly into Boston (90 minutes away) or Portland (35 minutes away). Transportation can be arranged by the inn, or you may rent a car.

The White Gull Inn - P.O. Box 160, Fish Creek, Wisconsin 54212
414-868-3517 / Fax: 414-868-2367

The White Gull Inn is open all year. Rooms range from $49 per night for a single, small room with a shared bath (most rooms have private baths) to $215 for an entire house that sleeps eight. No meals are included, but morning coffee is brought to all cottages and houses away from the main inn. All rooms in the inn are smoke free, but smoking is permitted on the porches and patio.No pets. Children welcome.

How to get there: You may fly into Milwaukee or Green Bay. Take I-43 from Milwaukee to Green Bay, then Hwy. 57 to Sturgeon Bay, then Hwy. 42 North to Fish Creek. Turn left at White Gull sign. Private planes may fly into the Fish Creek-Ephraim airport (call the inn for information). Staff will meet guests at this airport upon request.

Recipe Index